Evgeny Pashukanis

A Critical Reappraisal

Interest in the best-known Soviet legal scholar, Evgeny Pashukanis, today remains widespread. But how and why did Pashukanis emerge as the pre-eminent Soviet jurist from 1924 to 1930, come under only minor criticism from 1930 to 1936, and then be denounced and executed in 1937 as a 'Trotskyite saboteur'? And why have many Western scholars generally praised the quality and originality of Pashukanis' work, yet also drawn the conclusion that his fate illustrates the intrinsic impossibility of the entire communist project?

Answering these questions through a thorough examination of Pashukanis' relationship to the Stalinist regime, Head shows how Pashukanis' writings provide a rich source of material on the Marxist theory of law and the state, as well as attempts to apply that theory in Soviet Russia. It is, he argues, in a proper assessment of the historical and political context of Pashukanis' work that the striking contemporary relevance of his Marxist legal theory is revealed; particularly in view of the universal assault on civil liberties in the indefinite war on terror and the constant escalation of 'law and order' measures in Western societies.

Dr Michael Head is Associate Professor in the Law School at the University of Western Sydney.

Nomikoi: Critical Legal Thinkers, edited by **Peter Goodrich** and **David Seymour**.

Nomikoi: Critical Legal Thinkers

Series editors:
Peter Goodrich
Cardozo School of Law, New York

David Seymour
Lancaster University, UK

Nomikoi: Critical Legal Thinkers presents analyses of key critical theorists whose thinking on law has contributed significantly to the development of the new interdisciplinary legal studies. Addressing those who have most influenced legal thought and thought about law, the aim of the series is to bring legal scholarship, the social sciences and the humanities into closer dialogue.

Other titles in the Series
Judith Butler: Ethics, Law, Politics, Elena Loizidou

Evgeny Pashukanis

A critical reappraisal

Michael Head

Routledge
Taylor & Francis Group
LONDON AND NEW YORK

First published 2008 by Routledge-Cavendish

Published 2016 by Routledge
2 Park Square, Milton Park, Abingdon, Oxon OX14 4RN
711 Third Avenue, New York, NY 10017, USA

Routledge is an imprint of the Taylor and Francis Group, an informa business

Typeset in Times and Gill Sans by
RefineCatch Limited, Bungay, Suffolk

British Library Cataloguing in Publication Data
A catalogue record for this book is available from the British Library

Library of Congress Cataloging-in-Publication Data
Head, Michael, LL. B.
Evgeny Pashukanis : a critical reappraisal / Michael Head.
p. cm.
"Simultaneously published in the USA and Canada."
Includes bibliographical references.
ISBN 978–1–904385–76–9 (hardback : alk. paper) – ISBN 978–1–904385–75–2 (pbk. : alk. paper) 1. Law and socialism. 2. Sociological jurisprudence. 3. Law–Soviet Union–Philosophy–History. 4. Pashukanis, Evgenii Bronislavovich, 1891–1938? 5. Law teachers–Soviet Union–Biography. I. Title.
K357.H43 2007
340'.115–dc22

2007003289

ISBN13: 978–1–904385–75–2 (pbk)
ISBN13: 978–1–904385–76–9 (hbk)

Contents

Preface

My interest in Evgeny Pashukanis goes back to my university student days in the early 1970s. It was a period of considerable political tumult and ferment internationally – from the May–June 1968 general strike in France and the Soviet suppression of the 'Czechoslovakian Spring' later that year, to the massive movements against the Vietnam War, the ousting of Richard Nixon and the downfall of the dictatorships in Spain, Portugal and Greece.

Once I became acquainted with Marxism and the writings of Leon Trotsky, it was natural that, as a law student, I turned my attention to what had happened to the promise of the 1917 Soviet revolution, including in the field of law. I soon discovered considerable confusion surrounding the various attempts that were being made, mostly by 'left-wing' academics, to present Pashukanis as an enlightened alternative to Stalinism. This seemed incongruous because Pashukanis had risen to become one of the most prominent legal theorists after Stalin's victory over the Left Opposition in 1924. I was not able to pursue my intellectual curiosity, however, until my partial return to academic life in 1999, when I began teaching at the University of Western Sydney and launched into a PhD thesis on 'Marxism, revolution and law: the experience of early Soviet Russia'. Finally, the Glasshouse Press series 'Nomikoi: Critical Legal Thinkers' gave me the opportunity to transform part of my thesis into a reassessment of Pashukanis.

To my mind, the issues raised by the Soviet revolution and its pre-Stalinist achievements remain critical for the future of human civilisation. Far from being rendered redundant by the ultimate collapse of the thoroughly degenerated Soviet state in 1991, the principles that guided the early Soviet leaders and theorists have become all the more relevant following the disintegration of the Kremlin regime that many falsely called communist. In today's world of revived militarism, worsening inequality and intense popular dissatisfaction with the prevailing 'free market' agenda of global capitalism, nothing is more important than clearing up the widely misunderstood historical record of what went wrong in the Soviet Union. I hope this volume makes at least a small contribution to that task.

This is largely a work of analysis, not original research. It is based on the published anthologies and translations into English of the writings of Pashukanis and other early Soviet legal scholars. These materials are adequate for an overall assessment, but a more complete picture may emerge from future publications and translations of wider ranges of documents. In particular, this may be so with regard to the role of the Left and Joint Oppositions of 1923–27, and the complex interrelationship between their political challenges to the Kremlin leadership and the ongoing legal and jurisprudential debates. Hopefully, indeed, this volume may encourage other scholars, including Russian historians and legal theorists, to more fully explore the issues raised.

My thanks go to my students and colleagues in the Law School at the University of Western Sydney for their encouragement and interest. Over successive years, I have been repeatedly stimulated intellectually by the comments and suggestions of students in my Jurisprudence and Law Foundation classes, where we have touched upon the enigmas of Pashukanis. I have had the pleasure also of presenting several fruitful seminars on my work to my fellow academics at UWS and other universities. For their advice and rigour, I owe a special debt to the supervisors of my PhD thesis at UWS: Razeen Sappideen and Scott Mann.

Nor could this volume have been completed without the generous contributions of the staff and students of Osgoode Hall Law School at York University, Toronto, where I spent half a year in 2003 substantially completing my thesis. For their criticisms and support, I am indebted to two examiners of my thesis: Harold Berman and Gill Boehringer. I am also grateful to Harry Glasbeek and Frederick Choate for reading and commenting on draft chapters of this book. Needless to say, the responsibility remains entirely mine for the final outcome.

For their intellectual inspiration, I owe much to my colleagues in the Socialist Equality Party and at the World Socialist Web Site, for which I write regularly. Above all, this work would not be possible without the love and support of my darling partner, Mary, and children, Tom, Daniel and Kathleen. Finally, I wish to record my gratitude to my parents, Betty and Bill, for their care over the years. This book is dedicated to the memory of my father, William Neil Head, 1929–2006.

Michael Head
Sydney
May 2007

Chapter 1

Why Pashukanis?

[H]e claimed to go deeper into the nature of law than any Marxist hitherto.[1]

Why is it that nearly a century on, interest in the best-known early Soviet legal scholar, Evgeny Pashukanis (1891–1937), remains considerable? Both his detractors and admirers agree that his writings provide a rich source of material on the Marxist theory of law and the state, as well as the successes and failures of the attempts to apply that doctrine in Soviet Russia.

As we shall see, many of the debates surrounding his work retain profound contemporary relevance. More broadly, for all the defeats, disappointments and betrayals produced by the Stalinist perversion of Marxism, the legacies of Marx's analysis have proven enduring in the field of law, as in many others.

One reason for the lasting interest is that the Soviet Revolution of 1917 marked the first attempt internationally (apart from the short-lived and localised 1871 Paris Commune) to fundamentally reorganise economic, social and legal life along anti-capitalist, participatory and egalitarian lines. This record stands, notwithstanding the subsequent degeneration of the Soviet Union at the hands of Stalin's bureaucrats after 1923, which has been taken by many as proof that the aspirations of the Russian Revolution were hopelessly, even dangerously, utopian.

Among Western legal scholars, one tragic expression of that supposed misguided Marxist utopianism is often said to be the plight of Pashukanis. In 1924, Pashukanis published the first attempt to produce a general theory of Marxism and law.[2] He sought to go deeper than his contemporaries into the very nature of law itself, which he argued was a peculiar form of social regulation that reached its apogee under capitalism and was destined to fade away under genuine communism. Pashukanis rapidly became the best-known

1 Berman, 1963: 28.
2 Pashukanis' main treatise was published in a new English translation in 1978: Pashukanis, 1978.

early Soviet jurist, whose works were prescribed reading in university courses. Within a decade, however, one of the Kremlin's favourite legal theorists of the second half of the 1920s became officially reviled as a 'counter-revolutionary' and 'fascist agent'.

This book examines several enigmas thrown up by Pashukanis' work and his treatment, both by the Kremlin authorities and Western scholars. One question that looms large in the early history of Soviet legal theory and practice is: how and why did Pashukanis emerge as a pre-eminent Soviet jurist from 1924 to 1930, while still quite young – only in his thirties – come under only minor criticism from 1930 to 1936 and then be denounced and executed in 1937 as a 'Trotskyite saboteur'?

Another apparent enigma exists. Pashukanis came to prominence in 1924, just as Stalin's faction was opening its offensive against Trotsky's Left Opposition. He clearly aligned himself against the Opposition. Yet, Pashukanis has been considered by many Western academics – both those sympathetic to his views and those who are not – as a leading anti-Stalinist, or at least an exponent of an alternative, arguably more pure, version of Marxism to that adopted by the Stalinist bureaucracy.

A third, related, puzzle is this: Why have many Western scholars generally praised the quality and originality of Pashukanis' work, yet also drawn the conclusion that his fate illustrates the intrinsic impossibility of the entire communist project?

To answer these questions, Pashukanis' role has to be thoroughly reappraised. His contribution needs to be reassessed in the light of a number of key factors. First and foremost, Pashukanis must be placed in the context of the October 1917 Revolution itself. In relation to legal theory and practice, it launched the boldest and most sweeping experiment of the twentieth century. The Soviet government led by Vladimir Lenin dispensed with the previous courts, legal system and legal profession and sought to fashion a radically new approach to the state, law and legal theory, with some striking results in many fields, including criminal and family law. Moreover, it attempted to create the conditions for the fading away ('withering away') of law and the state.

Never before had a mass revolution placed in power an administration whose avowed intent was to dissolve itself into a classless, stateless society. One chronicler of the Russian Revolution, Isaac Deutscher noted that in October 1917, Lenin's Bolsheviks spoke of a 'great vision':

> Theirs was to be a state without a standing army, without police, without bureaucracy. For the first time in history, the business of government was to cease to be the professional secret and privilege of small groups of people, elevated above society. It was to become the daily concern of the ordinary citizen. . . . To be sure, this was the ideal state of the future, not the Russian state of 1917. But the Soviet republic, as it

> emerged from the revolution, was to be directly related to the ideal (Deutscher, 1954: 318).

This programme of state disappearance was soon enshrined as a constitutional principle. In the words of the first Constitution of the Russian Republic, adopted in 1918:

> The basic task of the Constitution . . . at the present transitional moment is the establishment of the dictatorship of the city and village proletariat and the poorest peasantry in the form of a powerful All-Russian state authority for the purpose of complete suppression of the bourgeois, the destruction of exploitation of man by man, and the installation of socialism, under which there will be neither division into classes nor state authority (cited in Berman, 1963: 30–31).

Such a heroic vision – the elimination of exploitation and the creation of a stateless society – should not be lightly dismissed as utopian. In many ways, it built upon, while necessarily taking far further, the epic aims of the great democratic revolutions of the seventeenth and eighteenth centuries in England, America and France. Each of these convulsions was influenced by the conceptions that emerged out of the Enlightenment, including the profoundly subversive idea that humanity's thinking, and therefore moral character, was, in the final analysis, a reflexive product of the material and cultural environment. Therefore, as outlined by Locke's 1689 *Essay Concerning Human Understanding*, the nature of humanity could be changed and improved upon by changing and improving the environment in which people lived.

These revolutions expressed the growing dissatisfaction of the emerging bourgeoisie with the suffocating political supremacy of the unproductive and parasitic monarchical and aristocratic layers. But they evoked universal themes of human solidarity and emancipation. The English Revolution, which began with the overthrow of Charles I in 1640 and culminated in the 1688 'Glorious Revolution' was a deeply-rooted social and economic upheaval, in which the forces of parliament and the City of London, representing the emerging British capitalist class, mobilised popular forces to end the remnants of the feudal-based absolute monarchy.[3] Some of the most fundamental democratic rights and civil liberties – such as freedom from arbitrary arrest and detention, and the right to silence – were won in a sweeping political and social revolution.[4]

By the time of the American Revolution of 1776, the advanced thinkers of

3 See Hill, 2001 and Hill, 1972.

4 On the democratic rights, see Robertson, 2005: 5.

the era proclaimed that all members of society were created equal, with 'unalienable rights', identified by Thomas Jefferson in the Declaration of Independence as 'life, liberty and the pursuit of happiness'. One noted historian of the American Revolution has described it as 'the greatest utopian movement in American history':

> The revolutionaries aimed at nothing less than a reconstitution of American society. They hoped to destroy the bonds holding together the old monarchical society – kinship, patriarchy, and patronage – and to put in their place new social bonds of love, respect, and consent. They sought to construct a society and government based on virtue and disinterested public leadership and to set in motion a moral movement that would eventually be felt around the globe (Wood, 1993: 229).

Just a decade later, the American Revolution helped inspire the French Revolution of 1789, which inscribed on its banners: 'liberty, fraternity, equality'. Among its influences was Rousseau's 1755 *Discourse on the Origin and Foundation of Inequality Among Men*, which insisted that the acquisition of private property, far from being a natural attribute of human existence, destroyed man's natural humanity and enslaved him.

Well before the Russian Revolution of 1917, however, it had been obvious to the advanced thinkers of the nineteenth century – Marx and others – that the capitalist society that had arisen out of these history-making transformations had proved organically incapable of delivering the promise of genuine liberty, democracy, equality and universal solidarity. Instead, the polarisation of society, through the creation of a wealthy elite monopolising the productive resources, on the one side, and the proletarianisation of the bulk of the population as wage labourers on the other, had become an inherent and insufferable obstacle to human liberation. The creation of a classless, stateless society was hence essential for the realisation of the great emancipatory message of the Enlightenment.[5]

The challenge of early Soviet jurisprudence

The early years of the Soviet Revolution and its social and legal reforms presented a fundamental challenge to Western capitalism and law.

- Where Western jurisprudence asserted the sanctity of private property, freedom of contract and the 'rule of law' itself, as supposed guarantors of liberty and formal equality, the Bolsheviks argued that these doctrines inherently produced economic and social inequality.

5 North, 1996: 6–18.

- While Western law enforced the stability of the nuclear family as an economic unit, the Soviet government called for genuine freedom of choice in undertaking and leaving marriage, and gender equality in family and social relations.
- Whereas Western legal systems largely declared miscreants punishable because of their alleged sinfulness of personality defects, Soviet law questioned the concept of individual 'guilt'. It treated 'crime' primarily as a product of social inequity and, accordingly, sought to replace 'punishment' with social improvement, education and other remedial measures.
- Western jurists insisted that law was an organic and indispensable method of governing society, essential to combat or curb the alleged deficiencies and aggressive tendencies of human nature. Early Soviet jurisprudence regarded humanity as capable of rising to a higher social and moral level, given the right conditions. It viewed the state and law as legacies of exploitative, class society and sought to create the social conditions for them to be supplanted by more participatory and democratic forms of administration.

Informed by this approach, Soviet law struck out in new directions, often setting benchmarks that Western governments later felt compelled to emulate. This was especially so concerning gender equality, domestic relations, labour protection and social welfare.[6] For example, Soviet law was the first in the world to give women equal rights in marriage, divorce and economic status. The 1918 Russian Socialist Federated Soviet Republic (RSFSR) family code instituted divorce on demand, without a separation period, and gave wives equal legal authority with husbands in decisions affecting their children. In Britain at that time, by contrast, divorce was only available on the ground of adultery and while a husband need only prove adultery, a wife had to prove cruelty or desertion in addition to adultery. According to the French Code Civil, a wife owed 'obedience to her husband' and was obliged 'to live with her husband and to follow him wherever he chooses to reside'.[7] In 1919, Lenin could state with some justification that:

> In the course of two years of Soviet power in one of the most backward countries of Europe, more has been done to emancipate women, to make her the equal of the 'strong' sex, than has been done during the past 130 years by all the advanced, enlightened, 'democratic' republics of the world taken together.[8]

6 Quigley, 1988.
7 Quigley, 1988: 135–9.
8 Ibid: 140.

There were similar groundbreaking achievements in labour protection (e.g. the eight-hour day), social welfare (e.g. social insurance) and housing (e.g. rent controls and rent-free public housing).[9] These developments reverberated around the world, politically compelling many governments to make social and economic concessions. Overall, the Soviet government sought to make a fundamental shift from private property and individual rights to social ownership and collective rights and responsibilities, underpinned by the nationalisation of land and key enterprises. This was accompanied by far-reaching efforts to develop more humane and civilised approaches to social problems.

The first Criminal Code of 1919 made criminal law hinge on 'social danger' and 'measures of social defence', replacing the notions of 'crime' and 'punishment'.[10] Soviet leaders drew the conclusion that the latter terms, together with 'guilt', functioned to obscure the social causes of crime.[11] The Communist Party programme of the same year looked ahead to when 'the entire working population will participate in administering justice and punishment will be replaced once and for all by educational measures'.[12] Thus, despite the primitive and difficult social and economic conditions that the Soviet government confronted after 1917, its early programmatic and legal instruments sought to lay the foundations for very different relations between members of society. Pashukanis' strengths and weaknesses should be viewed from this standpoint.

Is communism really dead?

But is any of this relevant today? Many of these early initiatives were reversed or abandoned under the Stalinist regime that took hold after the end of 1923. Moreover, it may be objected, doesn't that mean communism proved to be a failure? Since the collapse of the Berlin Wall in 1989, many writers have asserted that the demise of the Soviet Union and the Eastern European Stalinist regimes signalled the irrevocable triumph of the market over socialism and even the 'end of history', to use Francis Fukuyama's phrase.[13] This outlook has been summed up by the historian Eric Hobsbawm, a long-time member of the British Communist Party who for decades politically supported the Moscow regime. In his autobiography he wrote:

> Communism is now dead: The USSR and most of the states and societies built on its model, children of the October Revolution which inspired us,

9 Quigley, 1988: 141–51.
10 Berman, 1963: 35.
11 Bauer, 1959: 38.
12 Juviler, 1976: 25.
13 Fukuyama, 1992.

> have collapsed so completely, leaving behind a landscape of material and moral ruin, that it must be obvious that failure was built into the enterprise from the start (Hobsbawm, 2003: 127).

Others have gone further to assert that the experience of the Soviet Union proves the futility and indeed reactionary character of attempting to develop a higher form of human society than capitalism. Robert Conquest condemned 'the archaic idea that utopia can be constructed on earth' and 'the offer of a millenarian solution to all human problems'.[14] American historian Martin Malia elaborated upon this theme:

> [T]he failure of integral socialism stems not from its having been tried out first in the wrong place, Russia, but from the socialist idea per se. And the reason for this failure is that socialism as full noncapitalism is intrinsically impossible (Malia, 1994: 225).

Among the claims made is that Marxism has been discredited by the dissolution of the USSR because it failed to foresee the degeneration and ultimate disintegration of the Soviet state. According to Bryan Turner, for example, 'the authority of Marxist theory has been severely challenged, not least for the failure of Marxism to anticipate the total collapse of east European communism and the Soviet Union'.[15] Such statements ignore the analysis of the nature of the Stalinist regime made by Leon Trotsky and the Left Opposition, which warned as early as the 1930s that the policies of the Kremlin oligarchy would lead to the collapse of the Soviet Union, unless its privileged ruling caste was overthrown by the working class. In Trotsky's words, from *The Revolution Betrayed*, published in 1937:

> Will the bureaucrat devour the workers' state, or will the working class clean up the bureaucrat? Thus stands the question upon whose decision hangs the fate of the Soviet Union (Trotsky, 1937: 285).

Many in the West who rejected this prognosis falsely identified Stalinism with Marxism, or at least saw the Soviet Union as some kind of 'really existing socialism' even if they made criticisms of the Kremlin bureaucracy. One example is Raymond Aronson, who began his volume *After Marxism* with the statement that 'Marxism is over, and we are on our own'.[16] He wrote:

> The very immobility and ponderousness of the Soviet Union counted for

14 Conquest, 2000: 3.
15 Turner, 1993: 5.
16 Aronson, 1995: 1.

> something positive in our collective psychic space, allowing us to keep hope alive that a successful socialism might still emerge (Aronson, 1995: vii–viii).

Perhaps, now that Stalinism, regarded by many as a surrogate for socialism, has catastrophically imploded it is time to examine the possible lessons of the Soviet experiment more closely. As part of this project, we should assess the quality of the early (pre-Stalinist) Soviet legal debates and experiences, and identify any worthwhile features of this period. In the light of Stalinism's ignominious collapse, it may well be instructive to examine the contrast between the initial Soviet legal experiments and their subsequent degeneration.

Moreover, with the dawning of a new century it is apparent that many of the issues bound up with the Russian Revolution and which continued to plague humanity during the twentieth century – war, social inequality, economic exploitation, national oppression, colonialism, financial instability and environmental degradation – have not been resolved. Given the unleashing of market forces worldwide in the wake of the USSR's collapse, it may be no coincidence that there has been a marked growth in social inequality and wealth concentration in the richest 1 per cent (and especially the top 0.1 per cent) of the world's population. By 1998, according to the United Nations Human Development Report for that year, the average African household consumed 20 per cent less than 25 years earlier, and the world's richest 20 per cent of people accounted for 86 per cent of total private consumption expenditure, leaving a measly 1.3 per cent for the poorest 20 per cent.[17] The widening gap between rich and poor is also combining with economic globalisation and technological transformation to undermine the old political and legal certainties. The nation-state framework, through which most law-making has hitherto been conducted, is under mounting stress, as transnational corporations scour the globe for markets and ever-cheaper sources of labour and raw materials. It would seem myopic to dismiss the possible relevance of the early Soviet legal debates and experiences.

Towards a new assessment of Pashukanis

Lively and wide-ranging debates occurred on the future of the Soviet state and law throughout the early years of the Russian Revolution. This book advances a new paradigm for reconsidering Pashukanis' place in this phase of Soviet legal history, in which he was only the best-known protagonist. While much has been written in the West on his contributions, some fundamental flaws appear in the approaches that have been taken. A number of

17 United Nations, 1998: 2.

crucial factors have either been neglected or underestimated. They are essential for gaining an understanding of the wider significance of Pashukanis and the jurisprudential discussion with which he was associated, particularly during the initial decade of Soviet rule:

1. Broad-ranging legal debates

Above all, Pashukanis cannot be understood in isolation. Passionate conflicts erupted over the role of law in the early days of the Russian Revolution; debates that included, among others, Pashukanis and the first Soviet jurist, Peter Stuchka. Few Western scholars have examined the full scope and richness of these debates, the extent of which is still emerging in the wake of the collapse of the Soviet Union.[18] However, several well-known scholars, notably Kelsen, Hazard, Berman, Schlesinger and Fuller, surveyed aspects of the debates.[19]

After 1956, Khrushchev's attempts to distance the Kremlin bureaucracy from the most grotesque features of Stalinism, outlined in his secret speech to the 20th Congress of the Communist Party of the Soviet Union, led to renewed interest in the writings of Pashukanis and, to a lesser extent, Stuchka.[20] These studies, however, often paid insufficient attention to the wider jurisprudential discussion that flourished between 1917 and 1927, until they were extinguished by the Stalinist regime. Considering the austere and tense circumstances of the Soviet state, which had barely managed to survive the so-called civil war of 1918–21, these debates were remarkably open and spirited. To the extent that Pashukanis made an original contribution to Marxist legal theory, he owed much to this intellectual climate.

2. The social and historical context

With some exceptions,[21] existing Western academic works on the early phase of the Russian Soviet state are flawed by insufficient attention to the concrete historical and material circumstances facing the young workers' state after 400 years of suffocating and repressive authoritarianism and feudalism.[22]

18 Two valuable compilations of English language translations of extracts from the debates, both relied upon throughout this book, are: Jaworskyj, 1967 and Zile, 1970.
19 Berman, 1963; Kelsen, 1955; Hazard, 1951; Fuller, 1949; Schlesinger, 1951.
20 For example, Kamenka and Tay, 1970; Arthur, 1976–77; Redhead, 1978; Beirne and Sharlet, 1980; Balbus, 1977; Warrington 1981 (reprinted in Varga, 1993: 982–96); Norrie, 1982; Cotterrell, 1979; Sumner, 1981.
21 Notably Berman, 1963 and Schlesinger, 1951.
22 For example, Fuller, 1949 at p 1165 states that the causes that produced the shift in doctrine from Pashukanis to Vyshinsky, Stalin's principal legal spokesman in the late 1930s, 'are not, I think, obscure'. Rather than examine the economic and political conditions behind the

A basic contradiction lay at the heart of the October 1917 Revolution. Russia was not an advanced capitalist country, of the kind envisaged as the starting point for world revolution by Marx and Engels. The Russian Revolution occurred in one of the least developed countries of Europe, with an overwhelmingly peasant population, only formally freed from serfdom 50 years earlier. The leaders of the revolution, notably Lenin and Leon Trotsky, stated that socialism could not be built under such conditions, and that the survival and future of the Soviet state depended on the extension of the international revolution across Western Europe.

Instead, as it happened, the revolutionary upsurges in Germany, Italy and other European countries were suppressed. During the so-called civil war of 1918–21, Japan, Britain, the United States and other Western powers intervened behind the military opponents of the revolution, sending in more than half a million troops in an unsuccessful bid to overturn the revolution. Although the hastily assembled Red Army finally defeated the White armies, the victory came with huge human, social and economic costs. Many of the most active socialists were killed in the fighting, much of the country was devastated and production fell far below pre-World War I levels.

This was followed by the post-1921 New Economic Policy (NEP), under which Lenin's leadership, facing prolonged economic and political isolation in a capitalist world, felt compelled to restore private property rights and market relations to a certain degree in an attempt to revive domestic economic life. All these developments had a marked impact on legal practice and theory, as well as on Pashukanis' emergence and trajectory as one of the Kremlin's initially favoured legal theorists.

3. The legal record of Soviet Russia

It is impossible to properly assess the role of Pashukanis, and the wider legal debates, without placing them in the context of the actual legal record of the young Soviet government. For example, Pashukanis' best-known contribution, his so-called 'commodity exchange theory of law', was bound up with the contradictions thrust forward by the NEP, which necessitated a sweeping codification of law in order to protect revived economic property rights. Pashukanis' theory enabled him, for a period, to reconcile the Marxist theory of the 'withering away' of the state and law, with the greater recourse to legal sanctions. Yet, some authors have suggested that Pashukanis' thesis

circumstances, Fuller asserts, with little discussion, that the Soviet leaders rediscovered some 'ancient truths' about 'the very nature of the human animal'. This view undoubtedly flows from the assumptions and arguments underlying Fuller's entire procedural naturalist approach to the minimal requirements for a legal order (see Fuller, 1964) but Fuller did not substantiate his analysis in this context.

should be considered without reference to the requirements presented by the NEP.[23] This abstract approach has contributed to some romanticisation of Pashukanis.

4. The socialist opposition

Much of what has been written in the West makes no reference to the formidable socialist opposition to the post–1923 Stalinist regime, an opposition that Stalin sought to extinguish through repeated repression, from the 1927 expulsion of Leon Trotsky from the party leadership through to the great purges of 1936–39. It is of particular significance that Pashukanis lined up with Stalin's faction, and the publication of Pashukanis' initial volume, *The General Theory of Law and Marxism*, in 1924, coincided with the opening of the battle against the Left Opposition and with Stalin's proclamation of the quest to build 'socialism in one country'.

Some scholars, including the historian E.H. Carr, examine the impact of the suppression of the Left Opposition led by Trotsky on early Soviet legal developments. Others, however, make little or no mention of the Opposition.[24] It is impossible to assess the writings of Pashukanis, or the evolution of the legal discussion as a whole, outside the context of the Kremlin's struggle against the Opposition. Starting with the New Course, one of the first documents issued by the Left Opposition in late 1923, the Opposition demanded a return to a Marxist course: a democratic and participatory administration, designed to begin dissolving the state apparatus.

5. Classical Marxist legal theory

It is essential to analyse and measure the early Soviet legal debates by reference to classical Marxist theory on the relationship between economic development and law, the class role of law and the ultimate withering away of the state and law in a truly communist society. As will be explored in Chapter 2, the early Soviet legal theorists had a considerable Marxist heritage upon which to draw, including substantial writings on law and the state.

Some Western theorists display a limited or distorted understanding of Marxist theory, presenting it as mechanical economic determinism or class instrumentalism.[25] Others tend to dismiss its relevance or assert that it had

23 For example, Arthur, 1978: 28.

24 For example, none of the contributors to Beirne, 1990 refer to the Left Opposition. Fuller, 1949 makes no mention of the Left Opposition. Berman, 1963 refers to, or cites, Trotsky several times, and also mentions the Russian nationalist content of Stalin's measures, but does not explore the significance of the defeat of the Left Opposition.

25 Thus, Fuller, 1949 at p 1164 states: 'The orthodox communist conception regards law as the expression of the will of the ruling class.'

little to say on the practical issues facing the Bolsheviks.[26] Some go further, depicting existing Marxist theory as a serious barrier to the Bolsheviks developing a coherent view.[27] In reality, Marxist theory had much to say on these issues, but was perverted under Stalin. This book begins by examining, in outline form, the essential Marxist principles that existed to provide a guide for Soviet theorists and authorities.

6. *The axes of the early debates*

We need to better identify the essential axes of the conflicts over legal theory between 1917 and 1927. One chronicler of the debates, Jaworskyj, discerned the existence of at least four 'Marxist' schools: (a) sociological, (b) psychological, (c) social function and (d) normativist.[28] According to this classification, which is based on the categories adopted by some of the protagonists themselves, the so-called commodity-exchange theory of Pashukanis formed part of the predominant sociological school.[29]

While these classifications are sometimes helpful, they can obscure underlying differences of programme and perspective. The tendencies need to be analysed differently – primarily from the standpoint of their stances on the key interrelated issues of (1) the class character of the Soviet state – was it socialist or capitalist? (2) the role of law under socialism; and (3) the withering away of the state under communism.

This approach focuses on the function and nature of the state and law in the transition from capitalism to communism. Was the Soviet state apparatus socialist in character, or did it constitute a bourgeois hangover, or did it contain competing features of both? How, and at what pace, would the state wither away, and what factors would determine the outcome? What role would or should law play in the transition, and what would replace it as an instrument of social policy and regulation under genuine communism? Herein lay the nub of the jurisprudential and practical problems, from which flowed other issues.

The participants in the debates sought to elaborate a Marxist perspective by adapting, and criticising, various well-known schools of legal theory,

26 Fuller, ibid at p 1165 states: 'That doctrine [Marxism] gives no explicit guidance in conducting the transition from revolutionary terror to stability and legality, and such implicit guidance as can be deduced from it is fantastically wrong.' Likewise, Jaworskyj, 1967 at p 50 contends that Russian legal theorists found few answers in Marxist theory.

27 Beirne, 1990 at p ix states: [T]he Bolsheviks found themselves altogether lacking in theoretical direction for the role of law during the transitional period between capitalism and communism. For Bolshevik theorists of state and law the several strands of existing legal theory presented, in concert, a formidable obstacle to the development of a Marxist theory of law.'

28 Jaworskyj, 1967: 50–1.

29 See Chapter 6.

including the leading Western bourgeois writers. They did so, however, in the context of grappling with the contradictory requirements of the legal order posed by the successive phases of early Soviet Russia: (a) the consolidation of political power, October 1917 to mid-1918; (b) 'War Communism', mid-1918 to early 1921; (c) the New Economic Policy, from 1921; and (d) the emergence of Stalin's dominance after Lenin's death in early 1924. In particular, the NEP, with its concessions to market economic forces, necessitated the revival of discarded legal forms. From 1924, the ideological and practical needs of the Stalinist regime increasingly shaped and distorted the debates.

7. *The contrast with Stalinism*

There is a sharp contrast between the classical Marxist thesis that the state and the law will become redundant with the successful development of communism, and the increasingly authoritarian programme, dubbed 'socialist legality', imposed by the Stalinist dictatorship in the 1930s. Numbers of Western scholars have contended that the roots of, and the responsibility for, Stalinism lay in Marxist theory, or at least the unresolved problems of Marxist theory. Some have argued that Stalinism arose directly out of Marxism-Leninism, with disdain for the rule of law leading inexorably to Stalinist repression.[30] Others have suggested that the fragmentary character of Marxist writings about the nature of legal relations in the period of socialist transition between capitalism and communism created a theoretical vacuum that contributed to the intensification of authoritarian centralism during the late 1920s.[31]

This volume will suggest an alternative analysis, based on the antithesis between classical Marxism and Stalinist practice. The views mentioned above also underestimate two factors: the unfavourable material circumstances confronting the Soviet state, both internally and internationally, and the degree to which Stalinist authoritarianism intensified in direct response to the challenge of the Left Opposition, which fought for the continuation of a Marxist approach.

How the early debates evolved

The pre-Stalinist period between 1917 and 1923 saw free-ranging and scholarly discussion on legal theory. Debates began to emerge in the earliest days following the October Revolution, and continued during the difficult days of the civil war. More intense discussion arose over the complex issues raised by the NEP. The debates continued relatively unimpeded until after the final

30 For example, Cohen, 1985: 38–70.
31 Beirne and Hunt, 1990a and 1990b.

defeat of the Joint Opposition, led by Trotsky, Zinoviev and Kamenev, in 1927.

The ferment was part of a wider flowering of intellectual, artistic and cultural life generated by the 1917 Revolution. Many leading Bolsheviks, including Lenin and Trotsky, wrote on questions of religion, morality, philosophy, psychology, education, law, art and literature. Those seeking to dictate or suppress differences on such profound and intellectually rich issues were vigorously combated. To take the example of art and literature, intense debates arose in which Trotsky, Aleksandr Voronsky and other Left Oppositionists opposed the stifling doctrines of 'proletarian culture' and 'socialist realism'.[32]

After late 1923, the consolidation of the Stalinist regime increasingly meant an end to the open discussion of law and legal theory. From genuine debate, by the 1930s the dialogue became reduced to diatribes and denunciations. In essence, the regime's nationalist and bureaucratic programme, formalised by the adoption of Stalin's thesis of 'socialism in one country' in 1924 – after Lenin's death – collided with the basic Marxist understanding of the *international* basis of socialism, with terrible consequences for the role of the Soviet state. The basic perspective that had informed the October Revolution – that the destiny of the Russian Revolution hinged on the international overthrow of capitalism, without which genuine communism was inconceivable – was replaced by a programme based on building an authoritarian fortress state in the Soviet Union, with the prospect of communism delayed indefinitely.

These implications became more apparent over time. Initially, Pashukanis' 1924 so-called commodity theory of law became part of the regime's official doctrine. It helped reconcile the needs of the NEP, including the legal protection of private property rights, with the Marxist understanding of the withering away of the state. Nevertheless, his theory provided some profound insights into both the nature of the legal form and the concept of law under capitalism.

By the late 1920s, Pashukanis was under attack within the Soviet Union because he maintained, in keeping with authentic Marxism, that the law and indeed the state apparatus of the Soviet Union would ultimately disappear with the construction of a genuinely communist society. He initially resisted the Stalinist notion that the law and the state itself had become organically 'socialist' and therefore occupied a permanent place in social organisation. By 1936, his views were incompatible with the Kremlin line, which was based on the wholly self-contradictory claim that socialism had been built; yet the 'dictatorship of the proletariat' had been simultaneously strengthened.

Pashukanis made several efforts to 'correct' his 'errors', and joined the

32 See Voronsky, 1998; Deutscher, 1959: 164–200.

increasingly ritual denunciations of the 'Trotskyites' and then the 'Bukharinites' from the mid-1920s. His revisions became more grotesque by the mid-1930s, culminating in the almost complete repudiation of his basic theory in 1936, but this failed to save him. After a decade of opposing the Left Opposition, he ended up being denounced and executed as a 'Trotskyite' and 'fascist' in 1937, the year of Stalin's great terror.

His tragedy was bound up with that of his entire generation. Almost all those with any association with the 1917 Revolution, Marxist scholarship or creative intellectual or cultural development were put to death in 1936–37.[33] It is one of history's ironies that the country in which Marxism achieved its highest and widest influence, became the venue for the most ferocious assault on genuine Marxism – in the name of defending Marxism.

Such was the depth of the socialist opposition to his regime that Stalin undertook the Moscow show trials of 1934–37, the execution of Old Bolshevik leaders and mass purges of the 1930s in order to secure the survival of his rule. Stalin's extermination of his opponents was a political genocide, unparalleled in history. By framing-up and executing hundreds of thousands of socialist-minded workers and intellectuals, Stalin's regime sought to extinguish the Marxist heritage of the 1917 Revolution. Not only were the cream of the entire generation that led the revolution slandered in the most pernicious manner as 'saboteurs', 'counter-revolutionaries' and 'Nazi collaborators', they were forced to make ludicrous confessions and then put to death.[34] Trotsky and other leaders of the Left Opposition within the Soviet Union and worldwide were assassinated.

The extent of the repression was, however, also a measure of the power and grandeur of the ideas that the regime sought to silence. Although short-lived, the early pre-Stalinist period of Soviet Russia was living proof of the capacity of downtrodden people, informed by a progressive political perspective, to radically restructure economic, social and political life. This volume explores the possibility that some features of early Soviet legal thought and experience provide signposts for a future transition to a truly democratic and egalitarian society.

33 See Rogovin, 1998; Berman, 1963: 52.
34 Rogovin, 1998: 164–78.

Chapter 2

The Marxist view of law: socialism and democracy

> Law can never stand higher than the economic order and the cultural development of society conditioned by it.[1]

The neglected Marxist heritage

Pashukanis' endeavours and plight can be understood only in the light of the Marxist view of law. This book cannot attempt a full analysis of the Marxist concept of the state and law but two questions must be tackled. Is it true, as has been asserted, that there was no coherent Marxist heritage to guide Soviet legal theory and practice? Secondly, if such a legacy existed, what were the relevant propositions that Pashukanis attempted to elucidate?

Jaworskyj and other commentators assert that Russian legal theorists found themselves confronting uncharted waters for which Marxist theory had no answers.[2] It is certainly true that unprecedented challenges were posed in the years after 1917 that earlier Marxists could not have fully anticipated. None of the leading Marxists – Marx, Engels, Plekhanov, Lenin, Trotsky – attempted to set out a comprehensive model of society under socialism. They regarded such ventures as overly prescriptive, as well as premature and utopian. For them, socialism consisted of human self-emancipation and would be shaped by the actions and ideas of millions of working people, tempered by the concrete historical and international circumstances that prevailed. The classical Marxists were even less inclined to provide a detailed blueprint for the role of law and the state machinery in the transition from the overthrow of capitalism to socialism and then communism. They regarded law's role as being fundamentally bound up with and, in the final analysis, dependent upon the development of humanity's economic capacities and social well-being.

Karl Marx and his close collaborator, Frederick Engels, wrote considerably

1 Marx, 1970b:10.
2 Jaworskyj, 1967: 50.

on the role of law in contemporary society, but usually tangentially to their broader examinations of class structure and dynamics. With the exception of Marx's early *Critique of Hegel's Philosophy of Right*[3] and Engels' later *The Origin of the Family, Private Property and the State*,[4] they only addressed the issues of the state and law as subjects in themselves in several letters.[5] They wrote little on the post-revolutionary withering away of the state and law in the transition to genuine communism, but enough to provide a policy orientation. What they did not attempt, flowing from their analysis of law as ultimately derived from economic interests and the conquest of state power, was a general theory of law. Marx twice wrote of his intention to develop a theory of state and law,[6] but this project was set aside to concentrate on his study of political economy, presented in the three volumes of *Capital*.

Nevertheless, a Marxist heritage provided guiding principles. While Marx and Engels did not write systematic expositions on legal theory, many of their works examined the role of law in society.[7] Engels, in particular, commented on the state, law and legal theory in several major works, notably *The Origin of the Family, Private Property and the State* and *Ludwig Feuerbach and the End of German Classical Philosophy*. Taken as a whole, these passages provided a definite framework of analysis and orientation, as well as basic principles, which initially guided the early Soviet leadership. These principles were later betrayed under Stalinism.

It is worth noting that in the months preceding the October Revolution, while in hiding from the police of the Provisional Government, Lenin wrote a major work on the nature of the state, *The State and Revolution*.[8] In large measure, he worked over the relevant writings of Marx and Engels, particularly *The Origin of the Family, Private Property and the State*. He regarded this reworking as significant enough for the future of the revolution that in July 1917 he sent a note to Kamenev, asking him to publish his notes if he were assassinated.[9] In his August 1917 Preface to the First Edition, Lenin insisted that much-mystified questions of the state and law were of acute importance for the looming revolution and needed clarification in the minds of ordinary people. He also argued that the state and legality and their legitimacy in the eyes of the population could help determine the success and viability of the revolution. He wrote:

3 Marx, 1970a.

4 Engels, 1942.

5 See, for example, Marx's 23 November 1871 letter to F. Bolte in Marx and Engels, 1975: 328.

6 Marx, Letter to Wedermeyer (1 February 1859) in Marx and Engels, 1942: 119; Marx, 1973: 108.

7 See, for example, Marx, 1977 and Engels, 1978, especially part IV. For compilations, see Phillips, 1980, and Cain and Hunt, 1979.

8 Lenin, 1970.

9 Trotsky, 1977: 977.

> The question of the relation of the socialist proletarian revolution to the state is acquiring not only a practical political importance, but also the significance of a most urgent problem of the day, the problem of explaining to the masses what they will have to do before long to free themselves from capitalist tyranny (Lenin, 1964, vol 25: 388).

Fundamental conceptions

The two fundamental, underlying Marxist conceptions were (1) that, in general, all forms of law and the state were in the end derived from the development of the productive and hence cultural level of human society and (2) that law and the state would wither away in the process of arriving at a genuinely communist society. That is, the need for formal, bureaucratic and repressive instruments of rule would disappear with the creation of a bountiful, egalitarian and democratic world.

For all the major Marxist theoreticians the roles of law and the state, as key social institutions, were derivative and secondary, not primary, in the economic, social and political structure. Nevertheless, Marxists have not ignored the fact that law can play a critical part in shaping social development and consciousness under certain circumstances.

The starting point for understanding this historical materialist view is Marx's 1859 Preface to *A Contribution to the Critique of Political Economy*, where he tentatively described the following propositions, derived from years of research and experience, as 'a guiding thread for my studies':

> In the social production of their life, men enter into definite relations that are indispensable and independent of their will, relations of production which correspond to a definite stage of development of their material productive forces. The sum total of these relations of production constitutes the economic structure of society, the real foundation, on which rises a legal and political superstructure and to which correspond definite forms of social consciousness. The mode of production of material life conditions the social, political and intellectual life process in general. It is not the consciousness of men that determines their being, but, on the contrary, their social being that determines their social consciousness.
>
> At a certain stage of their development, the material productive forces of society come in conflict with the existing relations of production, or – what is but a legal expression for the same thing – with the property relations within which they have been at work hitherto. From forms of development of the productive forces these relations turn into their fetters. Then begins an epoch of social revolution. With the change of the economic foundation, the entire immense superstructure is more or less rapidly transformed.
>
> In considering such transformations, a distinction should always be

> made between the material transformation of the economic conditions of production, which can be determined with the precision of natural science, and the legal, political, religious, aesthetic or philosophical – in short, ideological forms in which men become conscious of this conflict and fight it out (Marx, 1969: 503–4).

Three themes can be discerned in this seminal passage. The first is that law, like other aspects of the political superstructure, arises from definite relations of production and the forms of social consciousness forged by those relations. The second is that those relations are not static but are inevitably shattered by the further development of technology and production itself, ultimately leading to social revolution. The third is that law is one of the ideological forms in which people become conscious of the underlying conflicts and 'fight them out'. Each of these three observations was reflected in the early Soviet legal debates.

This is not the place to enter into the disputes over the alleged dichotomy between the 'young' and 'mature' Marx and Engels and the supposed differences between Marx and Engels. Certain scholars have claimed to detect a contrast between the more 'humane' and less deterministic views of the young Marx and his later writings.[10] Other authors have argued that Engels was more mechanical, humanist and superficial in his views on law than Marx.[11] Some have argued that both Marx and Engels became amenable to the possibility of reforming, rather than removing, the legal and state apparatus of capitalism.[12] While this writer does not subscribe to any of these contentions, the existence of such debates underscores the fact that Marx and Engels left a body of writing on law that is capable of informing the struggle for socialism, even if different interpretations have been made of the legacy.

As to the alleged divergence between Marx and Engels, it is sufficient to point out that their intimate intellectual and political collaboration spanned 39 years, from 1844 until Marx's death in 1883. During that time, they maintained direct contact with each other either through written correspondence or personal meetings on virtually a daily basis. The contemporary edition of the *Marx–Engels Collected Works* includes 10 volumes (each containing between 500 and 600 pages) of correspondence. These letters, which allow the reader to follow the intellectual development and interaction of the pair over four decades, testifies to an exceptional degree of philosophical solidarity and theoretical agreement, not to speak of personal friendship. Where differences arose – whether over theoretical, political or personal matters – there exists a documentary record of the disputes. None concerned jurisprudence. In his

10 For example, Althusser, 1969: 221–47.
11 Cain and Hunt, 1979: 2.
12 Cain and Hunt, above: ix–xx; Thompson, 1975.

1859 Preface to *A Contribution to the Critique of Political Economy*, Marx emphasised the common intellectual development between the two, and the joint authorship of their seminal works:

> Friedrich Engels, with whom I maintained a constant exchange of ideas by correspondence since the publication of his brilliant essay on the critique of economic categories (printed in the *Deutsch-Französische Jahrbücher*) arrived by another road (compare his *Condition of the Working Class in England*) at the same result as I, and when in the spring of 1845 he too came to live in Brussels, we decided to set forth together our conception as opposed to the ideological one of German philosophy, in fact to settle accounts with our former philosophical conscience. The intention was carried out in the form of a critique of post-Hegelian philosophy. The manuscript, two large octavo volumes [*The German Ideology*] had long ago reached the publishers in Westphalia when we were informed that owing to changed circumstances it could not be printed. We abandoned the manuscript to the gnawing criticism of the mice all the more willingly since we had achieved our main purpose – self-clarification. Of the scattered works in which at that time we presented one or another aspect of our views to the public, I shall mention only the *Manifesto of the Communist Party*, jointly written by Engels and myself, and a *Speech on the Question of Free Trade*, which I myself published. The salient points of our conception were first outlined in an academic, although polemical, form in my *Poverty of Philosophy* ... (Marx and Engels, 1987, vol 29: 264).

As a young man, Marx studied law but soon rejected the 'metaphysics of law', which he saw as divorced from social reality. He turned initially to a study of the philosophy of law and then to the class and economic driving forces of social development. In his 1843 *Critique of Hegel's Philosophy of Law*, he criticised the 'speculative philosophy of law' for its disregard of 'real man'.[13] This notion was elaborated in the same Preface to his 1859 *A Contribution to the Critique of Political Economy*:

> Neither legal relations nor political forms can be comprehended whether by themselves or on the basis of a so-called general development of the human mind, but that on the contrary they originate in the material conditions of life, the totality of which Hegel, following the example of English and French thinkers of the eighteenth century, embraces within the term 'civil society'; that the anatomy of this civil society, however, has to be sought in political economy (Marx, 1977: 20).

13 Extracted in Cain and Hunt, 1979: 19.

This conception formed the kernel of his analysis of the role of law throughout his life, although his view was enriched by an exhaustive study of political economy. In *Capital*, his final work, he remarked upon Hodgskin's 1832 complaint that: 'The power of the capitalist over all the wealth of the country is a complete change in the right of property, and by what law, or series of laws, was it effected?'[14] Marx commented: 'The author should have remembered that revolutions are not made by laws.'[15] In other words, it was not abstract legality that determined property rights, but the taking of economic and political power by a definite social class, in this instance the capitalist class.

At the same time, the class role of law under capitalism was camouflaged in the language of formal equality and 'justice'. It also expressed productive and social relations in a necessarily mystified form. In *The German Ideology*, Marx and Engels examined the 'cult of concepts' that pervades jurisprudence:

> All relations can be expressed in language only in the form of concepts. That these general ideas and concepts are looked upon as mysterious forces is the necessary result of the fact that the real relations, of which they are the expression, have acquired independent existence. Besides this meaning in everyday consciousness, these general ideas are further elaborated and given a special significance by politicians and lawyers, who, as a result of the division of labour, are dependent on the cult of these concepts, and who see in them, and not in the relations of production, the true basis of all real property relations (Marx and Engels, 1976: 365).

These observations are bound up with what Marx and Engels termed commodity fetishism – an important conception that Pashukanis sought to develop – which is examined later in this chapter.

Essential propositions

Properly understood, the Marxist view of law includes a number of pivotal propositions. First, that socialism means democracy and the withering away of the state, not the bureaucratic 'command economy' that subsequently emerged under Stalin.

Second, that socialism cannot be achieved by seeking to reform the state machine of the old feudal or capitalist order. It requires a thoroughgoing popular revolution to establish a new kind of state, a genuinely democratic state (the dictatorship of the proletariat), as a transitional regime to create the ultimate conditions for a classless, stateless communist society.

14 Hodgskin, 1832: 98–9.
15 Marx, 1979c: 702–3.

Third, that law is not inherent or organic to society; rather it arises out of conflicting interests in society and primarily reflects the interests of the ruling layers. Therefore, in a classless society, the legal form of social regulation will become redundant. This withering away of the state and law can and must begin as soon as the socialist revolution has successfully wrested power from the old ruling class.

Fourth, that the relationship between law and socio-economic power is dialectical. Against crude materialism and class reductionism, Marxists explain that legal definitions and measures can, in some circumstances, exert a sharp influence on economic and social developments. In part, this arises from the mystified, ideological form in which law and legal theory present themselves.

Finally, the Marxist view of law rejects the notion that capitalism, based on private ownership of the means of production, is somehow natural while socialism is alien to human nature. Under capitalism, law plays an ideological role in disguising social inequality, dulling consciousness of class divisions and reinforcing 'commodity fetishism'. Thus, it helps to shape and distort what is often presumed to be 'human nature'.

Each of these propositions is essential for interpreting Pashukanis and the broader Soviet legal debates.

Socialism, democracy and the state

For Marx and Engels, a genuine socialist revolution must be a massive social movement, in which the working people themselves take control of society. It could not be a putsch, directed by an elite from above, which would then dictate the shape of social change. As Engels wrote in his 1895 Introduction to Marx's *Class Struggle in France*, the experience of previous failed or betrayed revolutions, including the European revolutions of 1848, as well as the ultimate defeat of the Paris Commune of 1871 indicated that:

> The time of surprise attacks, of revolutions carried through by small conscious minorities at the head of masses lacking consciousness is past. Where it is a question of a complete transformation of the social organisation, the masses themselves must also be in on it, must themselves already have grasped what is at stake, what they are fighting for, body and soul. The history of the last fifty years has taught us that (Marx and Engels, 1987, vol 27: 520).

This understanding is bound up with the underlying principle developed by Marx and Engels, that of the self-emancipation of the working class. Previously, in the writings of the utopian socialists, such as Saint-Simon and Robert Owen, socialism was conceived as the work of an enlightened elite, uplifting the downtrodden. Marx and Engels explained that the working class, which was created by industrial capitalism, was the only revolutionary class and could only liberate humanity from the irrationality and oppression of capitalism by freeing itself. This principle was enshrined as the first premise of the Rules of the First International in 1864: 'CONSIDERING, That the emancipation of the working classes must be conquered by the working classes themselves.'[16] Later, in a preface to the *Communist Manifesto*, Engels wrote: '[O]ur notion, from the very beginning, was that "the emancipation of the working class must be the act of the working class itself",' slightly varying the wording.[17] In his *Critique of the Gotha Program*, Marx regarded the principle of such importance that he objected to an 'improvement' of its formulation to say, 'the emancipation of labour must be the work of the working class'. Marx commented that the change rendered the principle unintelligible.[18] He did not elaborate, but clearly his concern was that the planned Gotha Program fudged or watered-down the proposition that no one could liberate the working class but the working class itself.[19]

This classical Marxist approach has profound implications for the transition to socialism after a revolution. Contrary to the 'command economy' view later imposed by the Stalinist bureaucracy in the Soviet Union, Marx insisted that the development of a socialist society would not take place according to a series of prescriptions and rules laid down by an individual, a political party or a governmental authority. Rather, it would develop on the basis of the activity of the members of society who, for the first time in history, consciously regulate and control their own social organisation as part of their daily lives, free from the domination and prescriptions of either the 'free market' or a bureaucratic authority standing over them.

In one of his earliest writings Marx stated:

> Only when man has recognised and organised his own powers as social forces, and consequently no longer separates social power from himself in the shape of political power, only then will human emancipation have been accomplished (Marx, 1976: 168).

This perspective guided him throughout his life. In one of his later writings, he explained that the significance of the Paris Commune of 1871 was that it involved

> . . . the reabsorption of state power by society as one of its own living forces instead of as forces controlling and subduing it, by the popular

16 Marx, 1964, vol 11: 288.

17 Engels, 1969: 28.

18 Marx, 1979b: 11.

19 On the historical development of the views of Marx and Engels on self-emancipation, see Draper, 1971: 81–109.

> masses themselves, forming their own force instead of the organised force of their own suppression – the political form of their social emancipation, instead of the artificial force appropriated by their oppressors (Marx and Engels, 1980: 153).

In Marx's view, the precondition for such a society is the development of the social productivity of labour to such a point that the vast bulk of humanity does not have to spend the greater portion of the day merely trying to obtain the resources to live. The overturn of capitalist rule would not see the overnight abolition of the market. The price mechanism would still be needed for a period as a guide in the provision of information regarding the relative costs of alternative production methods. But increasingly it would be made subordinate to and eventually replaced by the conscious regulation of the economy according to a plan, decided on, checked and altered to meet changing circumstances through the involvement of workers and the population as a whole in the process of economic decision-making.

The emergence of the Stalinist bureaucracy in the early 1920s, and its complete usurpation, by 1927, of political power meant that genuine socialist, that is democratic, planning, could never be carried out in the Soviet Union. Such democratic input would have immediately threatened the privileged social position of the bureaucracy and its monopoly of political power. Against the Stalinist bureaucracy, Trotsky argued that the demand for Soviet democracy was an economic necessity, not an abstract policy, much less the expression of a pure moral ideal. The establishment of a planned economy, he wrote, was

> . . . by its very nature insoluble without the daily experience of millions, without their critical review of their own collective experience, without their expression of their needs and demands and could not be carried out within the confines of the official sanctums (Trotsky, 1969: 96).

That is, bureaucratic planning would inevitably lead to terrible mismatches, dislocations, inefficiencies, crises and eventual economic collapse. Democratic participation was an essential prerequisite and ongoing requirement for the harmonious development of a genuinely socialist economy and the all-round growth of productive output, as well as social emancipation. This imperative has enormous implications for law, being a central component of the need to de-legalise social life as far as possible and facilitate the withering away of the state. As we will see in Chapter 5, one of the early acts of the Soviet government was to abolish the old courts, staffed by professional judges and serviced by lawyers, and introduce People's Courts, with lay assessors and lay advocates.

The transition to communism

Likewise, the concept of the dictatorship of the proletariat, in the writings of Marx and Engels, has a distinctly democratic content. It means the temporary and emergency political rule of the working class, as the first stage in the transition to a classless, stateless society. This political rule must include the control by the associated producers – the working class which constitutes the overwhelming majority of society – of the productive forces they themselves have created. In other words, the dictatorship of the proletariat means from the outset the establishment of genuine democracy, with the majority of the population exercising economic power.

The term 'dictatorship of the proletariat' as used by Marx and Engels does not mean tyranny or absolutism or rule by a single individual, a minority or even a single party but political rule exercised by the majority of the population. This is clear from their analysis of the Paris Commune of 1871, which ruled Paris for a period of 72 days before being militarily crushed. In his 1891 introduction to the re-issue of Marx's analysis of the Commune in *The Civil War in France*, Engels explained that the Commune, which was the first attempt at establishing the dictatorship of the proletariat, began with the 'shattering of the former state power and its replacement by a new and truly democratic one'.[20]

In *The Civil War in France*, Marx underscored its democratic character. The Commune abolished the 'whole sham of state mysteries and state pretensions' and made public functions the activities of working people instead of 'the hidden attributes of a trained caste'. Its tendency of development, Marx emphasised, was 'a government of the people by the people'. Marx declared the Commune to be a harbinger for a future communist society.

> When the Paris Commune took the management of the revolution in its own hands; when plain ordinary working men for the first time dared to infringe upon the governmental privilege of their 'natural superiors', and, under circumstances of unexampled difficulty, performed their work modestly, conscientiously, and efficiently – performed it at salaries the highest of which barely amounted to one-fifth of what, according to high scientific authority, is the minimum required for a secretary to a certain metropolitan school board – the old world writhed in convulsions (Marx, 1948: 58).

Lenin and Trotsky, like Marx before them, warned that in the transition to communism – which could be protracted – it would be impossible for the workers' government to immediately achieve the egalitarian goal: 'from

20 Marx, 1948: 17.

each according to his ability, to each according to his need.' Initially, the new order would have to fall back on incentives such as wage payments to spur production, giving rise to inequality that would continue to be enforced by the state.

In the *Critique of the Gotha Program*, Marx distinguished between the two stages of socialism. In the first, it would be impossible, given the economic, intellectual and moral birthmarks of the old capitalist order from whose womb socialist society emerged, to go beyond the 'narrow horizon of bourgeois right' – by which he meant the formal legal equality that invariably masks social inequality. 'Law can never stand higher than the economic order and the cultural development of society conditioned by it,' Marx wrote.[21] That is, the law would inherently reflect the fact that society could not provide a plentiful and satisfying life for all. Only after individuals were no longer enslaved by others, labour had become a meaningful and enjoyable pursuit rather than a burden, and the productive forces had increased abundantly would the communist ideal be realised.

Central to this view, as first expounded by Marx and Engels in the *Communist Manifesto* and later by Lenin in *The State and Revolution*, was that the state and law must begin to fade away as soon as the dictatorship of the proletariat was established. That is, inherent in the seizure of political power and the establishment of a workers' state was the creation of a unique kind of government that would immediately begin to transfer society's administration into the hands of the population at large.

In the *Communist Manifesto*, Marx and Engels put it this way:

> When, in the course of evolution, the class differences have disappeared and all production has been concentrated in the hands of the associated individuals, the public power will lose its political character. Political power, properly so called, is merely the organised power of one class for oppressing another. If the proletariat during its contest with the bourgeoisie is compelled, by the force of circumstances, to organise itself as a class, if, by means of a revolution, it makes itself the ruling class, and, as such, sweeps away by force the old conditions of production, then it will, along with these conditions, have swept away the conditions for the existence of class antagonisms generally, and will thereby have abolished its own supremacy as a class. In the place of the old bourgeois society, with its classes and class antagonisms, we shall have an association, in which the free development of each is the condition for the free development of all (Marx and Engels, 1952: 78).

Thus, after the socialist revolution, the state becomes an anachronism,

21 Marx, 1970b: 10.

retained only for the purpose of suppressing the former propertied classes, and immediately begins to fade away, to be replaced by a free association.

In *Anti-Duhring*, Engels described an evolving withering-away process. 'The interference of the state power in social relations becomes superfluous in one sphere after another and then becomes dormant of itself.'[22] He elaborated on this point in a letter to August Bebel in 1875, insisting that the dictatorship of the proletariat would be a state, but at the same time not a state, or, at least, it would be a self-dissolving state. Engels criticised the German Social-Democratic Party for advocating the formation of a 'free people's state':

> It would be well to throw overboard all this chatter about the state, especially after the Commune, which was no longer a state in the proper sense of the word. The anarchists have too long thrown this 'people's state' into our teeth, although already in Marx's work against Proudhon, and then in the *Communist Manifesto*, it was definitely stated that, with the introduction of the socialist order of society, the state will dissolve of itself and disappear. As the state is only a transitional phenomenon which must be made use of in struggle, in the revolution, in order to forcibly crush our antagonists, it is pure absurdity to speak of a 'people's free state'. As long as the proletariat still *needs* the state, it needs it, not in the interests of freedom, but for the purpose of crushing its antagonists; and as soon as it becomes possible to speak of freedom, then the state, as such, ceases to exist. We would, therefore, suggest that everywhere the word 'state' be replaced by 'community' (*Gemeinwesen*), a fine old German word, which corresponds to the French word 'commune' [italics in original] (Marx and Engels, 1942: 336).

Engels returned to this theme in his 1891 Introduction to Marx's *The Civil War in France*, which described the formation and suppression of the Paris Commune. Engels contrasted the Commune to all previous revolutions, which had replaced one oppressive state by another.

> From the very outset, the Commune was compelled to recognise that the working class, once come to power, could not go on managing with the old state machine; that in order not to lose again its only just conquered supremacy, this working class must, on the one hand, do away with all the old repressive machinery previously used against itself, and, on the other, safeguard itself against its own deputies and officials, by declaring them all, without exception, subject to recall at any time (Engels, Preface to Marx, 1948: 16).

22 Engels, 1975: 301.

Apart from the right of recall, Engels reviewed three other measures taken by the Paris Commune to prevent 'careerism': (1) election to all posts, administrative, judicial and educational; (2) restriction of the wages of all officials, high and low, to those paid to workers; and (3) binding mandates for delegates to representative bodies.

Engels scorned the reverence for the state as a font of eternal justice, cultivated under capitalism, and advocated reducing the role of the state as quickly as possible after a socialist revolution.

> In reality, however, the state is nothing but a machine for the oppression of one class by another, and indeed in the democratic republic no less than in the monarchy; and at best an evil inherited by the proletariat after its victorious struggle for class supremacy, whose worst sides the victorious proletariat, just like the Commune, cannot avoid having to lop off at once as much as possible until such time as a generation reared in new, free social conditions is able to throw the entire lumber of the state on the scrap heap (Engels, Preface to Marx, 1948: 18).

In other words, the state was an 'evil' remnant of class society, which had to be dispensed with in order to pave the way for the achievement of communism itself. This was not a late and heretic opinion of Engels. Marx expressed the same idea in an 1875 letter to Bracke, criticising the draft Gotha Program of the German Social-Democratic Party. Law would continue to exist in the transition from socialism to communism and, in spite of its progressive character as compared to bourgeois law, it would still be 'infected with a bourgeois barrier'.[23]

As will be explored in the next chapter, Lenin based himself on these principles in *The State and Revolution*. He described the proletarian state as a 'semi-state', being the 'transitional form of its disappearance (the transition from the political state to no state)'. Law and even the state itself remained 'bourgeois' in that they were capitalist legacies that could not be abolished immediately amid residual inequality. The state had to be so constituted that it began to wither way immediately and could not but wither away. Its coercive power must be exercised only against the bourgeoisie, not the working people:

> During the transition from capitalism to communism, suppression is still necessary; but it is the suppression of the minority of exploiters by the majority of exploited. A special apparatus, special machinery for suppression, the 'state' is still necessary, but this is now a transitional state, no longer a state in the usual sense (Lenin, 1970: 168, 194, 220).

23 Marx, Letter to Bracke (5 May 1875), cited in Kelsen, 1955: 33.

Dialectical interrelationship between law and social structure

In some Western academic writings, Marx and Engels are presented as mechanical economic determinists. This falsifies their analysis. It is true that they were determinists, in the following sense. For them, the driving forces of all economic, political and social life are the contradictions in material and economic life. Essentially, these contradictions arise from the conflict between the social forces of production and the relations of production – the class and property relations of society – within which those productive forces have hitherto developed.

More specifically, the development of capitalist economic relations shaped the content and structure of law in many ways. The most fundamental relate to the core concepts of private property and contract. Both required an essential break with feudal relations, based on communal and feudal property, fixed status and personal allegiance. Capitalism, as an expansionary economic system, demanded the unfettered accumulation of capital based on the private ownership of the means of production.

Past societies had developed concepts of property. What was new with capitalism was the development of *exclusive* private property. This involved a sharp shift from the previous conception that land and the fruits of the earth were originally given to mankind in common. Writing in the second half of the seventeenth century, the British political theorist John Locke for the first time nominated 'property' as an inalienable right of man and sought to provide a justification for its accumulation.[24]

Previous societies, including the Roman Empire, had also known commodity exchange. With capitalism, however, this became the predominant form of economy. Labour power itself was transformed into a commodity to be bought and sold on the market. The idea of contract, the supposed free and equal exchange of commodities, rose to dominance.[25] The notion of contract became central to the extraction of surplus value via the purchase and consumption of labour power as a commodity. The process was cloaked ideologically in the doctrine of freely given offers and acceptances, creating mutual agreements.

Of course, historical traditions and peculiarities played a part in shaping the particular forms taken by the law in different countries, but the essential form and content of bourgeois law was similar everywhere.

In *Ludwig Feuerbach and the End of German Classical Philosophy*, written in 1886, Frederick Engels commented on the universal content of law in Britain, France and Germany, notwithstanding certain notable variations. Comparing the French Civil Code with English and Prussian law, he contrasted the

24 Locke, 1984: Bk II, chap 7.
25 See Atiyah, 1990.

gradualist and pragmatic groping of the English common law – which substantially attempted to mould old feudal forms, particularly in the field of real estate – with French legal theory, which was radically overhauled in the wake of the 1789 Revolution:

> If the state and public law are determined by economic relations, so, too, is private law, which indeed in essence only sanctions the existing economic relations between individuals which are normal in the given circumstances. The form in which this happens can, however, vary considerably. It is possible, as happened in England, in harmony with the whole national development, to retain in the main the forms of the old feudal laws while giving them a bourgeois content; in fact, directly reading a bourgeois meaning into the feudal name. But, also, as happened in Western continental Europe, Roman Law, the first world law of a commodity-producing society, with its unsurpassably fine elaboration of all the essential legal relations of simple commodity owners (of buyers and sellers, debtors and creditors, contracts, obligations, etc.), can be taken as the foundation (Engels, 1978: 54).

Engels observed that the law could be developed through judicial practice (common law) or codified, sometimes badly, as in the case of the Prussian *Landrecht*.

> However, after a great revolution it was also possible for such a classic law code of bourgeois society as the French Code Civil to be worked out on the basis of Roman Law. If, therefore, bourgeois legal rules merely express the economic life conditions of society in legal form, then they do so well or ill according to circumstances (Engels, 1978: 54).

In an 1884 letter to Karl Kautsky, Engels explained the recourse of the French and other European governments to Roman Law as the foundation for their legal codes.

> Roman law was the consummate law of *simple*, i.e. pre-capitalist, *commodity production*, which however included most of the relations of the capitalist period. Hence precisely what our city burghers *needed* at the time of their rise and did *not* find in the local law of custom [italics in original] (Engels, Letter to K. Kautsky, 26 June 1884, in Marx and Engels, 1942: 451–2).

Marx and Engels concluded that the ultimate driving forces of all economic, political and social life are the contradictions in material and economic life. This analysis, however, is far from passive, lifeless and mechanical. While the decisive factors shaping law are economic relations, the legal system remains one of the arenas within which the class struggle is fought out. As Engels pointed out in his 1890 letter to Conrad Schmidt, Marx's section on the working day in *Capital* shows that legislation can have a 'drastic effect' on social conditions and the class struggle.[26]

This conflict is not automatically reflected in legal doctrines but refracted through the need to elaborate legal principles that have the appearance of internal coherence and universality and to continually adjust those doctrines to meet changing economic circumstances. On law, as other social phenomena, Marx and Engels demonstrated the dialectical interaction between the economic base of society and the ideological superstructure.[27] In a letter to J. Bloch, Engels emphasised that the economic situation is the 'ultimately determining factor in history' but:

> [T]he various elements of the superstructure – political forms of the class struggle and its results, such as constitutions established by the victorious class after a successful battle, etc., juridical forms, and especially the reflections of all these real struggles in the brains of the participants, political, legal, philosophical theories, religious views and their further development into systems of dogmas – also exercise their influence upon the course of the historical struggles and in many cases determine their *form* in particular [italics in original] (Engels, Letter to J. Bloch, 21 September 1890, in Marx and Engels, 1942: 394–5).

This analysis was also dynamic in relation to the continual contradictions produced by the further development of the productive forces and new forms of property rights. Further contradictions arose constantly from the ideological role of law – from the need of any modern ruling class in the epoch of mass politics to present its political order as just and impartial. In his letter to Schmidt, Engels stated:

> In a modern state, law must not only correspond to the general economic condition and be its expression, but must also be an *internally coherent* expression which does not, owing to internal conflicts, contradict itself. And in order to achieve this, the faithful reflection of economic conditions suffers increasingly. All the more, so the more rarely it happens that a code of law is the blunt, unmitigated, unadulterated expression of the domination of a class – this in itself would offend the 'conception of right' (Engels, Letter to Conrad Schmidt, 27 October 1890, in Marx and Engels, above: 399–402).

26 Engels, Letter to Conrad Schmidt, 27 October 1890, in Marx and Engels, 1942: 402.

27 For a general presentation of Marx and Engels' writings on this dialectical relationship, see Cain and Hunt, 1979: chapter six, 'Law and Politics'.

In particular, Marx and Engels recognised the decisive role that could be played by control over the state apparatus, including the legal system, at critical junctures in history, most notably during revolutionary struggles. He concluded his letter to Schmidt by posing the question: 'Why do we fight for the political dictatorship of the proletariat if political power is economically impotent? Force (that is, state power) is also an economic power!'[28]

This active materialist conception provided the Russian Marxists with some understanding of the role that law could play in the transition to a future communist society. Soviet law could not rise higher than Soviet Russia's, initially primitive, economic development. At the same time, it could assist in clarifying the political and economic tasks at hand. Moreover, in a society that was conscious of law's ideological role, the transitional legal system could perform educational and normative functions.

Law and ideology

While Marx and Engels recognised that under capitalism, ideological factors could determine the form of legal development, the resulting process produced a mystification, by presenting economic interests as philosophical principles. In his 1890 letter to Schmidt, Engels wrote:

> Economic, political and other reflections are just like those in the human eye. They pass through a condensing lens and therefore appear upside down, standing on their heads. Only the nervous system, which would put them on their feet again for representation, is lacking . . . The reflection of economic relations as legal principles is necessarily also a topsy turvy one: it happens without the person who is acting being conscious of it; the jurist imagines that he is operating from *a priori* principles, whereas they are really only economic reflexes; so everything is upside down. And it seems to me obvious that this inversion, which, so long as it remains unrecognised, forms what we call ideological conception, reacts in its turn upon the economic basis and may, within certain limits, modify it (Engels, Letter to Conrad Schmidt, 27 October 1890, in Marx and Engels, 1942: 482).

Precisely because law was a distorted reflection of economic reality, the distortion could, to the extent that the deformation went unrecognised, impact on the underlying economic relations. This view has a number of implications. In the first place, the mystified distortion served to legitimise exploitation. By reproducing in legal form the commodification of all relations, law presented these relations in an 'inverted' way, camouflaging their real

28 Engels, Letter to Conrad Schmidt, 27 October 1890, in Marx and Engels, 1942: 402.

content. This was not simply a conspiracy or confidence trick perpetrated by the ruling class, aided by legal theorists and lawyers. Because law was shaped by the objective requirements of the capitalist mode of production, it was organically shrouded in a distorted view of social relations. Bourgeois legal theorists were themselves trapped in an ideological inversion, mistakenly regarding their ideas as the source of jurisprudential development.

While much of their work concentrated on tracing the impact of productive and class relations on political life, Marx and Engels recognised the influence of ideology in shaping the forms in which this impact made itself known. This was particularly evident in both their early and late writings. In one of their early works, *The German Ideology*, Marx and Engels stated:

> In direct contrast to German philosophy which descends from heaven to earth, here we ascend from earth to heaven. That is to say, we do not set out from what men say, imagine, conceive, nor from men as narrated, thought of, imagined, conceived, in order to arrive at men in the flesh. We set out from real, active men, and on the basis of their real life-process we demonstrate the development of the ideological reflexes and echoes of this life-process. The phantoms formed in the human brain are also, necessarily, sublimates of their material life-process, which is empirically verifiable and bound to material premises. Morality, religion, metaphysics, all the rest of ideology and their corresponding forms of consciousness, thus no longer retain the semblance of independence (Marx and Engels, 1976: 42).

Marx later traced the ultimate source of this distortion of reality to commodity fetishism, a concept that he fully developed in Chapter One of *Capital*, Volume 1.[29] At the heart of production and exchange under capitalism was a perverted appearance of social relations.

> It is a characteristic feature of labour which posits exchange-value that it causes the social relations of individuals to appear in the perverted form of a social relation between things. The labour of different persons is equated and treated as universal labour only by bringing one use-value into relation with another in the guise of exchange-value. Although it is correct to say that exchange-value is a relation between persons, it is however necessary to add that it is a relation hidden by a material veil . . . All the illusions of the monetary system arise from the failure to perceive that money, though a physical object with distinct properties, represents a social relation of production (Marx, 1977: 34–5).

29 Marx, 1970c: vol 1, 76–87.

(One contemporary writer who provided a useful, if somewhat pretentious, summation of the concept of commodity fetishism and its relation to law is Balbus:

> [T]he masking of the link between commodities and their human origins gives rise to the appearance, the ideological inversion, that commodities have living, human powers. Products appear to take on a life of their own, dominating the very human subjects who in fact bring them into existence but who no longer 'know' this. Commodity fetishism thus entails a profound reversal of the real causal relationship between humans and their products: humans, the subjects who create or cause the objects, become the object, i.e., are 'caused' by the very objects which they have created and to which they now attribute subjectivity or causal power (Balbus, 1977: 574–5).

According to Balbus, this process led to life being dominated by the passion to possess the power of the one commodity, money, that made possible the accumulation of all other commodities. Ultimately, 'money is transformed from a means of exchange into the very end or goal of human life itself'.[30] Likewise, legal fetishism, which parallels commodity fetishism, regards the legal form as independent or autonomous from the power or will of the human subjects who originally set law in motion.[31])

Engels elaborated on the role of ideological factors in several of the letters written in the final years of his life. In an 1893 letter to Franz Mehring, Engels sought to correct a 'mistake' that he and Marx may have made in focusing mainly on the basic economic facts while neglecting the ideological forms through which the economic factors were expressed.

> Ideology is a process accomplished by the so-called thinker consciously, indeed, but with a false consciousness. The real motives impelling him remain unknown to him; otherwise it would not be an ideological process at all. Hence, he imagines false or apparent motives. Because it is a process of thought, he derives both its form and its content from pure thought, either his own or that of his predecessors. He works with mere thought material which he accepts without examination as the product of thought; he does not investigate further for a more remote process independent of thought; indeed, its origin seems obvious to him, because, as all action is produced through the medium of thought, it also appears to him to be ultimately based upon thought (Engels, Letter to Mehring, 14 July 1893, in Marx and Engels, 1942).

30 Balbus, 1977: 574–5.
31 Ibid, 584.

These issues became frequent points of contention during the early Soviet debates. Broadly speaking, Pashukanis opposed those writers who depicted law as a mere ideological construct. He emphasised the inner connection between the legal form and commodity production. His initial protagonists expressed two tendencies. One, the 'social function' school, personified by Goikhbarg, saw law as a form of ideological deception that could be dispensed with under socialism. Others in the 'psychological' school, such as Reisner, stressed that, to be effective, law had to correspond to a public sense of justice. Later in the debates, figures such as Naumov decried both schools as evincing a disregard for 'Soviet legality'.

Law and 'human nature'

The proponents of the free market and capitalist ownership of the means of production argue that socialism is unnatural and therefore doomed to failure because it violates the inherent drive in every human being towards the exclusive ownership of property. Children, it is often argued, are either born with, or quickly acquire, a drive to gain their 'own' possessions. This conception is filled with unstated assumptions.

In the first chapter of *Capital*, in his analysis of commodity fetishism, Marx explained that one of the great difficulties in coming to an understanding of society is that it has already undergone a considerable development:

> Man's reflections on the forms of social life and consequently, also, his scientific analysis of those forms, take a course directly opposite to that of their actual historical development. He begins, post festum, with the results of the process of development ready to hand before him. The characters that stamp products as commodities, and whose establishment is a necessary preliminary to the circulation of commodities, have already acquired the stability of natural, self-understood forms of social life, before man seeks to decipher, not their historical character, for in his eyes they are immutable, but their meaning (Marx, 1970c: vol 1, 80).

In other words, analysis begins with categories and forms of thought already at hand, under conditions where the historical processes that gave rise to these forms is obscured from view. Hence these forms of thought are not understood as the product of historical processes, but seem to spring from the 'inner nature' of man himself. Marx was examining this deep methodological problem in relation to the mystery that surrounds commodities, in which the relations between people appear as relations between things, the products of labour. We will return to this fetishism of commodities later, in reviewing and assessing Pashukanis' theoretical accomplishments. But similar considerations arise with the supposedly natural and stable character of what is labelled 'human nature'.

What needs to be investigated is the manner in which social values and even human personality have been changed, shaped and forged over centuries through definite changes in the underlying socio-economic relations. One elementary example is the transformation that took place in the overturning of feudal society and its replacement by capitalism. Throughout the feudal period it was undoubtedly considered 'natural' that serfs occupied a subservient place in the social order, assigned to them for life by dint of their birth, with their labour predominantly allocated to the benefit of their lord. Far from being thought to have a natural desire to accumulate private property, they were regarded as being intrinsically bound to the land of the lord. And, in return, the lord owed them obligations that also flowed from his custodianship of the land.

In capitalist society, by contrast, the extraction of surplus labour does not take place through fixed status or political means, but economically. That is, while there were a myriad of laws in feudal society, which spelt out the obligations of the peasant, there are no such laws under capitalism. There is no statute that compels the worker to sell his or her labour power to the owner of capital. In the final analysis, he or she is forced to do so by the pressure of economic necessity. And that compulsion arises from the fact that, unlike the peasant or small producer in feudal society, who retains a relationship to the land, the worker in capitalist society has been separated from the ownership of the means of production.

Therefore, the crucial question to be examined in the transition from feudalism to capitalism is how this transformation took place. That is, how it was that a class of free wage labourers emerged – free both from feudal obligations and from the means of production – with nothing to sell but their labour power. History shows that this transformation did not result from some innate human nature, but was the outcome of new forms of social organisation based on the market. Those who maintain that the emergence of capitalism is the result of some inherent drive to own private property can never answer the question of why the transition to capitalism took place between the sixteenth and eighteenth centuries, rather than earlier. Capitalism could only emerge once society's technology and productive capacity – for example, steam power – had developed to the point where large-scale manufacturing could arise.

One of the most important battles in the development of capitalism was the establishment of *exclusive* property rights, above all in land, over the common property rights that had played such a central role in the lives of the peasantry under feudalism. Far from expressing some inherent human characteristic, manifesting itself in childhood, this new form of property had to establish itself against the conception that land should be held in common and its fruits available to all. John Locke, in particular, had to argue strenuously for the right to individual property, against the conception of common property and custodianship. Locke identified certain inalienable rights – the right to life, liberty and property. According to Locke, every man was the sole proprietor of his own person and capacities. His right to property derived from his right to enjoy the fruits of his own labour.

C.B. Macpherson has pointed out that the political concepts developed by Locke were intimately bound up with the rise of the free market and individual property rights. Locke provided the ideological basis for exclusive private property, so essential to the development of the new mode of production.

> [I]f the new kind of property required by the capitalist market society, i.e. property as exclusive, alienable rights to all kinds of material things including land and capital, was to be thought to be justified, the right would have to be based on something more universal than the old feudal or customary class differentials in supposed needs and capacities. The universal basis was found in 'labour'. Every man had a property in his own labour. And from the postulate that a man's labour was peculiarly, exclusively his own, all that was needed followed. The postulate reinforced the concept of property as exclusion. As his labour was his own, so was the land with which he had mixed his labour, and the capital that he had accumulated by means of applying his labour. This was the principle that Locke made central to the liberal concept of property (Macpherson, 1990: 129–30).

Later, Macpherson observed:

> Locke begins by accepting, as the dictate both of natural reason and of Scripture, that the earth and its fruits were originally given to mankind in common. This was of course the traditional view, found alike in Medieval and in seventeenth-century Puritan theory. But Locke accepts this position only to refute the conclusions previously drawn from it, which had made property something less than a natural individual right. 'But this [that the earth was given to mankind in common] being supposed,' Locke wrote, 'it seems to some a very great difficulty, how any one should ever come to have a *Property* in any thing . . . I shall endeavour to shew, how Men might come to have *property* in several parts of that which God gave to Mankind in common, and that without any express Compact of the Commoners' (Macpherson, 1962: 199–200).

In other words, men could rightfully assert individual property ownership without any specific social contract or agreement. Locke's concerns demonstrate that the forms of property, based on exclusion, which are considered as emanating from human nature today, were once regarded as so unnatural that they had to be argued for. One could go back further historically and examine earlier societies such as the Australian Aboriginal, where there was no conception of private ownership of land or any other means of production. Moreover, even in today's capitalist society, despite centuries of economic transformation and social conditioning, examples abound of ordinary people willingly acting for the benefit of others, or society as a whole, rather than for the acquisition of private wealth – from volunteering for community services to mentoring younger people.

In considering these issues of property and human nature, it is important to understand that socialism does not mean the abolition of personal property. Marx wrote in the *Communist Manifesto*, 'The distinguishing feature of Communism is not the abolition of property generally, but the abolition of bourgeois property.' By that, Marx meant the abolition of the private ownership of the means of production, not all individual private property. He stated, 'Capital is a collective product, and only by the united action of many members, nay, in the last resort, only by the united action of all members of society, can it be set in motion.'[32]

The theory that identifies freedom with private ownership is based on the claim that each individual has the natural right to the fruits of their own labour and that private property is the means through which this right is secured. But concentration of ownership and the separation of the mass of the population from the means of production with nothing to sell but their labour power to the owners of capital means that private property itself has long ago undergone a transformation. No longer is it a social mechanism through which individuals secure the fruits of their *own labour*, it is rather the mechanism through which capital secures the fruits of *other people's labour* in the form of profit.

Finally, it must be noted that the Marxist movement did not regard the development of a truly human nature as a spontaneous process that simply could take place unaided under the immense pressures of everyday life. The working masses had to build a political party that would consciously fight for their true interests, on the basis of a scientific understanding of the objective driving forces of human society. Flowing from Marx's theory of commodity fetishism, it was not possible for a worker, even if convinced that he or she was being exploited, to perceive the underlying socio-economic mechanism of that exploitation on the basis of his or her own bitter personal experience.

Moreover, the concept of exploitation was not easily understood, let alone derived directly from the instinctive sense of not being paid enough. Workers did not automatically understand that they were selling their labour power, or that the unique quality of that labour power was its capacity to produce sums of value greater than the prices (the wages) at which it had been purchased; and that profit was derived from this differential between the cost of labour power and the value that it created. It was not, and could not be apparent to

32 Marx and Engels, 1952.

workers, on the basis of sense perception and immediate experience, that any given commodity's value was the crystallised expression of the sum of human labour expended in its production.

Nor were working people in a position to grasp spontaneously, on the basis of immediate experience, capitalism's origins, internal contradictions and the historically limited character of its existence. The understanding of the exploitative relationship between capital and wage-labour, of the inevitability of class struggle and its revolutionary consequences, arose on the basis of intense theoretical work, summed up in *Capital.* The resulting knowledge, and the method of analysis involved in achieving and extending this knowledge, had to be introduced into the working class by a revolutionary party. Against the vulgar public opinion shaped through commodity fetishism, reinforced under the bombardment of the propaganda organs of the capitalist mass media, this socialist party would have to create a different, non-bourgeois form of public opinion, in which the real political and historical interests of the working class found expression.

This understanding, often falsely branded elitist, also informed the Marxist approach to law. Law's true role had to be analysed historically, and ordinary people had to be informed and educated as to its functions, freed from the mystifications that had arisen over centuries. An enlightened attitude to law, including the understanding that society and its members could harmoniously flourish without an apparatus of 'law enforcement', could only be developed with an historical materialist method. In turn, the explanation and application of a Marxist approach would contribute towards the emergence of a liberated human nature, used to living without constant policing.

Chapter 3

The Russian Marxists and law

> The socialist culture implies the utmost development of the human personality.[1]

In considering the legacy that Pashukanis had to work with, we cannot ignore the contributions made by the leading Russian Marxists. How did they seek to elaborate and apply the Marxist tenets on the state and law? To what extent did their efforts clarify or modify Marxist jurisprudence? To what degree did they shape or influence the context in which Pashukanis developed his *General Theory*? A starting point in answering these questions is to examine the views of the three foremost Russian Marxist theoreticians – George Plekhanov, Lenin and Trotsky. Each of their views had a substantial, but generally ignored or underestimated, impact on Pashukanis – albeit in quite different ways.

George Plekhanov's contribution

George Plekhanov is regarded as the father of Marxism in Russia, because he co-founded the first Russian Marxist group, Emancipation of Labour, in 1883. Throughout his five volumes of *Selected Philosophical Works* on Marxist philosophy and historical analysis can be found some important insights on the role of law. Plekhanov ended up opposing the October 1917 Revolution, in part because he held to a mechanical conception that Russia first had to proceed through a protracted capitalist stage. Nonetheless, his earlier writings contained much of value and were sometimes referred to during the early Soviet legal debates, notably by Pashukanis.[2]

Plekhanov elaborated the basic thesis that law cannot rise higher than the socio-economic order, whether it is feudal, capitalist or socialist. This remains

1 Trotsky, 1975: 9.
2 For example, Pashukanis, 1978: 54.

crucial for understanding the contradictions of Soviet Russia. He summed up the Marxist view as follows: 'In the opinion of the economic materialists, legal concepts develop, *not of themselves* but under the influence of the mutual relationships entered into by producers under the impact of economic necessity.'[3] Only one of two things was possible: 'either the legal institutions of a given country are in accord with its economic needs, or they are not in accord.'[4] Plekhanov pointed out that a legal system may lag behind technological and other rapid changes in production, but this gave rise to a striving to overcome the discrepancies.

Plekhanov explained that new stages in society's economic development must be translated into political and legal concepts, highlighting the deep interaction between the economy – the primary historical driving force – and the political and legal superstructure. Referring to different stages of economic development, Plekhanov stated:

> Mankind's advance from point A to point B, from point B to point C and so on, right up to point S, *never takes place on the plane of the economy alone . . . The road from one turning point to another always lies through the 'superstructure'* . . . What do a country's political institutions hinge on? We already know that they are an expression of economic relations. For that practical expression, however, these economically prompted institutions must first pass through the minds of people in the shape of certain concepts [italics in original] (Plekhanov, 1976, vol II: 202).

Interestingly, given Pashukanis' later focus on the legal form, Plekhanov distinguished between legal form and content, pointing out that it took centuries for law to emerge from religion as a separate form of social regulation:

> *At various stages of social development, any given ideology experiences in a highly unequal degree the influence of other ideologies.* Thus, in ancient Egypt and partly in Rome, law was subordinate to religion; in recent history, law has developed (in the *formal* aspect – we would underscore that and ask for due note to be taken) under the strong influence of philosophy [italics in original] (Plekhanov, 1976, vol II: 245).

Plekhanov emphasised the point made by Engels in his letters of 1890 and 1895, refuting the caricatured view of mechanical economic determinism attributed by some critics to Marx: 'Political development rests on the economic development but at the same time reacts on the economic base.'[5] In

3 Plekhanov, 1976, vol II: 186–7.
4 Ibid, vol II: 187.
5 Plekhanov, 1976, vol II: 460.

particular, Plekhanov noted an important passage in Marx's critique of Hegel's philosophy of law, in which Marx remarked upon the ideological and political need for any ruling class to gain legitimacy in the eyes of the rest of society:

> No class . . . can play this role without arousing a moment of enthusiasm in itself and in the masses, a moment in which its demands and rights are truly the rights and demands of society itself; a moment in which it is truly the social head and the social heart (Plekhanov, 1976, vol II: 461, quoting Marx and Engels, 1975b, vol III: 184).

Plekhanov, like Marx and Engels, noted that while law was fundamentally determined by economic factors, law and legal ideology could have a critical impact on social consciousness.

> The legal and political relations engendered by a given economic structure exert a decisive influence on social man's entire mentality. 'Upon the different forms of property, upon the social conditions of existence,' says Marx, 'rises an entire superstructure of distinct and peculiarly formed sentiments, illusions, modes of thought and views of life' (Plekhanov, 1976, vol III: 149, quoting from Marx and Engels, 1973, vol I: 421).

Plekhanov, following Marx and Engels, also emphasised that historical materialism provided a method of analysis, not a 'key to all riddles'. That is, Marxism provided a method of approach to the role of law in society, not a recipe for predicting every legal twist and turn under capitalism, nor for detailed law-making in the transition to socialism. This observation is helpful in assessing the later Soviet experience.

Lenin and law

A brief review of Lenin's positions on the state and law is essential to understanding the debates over early Soviet law and Pashukanis' contribution, as well as the subsequent degeneration under Stalin. Between 1917 and 1923, Lenin intervened continuously on issues large and small that impinged on legal policy and administration, often cutting across the niceties of the theoretical discourse. More generally, his views shaped the overall theoretical and practical terrain within which the debates occurred.

Lenin was undoubtedly the most important figure in the Russian Revolution. Arguably, Trotsky had a more profound impact by elaborating the international paradigm – the theory of permanent revolution – that clarified the necessity for a socialist revolution in Russia, as we shall see in Chapter 4. But Lenin provided the pivotal theoretical, political and practical leadership in the establishment and administration of the Soviet government. This was not simply a product of his formal position as chairman of the Council of People's Commissars. His protracted record since the 1890s, his leadership in forging the Bolshevik tendency from 1903, combined with his exacting attention to the strategic experiences of the international working class movement, gave him enormous political authority within the ruling party. While he strenuously opposed all forms of formal glorification and personal deference, he exercised critical intellectual authority, backed by widespread popular support.[6]

Lenin's pre-eminent role continued until his first stroke in May 1922, and resumed before his second stroke of December that year. That is not to say that Lenin's views prevailed automatically. They were invariably the topic of considerable discussion and subject to variations in implementation. The Bolshevik Party was far from the monolithic apparatus that it later became under Stalin, and Lenin often had to overcome deep differences and sharp resistance within the government.[7] But time and again, he would write an article, deliver a speech or give a lecture that would lead to definite policy shifts. On occasions, he would write or amend decrees or other declarations himself.

More fundamentally, Lenin's capacity to direct the trajectory of Soviet Russia was deeply limited by the underlying and often dire circumstances of the Russian Revolution (explored in Chapter 4) that were rooted in the primitiveness and isolation of the first socialist-inspired state. These problems particularly dominated the last part of his active political life, from January to March 1923, when he suffered a third stroke that virtually incapacitated him until he died in January 1924. During that period, in alliance with Trotsky, he fought to combat the Russian nationalism and bureaucratism that he saw imperilling the entire revolution.[8]

Interestingly, Lenin was a lawyer by training. In fact, he received a 'first' in the state law examination of 1891 and practised law for a year before devoting himself full-time to revolutionary politics.[9] Like Marx before him, he drew the conclusion that the ills of society could not be resolved through legal practice but only through a more systematic overturn of the existing legal order itself. But Lenin was certainly well acquainted with legal theory and practice and, as Stuchka later related, took a lively interest in legal matters at times.[10]

Much has been written, or speculated upon, regarding Lenin's alleged disdainful and manoeuvring positions on law and the state.[11] In particular, Lenin was supposedly duplicitous in arguing for the withering away of the

6 Trotsky, 1925.
7 See Chapter 5.
8 See generally Lewin, 1969: Carr, 1969.
9 Berman, 1963: 25.
10 Sharlett, Maggs and Beirne, 1988: 89.
11 For example, Kucherov, 1970: 3–13, 662–74; Lapenna, 1968: 42–9.

state and law under communism, while often energetically strengthening the state apparatus under Soviet rule. Some authors have suggested that Lenin's views on de-legalising society were fatally compromised by a letter he wrote to the Political Bureau in May 1922, in which he called for greater respect for law as an essential element of culture.[12]

These assertions are bound up with wider debates over Lenin's responsibility for the subsequent degeneration of the Soviet state into authoritarianism under Stalin. According to the widely held traditional and social democratic interpretation, Stalinism arose directly out of Leninism – Lenin's alleged ruthlessness, centralism and contempt for the rule of law led inexorably to Stalinist repression.[13] Importantly, in two detailed reviews of Lenin's writings on law and the state, Beirne and Hunt take a different view.[14] They argue that Lenin's diverse and fragmented views about the nature of legal relations in the period of socialist transition between capitalism and communism unintentionally created a theoretical vacuum that contributed to the intensification of authoritarian centralism during the late 1920s. Above all, they contend, Lenin failed to establish an institutional separation of powers or juridical or other means of maintaining limits on the powers exercised by Soviet authorities. They specifically suggest that in the field of crime and penal policy, Lenin combined both libertarianism and authoritarianism in a manner that opened the door for Stalinist abuse. Beirne and Hunt sum up their argument as follows:

> Our underlying thesis is that the origins of authoritarianism in general, and of authoritarian penal practices in particular, were intrinsic neither to the early Bolshevik project nor to Lenin's discourse as its major exponent. Rather, authoritarianism was the unintended consequence of the silences, omissions, and absences in Lenin's political theory and practice, including its libertarian tendencies. Specifically, it derived from the absence of any sustained theory of what we have designated as the constitution of Soviet society (Beirne, 1990: 100).

While there is some truth in Beirne and Hunt's thesis, it underestimates the extent to which the unfavourable material circumstances confronting the Soviet state, both internally and internationally, weighed down upon Lenin's programme. Beirne and Hunt's analysis also ignores the degree to which Stalinist authoritarianism heightened in reaction to the challenge of the Left Opposition, led by Trotsky, which fought for the continuation of the emancipatory theory and practice of Lenin against the emergent bureaucratic layers

12 ' "Dual" Subordination and Legality', in Lenin, 1964, vol 33: 363–7.
13 For example, Cohen, 1985: 38–70; Gouldner, 1977: 7–11.
14 Beirne and Hunt, 1990a and 1990b.

upon which Stalin rested. Their assessment makes no mention of Lenin's 1922 bloc with Trotsky, the existence of the Left and Joint Oppositions of 1923 and 1926, and the Stalinist response to these developments.

Before examining these issues, it is helpful to recall that Lenin's *Collected Works*,[15] setting out his political views, run to 55 volumes. It is best to make them the starting point of any objective examination of his positions on law and the state. Beirne and Hunt attempt to systematically review the content of Lenin's voluminous writings. Although they regard Lenin's views on the subject as often contradictory, they ascribe to his outlook a coherence that can be expressed in the form of five theses, which I have simplified as follows:

(1) Bourgeois law, albeit founded on unequal relations, provided a significant arena of struggle to secure concessions from the ruling classes.
(2) Law is a minor but useful educative vehicle in disseminating the socialist programme under the dictatorship of the proletariat.
(3) Under the dictatorship of the proletariat, 'socialist legality' – characterised by informality, flexibility and political content – can help realise the emancipatory capacity of the popular masses.
(4) For both the immediate and long-term achievement of the transition to communism, there must be a complete rupture with the political and legal institutions of capitalism, and their replacement by soviets and other forms of socialist democracy.
(5) Because communism abolishes the conditions that produce law and also greatly simplifies and extends participation to all citizens, communist society will be a non-legal social order.[16]

Beirne and Hunt argue that within this coherence lay a serious tension, produced by Lenin's repeated emphasis, most notably expressed in *The State and Revolution*, of the need for the disappearance of the state and law under communism. This tension, they contend, led to and was part of an inadequate constitutionalism in Lenin's view of law, which thereby lacked a distribution of powers, checks and supervisory mechanisms. By taking this view, they blame the central feature of Lenin's conception – the necessity for the withering away of the state – for the subsequent rise of a totalitarian state under Stalin.

While Lenin's views had an overriding coherence along the lines Beirne and Hunt suggest, their summation is questionable in three key respects. First, Lenin did not use the term 'socialist legality', which implies at least a semi-permanent role for law, as well as a specifically 'socialist' role for law. Instead, he referred to the need for 'greater revolutionary legality' during the

15 Lenin, 1964.
16 Beirne, 1990: 63.

NEP, in order to develop relations with the peasantry and to promote trade.[17] In general, Lenin regarded law as a residual, essentially bourgeois, instrument that a socialist state was obliged to use as long as it remained incapable of achieving the conditions for genuine communism. Second, Lenin emphasised in *The State and Revolution* that the state formed after a socialist revolution must begin to wither away immediately. To the extent that a coercive and distributive state apparatus continued to exist, it remained a 'bourgeois' state. Third, Lenin arrived at that position during the course of 1917, following the February Revolution and his April Theses, where he revised his strategic conception of the Russian Revolution. Until then, he conceived of the Russian Revolution as a radical bourgeois democratic revolution led by the working class, not as a socialist revolution.[18]

The single most consistent theme running through Lenin's relevant writings is that law and the state machinery are not neutral and necessary instruments of social regulation but historical products of class society. They are essentially mechanisms whereby the most powerful social class enforces its economic and political rule. From the moment of the revolutionary taking of power by the working class and other oppressed masses, leading to the eventual creation of a classless society, the need for law and an enforcing state apparatus begin to fade away.

In his early writings on law, Lenin focused on the class nature of the Tsarist legal order, pointing out, for example, how the majority of the government's legislation served the practical needs of the emerging capitalist class or the Tsarist state machinery itself.[19] He polemicised against police brutality,[20] denounced the penal servitude regulations and forced labour,[21] and demanded basic democratic reforms.[22]

These views, full of contempt for the authoritarian apparatus, reverberate in *The State and Revolution*, written during the months following the February 1917 Revolution that ended the Tsarist dictatorship. Lenin saw the factory and soldiers committees, the workers' militia and the soviets of workers, soldiers and peasants deputies thrown up by the revolution as the seeds of a future socialist society. This new social order would be 'no longer a state in the proper sense of the term, for . . . these contingents of armed men are the masses themselves, the entire people'. In the future, it would be possible to 'cast "bossing" aside and to confine the whole matter to the organisation of the proletarians (as the ruling class), which will

17 'Ninth All-Russia Congress of Soviets', in Lenin, 1964, vol 33: 176.
18 See Chapter 4.
19 'Objective Statistics', in Lenin, 1964, vol 4: 408–12.
20 'Beat – But Not to Death', in Lenin, ibid: 387–402.
21 'Penal Servitude Regulations and Penal Servitude Sentences', in Lenin, 1964, vol 5: 243–9, and 'Review of Home Affairs', vol 5: 251–301.
22 'The Drafting of 183 Students Into the Army', in Lenin, 1964, vol 4: 414–19.

hire "workers, foremen and bookkeepers" in the name of the whole of society'.[23]

After the October Revolution, Lenin continued to argue for the democratic superiority of the Soviet system. Responding to German Social Democrat Karl Kautsky's 1918 condemnation of the 'dictatorial' methods of the Soviet government, Lenin questioned Kautsky's claim that, by contrast, modern capitalist states provided 'democracy':

> Take the fundamental laws of modern states, take their administration, take freedom of assembly, freedom of the press, or 'equality of all citizens before the law,' and you will see at every turn evidence of the hypocrisy of bourgeois democracy with which every honest and class-conscious worker is familiar. There is not a single state, however democratic, which has no loopholes or reservations in its constitution guaranteeing the bourgeois the possibility of dispatching troops against the workers, of proclaiming martial law, and so forth, in case of a 'violation of public order,' and actually in case the exploited class 'violates' its position of slavery and tries to behave in a non-slavish manner (Tucker, 1975: 468).

Lenin returned to this issue in a lecture on 'The State' delivered to students at the Sverdlov Communist University in July 1919:

> One of the most democratic republics in the world is the United States of America, yet nowhere is the power of capital, the power of a handful of multi-millionaires over the whole of society, so crude and so openly corrupt as in America. Once capital exists, it dominates the whole of society, and no democratic republic, no franchise can change its nature ('The State', in Lenin, 1964, vol 29: 485–6).

In the same lecture, he reiterated the need for the role of the state and law to be demystified, given that the state was often presented as something divine and supernatural, and as impartial. Under class society, 'the state is a machine for maintaining the rule of one class over another'.[24] Socialism meant the abolition of classes, and only then could the state wither away:

> We reject all the old prejudices about the state meaning universal equality – for that is a fraud: as long as there is exploitation there cannot be equality. The landowner cannot be the equal of the worker, or the hungry man the equal of the full man . . . So far we have deprived the capitalists of this machine and have taken it over. We shall use this [state] machine,

23 Lenin, *The State and Revolution*, in Lenin, 1964, vol 33: 86–95.
24 'The State', in Lenin, 1964, vol 29: 478.

> or bludgeon, to destroy all exploitation. And when the possibility of exploitation no longer exists anywhere in the world, when there are no longer owners of land and owners of factories, and when there is no longer a situation in which some gorge while others starve, only when the possibility of this no longer exists shall we consign this machine to the scrap-heap. Then there will be no state and no exploitation ('The State', in Lenin, 1964, vol 29: 488).

This lecture has assumed added significance because of the interpretations placed upon it. Beirne and Hunt regard it as a statement by Lenin, albeit an aberrational one, that the Bolsheviks should use the old bourgeois state against the bourgeoisie.[25] But Lenin's consistent view, both before and after this lecture, was that the old state had been shattered and a new one created, albeit with bourgeois distortions, which would ultimately disappear.

Kelsen, a prominent scholar, and opponent, of Marxist legal theory, asserted that this lecture amounted to a first attempt to modify the doctrine of the withering away of the state. There was a 'hint' that Lenin had changed his opinion, by declaring that exploitation must disappear everywhere, and not just in one country, before 'we' – which could only mean the Soviet government, according to Kelsen – would consign this machine to oblivion. Kelsen argues that this abandons the conception of the state gradually and automatically withering away.[26] But, in the first place, Lenin's 'we' seems to refer to the Soviet people, not just the government or the party. Secondly, Lenin, following Marx and Engels, never portrayed the withering away of the state as a purely objective or spontaneous process. That is why they proposed definite measures, such as instant recall of elected representatives, to guard against the dangers of careerism and the usurpation of power. They did insist that the very nature of the proletarian state had to be such that it would ensure its own dissolution. But they recognised that this unprecedented task presented considerable political challenges.

Lenin and the withering away of the state

These conclusions can be supported by a further review of the evolution of Lenin's writings. In *The State and Revolution*, quoting extensively from Marx and Engels, Lenin insisted that a socialist revolution could not adapt the old state machinery of capitalist society to its needs but would have to abolish the existing legal and bureaucratic apparatus and create a unique new system. This regime would be required to overcome the resistance of the old ruling class, but it would be democratic for the majority of the

25 Beirne, 1990: 91, fn 5.
26 Kelsen, 1955: 54–5.

population and it would be transitional, leading to the emergence of a classless society.

Beirne and Hunt postulate the existence in Lenin's texts of three distinct forms of the dictatorship of the proletariat. The first was the exceptional, quasi-military form required for the immediate seizure and defence of state power. The second was based on the need to completely abolish (smash) and replace the previous state machinery. The third was to actively promote and popularise the social relations and institutions needed for the transition to communism.[27] With this categorisation, they suggest a tension or contradiction between the first two, 'negative' strands in Lenin's conception and the third, more long-term form.

Yet, Lenin emphasised that even under the temporary dictatorship of the proletariat, the state would immediately *begin* to die away and would *ultimately* 'wither away' altogether when communism was really achieved, that is, when the productive forces of man had developed and been rationally planned to the point where, for all practical purposes, scarcity and inequality were eliminated and along with it, the struggle for individual existence.

'According to Marx, what the proletariat needs is only a state in process of withering away, i.e., so constituted that it will *at once* begin to wither away and cannot help wither away.' Further on he added: 'The proletarian state will begin to wither away *immediately* after its victory, since in a society without class contradictions, the state is unnecessary and impossible.'[28] [My emphasis.]

Lenin did not expect an isolated revolution in backward Russia, followed by a prolonged capitalist encirclement. Nevertheless, even in the most favourable circumstances, he did not expect the process of withering away to be automatic. Drawing from Marx's writings on the Paris Commune, he advocated the introduction of definite protections against the misuse of official power: political representatives would be paid no more than the average workers' wage; they would be subject to instant recall by their electors; and representatives would be obliged to participate in administrative work.[29]

Only with the advent of true communism, would the root causes of social antagonisms – private and conflicting ownership of the productive forces, the division of the globe into nation-states and the inherent social inequality produced by the capitalist market – be overcome. By then, the great majority of working people would be accustomed to administering their own affairs and those of society without the need for legal and physical coercion. This would eventually dispense with the need for a state – that is, a separate body of politicians, bureaucrats, judges and armed personnel.

27 Beirne, 1990: 62.
28 Lenin, 1970: 37, 43.
29 Ibid: 62–3.

Lenin drew a further remarkable conclusion from Marx's analysis – that not only law, but the workers' state itself would be 'bourgeois' in the period of transition to communism.

> As regards the distribution of products of consumption, bourgeois law, of course, inevitably presupposes the *bourgeois* state as well, because law is nothing without a mechanism capable of *compelling* the observance of legal norms. It follows that under communism not only does bourgeois law remain for a certain time but so does the bourgeois state, without the bourgeoisie! [emphasis in original] (Lenin, 1970: 138).

This passage generated intense debate among Soviet legal theorists and caused difficulty for the emerging Stalinist bureaucracy in justifying the ever-greater gathering of power in the hands of the state apparatus. Lenin's analysis of the state remaining bourgeois, at least as regards the unequal distribution of production, provides a key to understanding the rise of privileged layers under Stalin, presiding over gross inequality. It points to the inherent danger that the state apparatus, as well as the law it enforces, will be used by a new elite against the interests of the broad masses of people.

Lenin insisted that this danger had to be consciously combated. In 1919, he wrote in his *Theses on Bourgeois Democracy and the Dictatorship of the Proletariat*, which was presented to the founding conference of the Communist International:

> Only the soviet organisation of the state can really effect the immediate breakup and total destruction of the old, i.e., bourgeois, bureaucratic and judicial machinery, which has been, and has inevitably had to be, retained under capitalism even in the most democratic republics, and which is, in actual fact, the greatest obstacle to the practical implementation of democracy for the workers and the working people generally. The Paris Commune took the first epoch-making step along this path. The soviet system has taken the second. Destruction of state power is the aim set by all socialists, including Marx above all. Genuine democracy, i.e., liberty and equality, is unrealisable unless this aim is achieved. But its practical achievement is possible only through soviet, or proletarian democracy, for by enlisting the mass organisations of the working people in constant and unfailing participation in the administration of the state, it immediately begins to prepare the complete withering away of any state (Pathfinder, 1987: 157–8).

Lenin, the NEP and 'socialist law'

A critic of the Soviet system, Schlesinger, cited a 1922 letter sent by Lenin to Justice Commissar Kursky as evidence that Lenin viewed Soviet law as socialist in character, and not as a bourgeois remnant. Schlesinger asserted that Lenin's view contrasted with the early theorising of Pashukanis and Stuchka about the capitalist nature of law. The letter in question was written in the discussions preceding the enactment of the Civil Code, giving effect to the New Economic Policy. The passage from Lenin's letter to Kursky quoted by Schlesinger is as follows:

> We do not recognise any 'private' thing, with us, in the field of economics, there is only public, and no private law. The only capitalism we allow is that of the State . . . For this reason, we have to widen the sphere of state interference with 'private' legal relations, and to enlarge the right of the State to abolish 'private' agreements. Not the *corpus juri Romani*, but our revolutionary consciousness of Justice ought to be applied to 'Civil Law relations' (Schlesinger, 1951: 150).

It is difficult to justify the conclusions that Schlesinger drew from this extract. In the first place, it is clear that the letter was written in the context of being forced to make legal concessions for the purposes of the NEP. The letter is entitled 'On the Tasks of the People's Commissariat of Justice Under the New Economic Policy'. Secondly, Schlesinger omitted to quote the preceding sentences, where Lenin emphasised the need to curtail the return to bourgeois law as much as possible, given the necessities of the NEP:

> The new civil legislation is being drafted . . . [T]he task [of the People's Commissariat of Justice] is to create a new civil law, and not to adopt (rather, not to allow itself to be duped by the old and stupid bourgeois lawyers who adopt) the old bourgeois concept of civil law (Beirne, 1990: 78).

Thirdly, Schlesinger did not refer to the previously cited passage from *The State and Revolution*, where Lenin warned that not only law, but also the state, would remain 'bourgeois' in the transition to communism. (Schlesinger dismissed the relevant sections of *The State and Revolution* as 'vague sayings of Lenin'.[30]) Given Lenin's record of rigorous attention to all matters theoretical and doctrinal, it is likely that if he were seriously reappraising or abandoning in 1922 the analysis he made in 1917, his reconsideration would be explicit.

Rather, Lenin's letter indicates his desire to limit as far as possible the concessions made to bourgeois law under the NEP. It underscores his concern about the political and economic pressures produced by the operation of capitalist law under the NEP. While it was necessary to restore 'private legal

30 Schlesinger, 1951: 150.

relations' in order to sustain the NEP, in drafting the Civil Code the government had to retain the maximum scope for socialist principles and state ownership. Lenin was not saying that bourgeois law would cease to exist, but that its domain should be constrained. While Lenin referred scornfully to Roman law, the final draft of the Civil Code did in fact borrow from Roman law – but reserved the power of courts to overrule private property rights to prevent injustice or harm to the Soviet economy.[31]

In another letter to Kursky during the same period of discussion, Lenin reiterated the need to 'move farther in intensifying state interference in "private legal relations" in civil affairs'. Lenin emphasised the importance of not showing 'a lack of spirit' on the eve of the Genoa conference, where a Soviet delegation was about to meet the representatives of 29 countries to discuss economic cooperation.[32] This latter consideration demonstrates Lenin's recognition of the intense international economic pressure on the Soviet state and the need for Soviet economic regulation to play a part in combating that pressure. Again, Lenin did not see 'law' as an independent entity but as an aspect of economic and social policy, both domestic and international.

Lenin and the political role of law

Lenin often saw laws and decrees as instruments of social policy and political communication, whose importance and role varied according to the stage of development. In 1922 at the Eleventh Party Congress, he said:

> Passing laws, passing better decrees, etc., is not now the main object of our attention. There was a time when the passing of decrees was a form of propaganda. People used to laugh at us and say that the Bolsheviks do not realise that their decrees are not being carried out; the entire white guard press was full of jeers on that score. But at that period this passing of decrees was quite justified. We Bolsheviks had just taken power, and we said to the peasant, to the worker: 'Here is a decree; this is how we would like to have the state administered. Try it!' From the very outset we gave the ordinary workers and peasants an idea of our policy in the form of decrees. The result was the enormous confidence we enjoyed and now enjoy among the masses of the people (Lenin, 1964, vol 33: 94).

At times, Lenin intervened forcefully into the legal system, using his position as Chairman of the People's Commissars to propose specific changes to legislation. One constant theme was that harsh and exemplary measures

31 See Chapter 5.
32 Lenin, 1964, vol 33: 203–4.

should be taken against state and party officials who abused their positions. In May 1918, he instructed Kursky, the Justice Commissar, to draft a bill imposing a minimum sentence of 10 years' imprisonment for bribery, an offence that went to the heart of protecting the young Soviet state from corruption:

> It is essential *immediately*, with demonstrative speed, to introduce a Bill stating that the penalty for bribery (extortion, graft, acting as an agent for bribery, *and the like*) shall be *not less than* ten years' imprisonment and, in addition, ten years of compulsory labour [emphasis in original] (Lenin, 1964, vol 35: 331).

Lenin wrote the letter after the Moscow Revolutionary Council passed a sentence of only six months' imprisonment on four members of the Moscow Commission of Investigation convicted of bribery and blackmail. Lenin also proposed to the party Central Committee that the tribunal members who passed the lenient sentence be expelled from the party. Acting on Lenin's letter, the Council of People's Commissars adopted a decision obliging the Commissariat of Justice 'immediately' to draft a Bill stipulating a 'heavy minimum sentence for bribery and any connivance in bribery'. The Bill was discussed by the Council of People's Commissars four days later and amended by Lenin before coming into effect.[33]

Beirne and Hunt catalogue similar instances in which Lenin condemned and called for action against what they term 'red-collar crimes'.[34] Notably, in 1922 he demanded that differential penalties be imposed on party members. 'Triple penalties should be inflicted on Communists, as compared with non-Party people,' he insisted.[35]

Lenin's regard for legality in this context was bound up with a strict sense of correctness and equality. This is illustrated by an indignant letter he wrote in May 1917 rebuking V.D. Bonch-Bruyevich, office manager of the Council of People's Commissars, for unlawfully increasing Lenin's salary:

> In view of your failure to fulfil my insistent request to point out to me the justification for raising my salary as from March 1, 1918, from 500 to 800 rubles a month, and in view of the obvious illegality of this increase, carried out by you arbitrarily by agreement with the secretary of the Council, Nikolai Petrovich Gorbunov, and in direct infringement of the decree of the Council of People's Commissars of November 23, 1917, I give you a severe reprimand (Lenin, 1964, vol 35: 333).

33 Lenin, 1964, vol 35: 604 (fn).

34 Beirne, 1990: 109–11.

35 'On the Tasks of the People's Commissariat of Justice under the New Economic Policy', in Lenin, 1964, vol 36: 562.

Lenin's objection was not a purely personal one. The November 1917 decree had set a maximum monthly salary for Commissars at 500 rubles, with an allowance of 100 rubles for each member of the family unable to work.[36] This was in line with the proposition, derived from Marx's writings on the Paris Commune, that socialist leaders should not be paid more than the average wage. Lenin had emphasised the importance of this principle, as a safeguard against careerism, in *The State and Revolution*.

Lenin consistently argued that Marxists must operate with a definite ethical and moral compass, centring on the active and informed involvement of ordinary people in shaping a society free of economic exploitation. He strenuously denied the allegation, levelled by critics of the revolution, that communism was amoral. In a 1920 address to the Russian Young Communist League congress, he stated:

> The old society was based on the principle: Rob or be robbed, work for others or make others work for you, be a slave owner or a slave. Naturally, people brought up in such a society imbibe with their mother's milk, so to speak, the psychology, the habit, the concept: You are either a slave owner or a slave, or else a small owner, a small employee, a small official, an intellectual – in short, a man who thinks only of himself, and doesn't care a hang for anybody else . . . [Communist] Morality serves to help human society rise to a higher level and get rid of the exploitation of labour (Selsam and Martel, 1963: 273–4).

Another occasion on which Lenin intervened directly into legal affairs illustrates a further important aspect of his political approach to law. Under the NEP, Lenin wrote a May 1922 letter 'On Dual Subordination and Legality' to the Political Bureau, opposing 'dual' subordination of the proposed new central procuracy (a legal and judicial supervisory body) to local authorities as well as the People's Commissariat of Justice. Lenin criticised a recommendation by a commission of the All-Russian Central Executive Committee that local procurators be subordinate to regional executive committees. 'The law must be uniform and the basic evil in our life and in our lack of culture is our toleration of the primordial Russian view and the habit of semi-savages to the effect that legality in Kaluga may be different from legality in Kazan,' he wrote. Lenin emphasised that the procuracy's duties were purely supervisory. 'The procurator has both the right and the duty to do just one thing: to pursue a truly uniform understanding of legality throughout the republic, irrespective of any local differences and contrary to any local influences.'[37]

36 Lenin, 1964, vol 35: 605 (fn).
37 Lenin, 1964, vol 33: 364–5.

In elaborating his argument further, Lenin provided an insight into how the Soviet government conceived of the role of the people's courts in balancing between strict enforcement of national laws and local circumstances. His approach confirms that his concern for legal uniformity was modulated by a sensitivity to local conditions. Whereas the procuracy was obliged to pursue uniform legal standards, the people's courts, elected by local soviets, could take into account local sentiment:

> The only right and duty of the procurator is to take the matter before the court. What sort of court? Our courts are local courts. Our judges are elected by the local Soviets. Hence, the authority to which a procurator submits a case of infringement of the law is a local authority which, on the one hand, must strictly abide by the laws uniformly established for the whole Federation and, on the other hand, in determining the penalty, must take all local circumstances into consideration. And it has the right to say that although there has been a definite infringement of the law in a given case, nevertheless, certain circumstances, with which local people are closely familiar, and which come to light in the local court, compel the court to mitigate the penalty to which the culprit is liable, or even acquit him. Unless we strictly adhere to this most elementary condition for maintaining the uniformity of the law for the whole Federation, it will be utterly impossible to protect the law, or to develop any kind of culture (Lenin, 1964, vol 33: 364–5).

Lenin's references to developing culture are an important indicator of his motives. He regarded law as an instrument in elevating social and cultural consciousness. He was seeking to overcome centuries of backwardness imposed by Tsarism – hence his scorn for the 'primordial Russian view'. In a statement sometimes taken as a repudiation of the Marxist outlook on law, Lenin continued: 'There can be no doubt that we live in a sea of lawlessness and that local influences are one of the greatest, if not the greatest, enemy of the establishment of legality and culture.'[38] In associating legality with culture, however, Lenin was not ascribing an ahistorical permanence to legality. He was pointing to its function in the struggle against local prejudice, privilege and bureaucratism. He referred to the need to overcome 'local and personal influences' and 'the interests and prejudices of local bureaucrats and local influences'.[39]

In summary, Lenin's concern for legality in the transition to communism flowed from several considerations: ensuring equal treatment of all citizens, and informing and educating the public on the principles of the Soviet order,

38 Zile, 1970: 70.
39 Lenin, 1964, vol 33: 366–7.

as well as strengthening the authority and efficiency of the state machinery. His views were later distorted by the Stalinist regime to proclaim the necessity of 'socialist legality' as a permanent institution, justifying the establishment of a draconian and repressive state.

Lenin and bureaucratism

In the final period of Lenin's active life he was increasingly preoccupied with fighting bureaucratism, which he sometimes labelled 'red tape', and making the Soviet administration more accessible to ordinary people.[40] In September 1921, after receiving a complaint from Professor Graftio, a hydro-electricity project chief engineer, about bureaucratic attitudes towards the project, Lenin wrote to Kursky instructing the Justice Commissariat to take more public and energetic measures to combat 'red tape': 'This red tape is just what is to be expected, especially in the Moscow and central institutions. But all the more attention should be given to fighting it.'[41]

This letter is instructive in several respects. It displays Lenin's keen awareness of the problem of bureaucratism – 'just what is be expected' – and his determination to stamp it out. His realism stands in contrast to the later rosy pictures painted of the Soviet state machinery under Stalin. The letter demonstrates Lenin's highly political approach to the use of legal measures, rejecting a formalist stance of separating the justice system from political considerations. It also shows Lenin's recognition of the limitations of law enforcement and the need to combine punitive measures with remedial programmes, including a plain language circular alerting the general public to the problem and the government's attitude.

Four months later, in January 1922, Lenin again wrote to Kursky, expressing his dissatisfaction with the latter's response. Kursky had written to Lenin stating that the campaign against 'red tape' was slow-moving and difficult because 'red tape is the result of the activity of persons, and not an objective consequence of the insufficiently smooth working of our apparatus'. A second communication from the Justice Commissariat had, Lenin complained, 'set forth platitudes about bureaucracy, complexity of apparatus, etc., etc.' Lenin rejected this approach, insisting that the source of the problems lay in 'organisational defects' for which 'responsible persons' were to blame. He urged Kursky to re-examine the question and organise a war-like campaign. Lenin called for an exhaustive reply to the tasks he had set earlier and instructed Kursky to send monthly reports on the course of the campaign.[42]

40 For another summation of Lenin's interventions against bureaucratism, see Beirne, 1990: 80–3.
41 Lenin, 1964, vol 35: 521–2.
42 Lenin, 1964, vol 35: 533–4.

Lenin clearly intended to monitor this campaign closely but was incapacitated by a stroke within weeks of this letter.

As soon as Lenin recovered partially, he wrote his last article, 'Better Fewer, But Better,' published in February 1923, roundly criticising the Soviet state apparatus as 'deplorable' and 'wretched'.[43] It was written as a campaign, including the drastic revamping of the Workers and Peasants Inspection (WPI), established at Lenin's insistence in 1919 to combat Soviet and Party bureaucracy. 'We have bureaucrats in our Party offices as well as in Soviet offices,' Lenin emphasised.[44] His remarks were intended as an unmistakable criticism of Stalin, who was responsible for the activities brought under the scrutiny of the Inspection.

Beirne and Hunt, however, accuse Lenin of pursuing a 'myopic strategy' of seeking to remedy the deficiencies of the existing institutions by creating new ones. These mechanisms, including the WPI, became bureaucratised and further ossified the whole system. 'His strategy was therefore doomed,' the authors conclude.[45] This criticism is not easily reconciled with their underlying contention that Lenin's chief fault was a failure to establish an institutional separation of powers or juridical or other means of maintaining limits on the powers exercised by Soviet authorities. The WPI was an attempt to create such a mechanism. To understand its failure to halt the emergent Stalinist layer it is necessary to focus on the extraordinarily unfavourable circumstances confronting Soviet Russia by late 1923, especially after the defeat of the German revolution of October 1923, as well as on the ferocious campaign launched by Stalin's faction against the newly-formed Left Opposition. These circumstances are explored in the next chapter.

Leon Trotsky's observations

No discussion of the Marxist conception of law and Pashukanis' contribution can be complete without considering the writings of Trotsky, one of the foremost leaders of the October 1917 Revolution and of the fight against Stalin's bureaucratisation of Soviet society. The impact of Trotsky and the Left Opposition on the early Soviet legal debates is examined in Chapter 10 but Trotsky's views are also significant in elucidating the classical Marxist view of the state and law.

Like other central figures in the Marxist movement, Trotsky did not attempt to present a systematic analysis of the role of law in society. Moreover, unlike Marx and Lenin, Trotsky had no formal training in law. His most complete exposition of the relationship between law and the state was written

43 Tucker, 1975: 734.
44 Lenin, 1964, vol 33: 494.
45 Beirne, 1990: 83.

as part of his analysis of the degeneration of the Soviet Union, in *The Revolution Betrayed.* Chapter 3 of that work, entitled 'Socialism and the State', contrasts the evolution of the Soviet state into an ever more totalitarian regime under Stalin with the classical Marxist conception of the withering away of the state.

While basing himself on the writings of Marx, Engels and Lenin on law and the state (quoting several of the passages cited in Chapter 2) Trotsky developed their conceptions by examining them in the context of both the acute contradictions of the Russian Revolution and the increasingly integrated character of world economic life. Trotsky first set out to explain the unavoidable necessity for a socialist revolution to pass through a transitional regime in 'the lowest stage of communism' before the material and political conditions arose for genuine communism:

> The material premise of communism should be so high a development of the productive forces that productive labor, having ceased to be a burden, will not require any goad, and the distribution of life's goods, existing in continual abundance, will not demand – as it does not now in any well-off family or 'decent' boardinghouse – any control except that of education, habit and social opinion (Trotsky, 1937: 39–40. See also Trotsky, 1975: 51–68).

In doing so, Trotsky pointed to the tension at the heart of early Soviet Russia.

> Capitalism prepared the conditions and forces for a social revolution: technique, science and the proletariat. The communist structure cannot, however, immediately replace the bourgeois society. The material and cultural inheritance from the past is wholly inadequate for that. In its first steps the workers' state cannot yet permit everyone to work 'according to his abilities' – that is, as much as he can and wishes to – nor can it reward everyone 'according to his needs,' regardless of the work he does. In order to increase the productive forces, it is necessary to resort to the customary norms of wage payment – that is, to the distribution of life's goods in proportion to the quantity and quality of individual labor (Trotsky, 1937: 46).

This would be the case, Trotsky argued, even in an American socialist state, based on the most advanced capitalism. Even under those favourable circumstances, it would not be possible to immediately provide everyone with as much as he needed, and therefore everyone would initially have to be spurred or encouraged to produce as much as possible. Moreover, Trotsky noted that Marx had expected the social revolution to commence in the most economically advanced capitalist countries, such as Germany and Britain. Instead, Russia, one of the least developed countries, had been thrust into the lead. By itself, Russia could not even reach socialism, that is, 'the lowest stage of communism', because it was still trying to catch up with the capitalist powers. From this, Trotsky drew the conclusion that Soviet Russia could not be classified as a socialist regime, 'but a preparatory regime transitional from capitalism to socialism':

> If Marx called that society which was to be formed upon the basis of a socialisation of the productive forces of the most advanced capitalism of its epoch, the lowest stage of communism, then this designation obviously does not apply to the Soviet Union, which is still today considerably poorer in technique, culture and the good things of life than the capitalist countries (Trotsky, 1937: 47).

Trotsky insisted that an essential task of the transitional proletarian dictatorship was to prepare for its own dissolution. Success in this 'fundamental mission' was bound up with overcoming both class distinctions and material contradictions.[46] In *Anti-Duhring*, Engels had written that in order for the state to fade away, 'class domination and the struggle for individual existence' must disappear. But these two preconditions would not necessarily be achieved simultaneously. As the Russian experience demonstrated, the socialisation of the means of production did not automatically remove the struggle for individual existence. In order to stimulate production, the state had been obliged to resort to the methods of labour payment worked out by capitalism. Hence the relevance of Marx's warning that 'bourgeois law' was inevitable in the first socialist phase, and Lenin's added warning that even a bourgeois state would persist, albeit without a bourgeoisie.

> We have thus taken the first step toward understanding the fundamental contradiction between Bolshevik program and Soviet reality. If the state does not die away, but grows more and more despotic, if the plenipotentiaries of the working class become bureaucratised, and the bureaucracy rises above the new society, this is not for some secondary reason like the psychological relics of the past, etc. but is a result of the iron necessity to give birth to and support a privileged minority so long as it is impossible to guarantee genuine equality (Trotsky, 1937: 55).

Trotsky conceded that the first attempts to create a state cleansed of bureaucratism had suffered from the 'unfamiliarity of the masses with self-government' and 'the lack of qualified workers devoted to socialism'. At the same time, he pointed to more profound difficulties that soon emerged, arising out of the unfavourable global situation.

46 Trotsky, 1937: 52.

> That reduction of the state to functions of 'accounting and control,' with a continual narrowing of the function of compulsion, demanded by the party program, assumed at least a relative condition of general contentment. Just this necessary condition was lacking. No help came from the West. The power of the democratic Soviets proved cramping, even unendurable, when the task of the day was to accommodate those privileged groups whose existence was necessary for defence, for industry, for technique and science. In this decidedly not 'socialistic' operation, taking from ten and giving to one, there crystallised out and developed a powerful caste of specialists in distribution (Trotsky, 1937: 59).

This clearly had immense implications for the legal system, whose function became, in large measure, the enforcement of social disparities. Trotsky related that the Left Opposition had warned in the early 1930s against accepting the predictions of the Soviet bureaucracy that within five years, 'the last relics of capitalist elements in our economy will be liquidated'.

> You must not limit yourself to the socio-juridical form of relations which are unripe, contradictory, in agriculture still very unstable, abstracting from the fundamental criterion: level of the productive forces. Juridical forms themselves have an essentially different social content in dependence upon the height of the technical level. 'Law can never be higher than the economic structure and the cultural level conditioned by it' (Marx) (Trotsky, 1937: 60–1).

This passage encapsulates Trotsky's adherence to the Marxist analysis of law as conditioned and shaped by the level of economic development. In the course of seeking to apply this analysis to the degeneration and betrayal of the Russian Revolution, he arguably enhanced the analysis. He suggested that legal forms themselves, while retaining their formal outer appearance, would have varying social content, depending on the economic, technical and cultural level of society.

In earlier writings, Trotsky consistently defended the October 1917 Revolution and the initial actions of the Bolsheviks, including the seizure of power, the dissolution of the Constituent Assembly, the banning of parties that took up arms against the revolution and other measures taken during the civil war of 1919–21. In *Terrorism and Communism – A reply to Karl Kautsky*, Trotsky responded to Kautsky, previously a major figure in the Marxist movement, who accused the Bolsheviks of proceeding undemocratically.[47] Members of the Austro-Marxism school, who, in some instances, claimed to be Marxist legal theorists, joined Kautsky's denunciation of the revolution. They included

47 Kautsky, 1920.

Karl Renner, Otto Bauer, Max Adler, Rudolf Hilferding and Friedrich Adler.[48]

Trotsky insisted that the Soviet revolution was far more democratic than the parliamentary apparatus defended by Kautsky. He pointed to the innate fraud of capitalist democracy, which leaves the economic power and control over the state apparatus in the grip of a ruling elite. Trotsky argued that this reality gave the working masses no other way but revolution to take charge of society:

> Violent revolution has become a necessity precisely because the imminent requirements of history are helpless to find a road through the apparatus of parliamentary democracy. The capitalist bourgeois calculates: 'while I have in my hands lands, factories, workshops, banks; while I possess newspapers, universities, schools; while – and this is most important of all – I retain control of the army: the apparatus of democracy, however you reconstruct it, will remain obedient to my will . . .' To this the revolutionary proletarian replies: 'Consequently, the first condition of salvation is to tear the weapons of domination out of the hands of the bourgeoisie. It is hopeless to think of a peaceful arrival to power while the bourgeoisie retains in its hands all the apparatus of power. Three times hopeless is the idea of coming to power by the path which the bourgeoisie indicates and, at the same time, barricades – the path of parliamentary democracy. There is only one way: to seize power, taking away from the bourgeoisie the material apparatus of government. Independently of the superficial balance of forces in parliament, I shall take over for social administration the chief forces and resources of production (Trotsky, 1975: 58).

Trotsky examined democracy from a theoretical and historical standpoint. He pointed to the degeneration of the democratic conception in the hands of the capitalist class and its jurisprudential theorists.

> As a battle cry against feudalism, the demand for democracy had a progressive character. As time went on, however, the metaphysics of natural law (the theory of formal democracy) began to show its reactionary side – the establishment of an ideal standard to control the real demands of the labouring masses and the revolutionary parties . . . Natural law, which developed into the theory of democracy, said to the worker: 'all men are equal before the law, independently of their origin, their property, and their position; every man has an equal right in determining the fate of the people.' This ideal criterion revolutionised the consciousness

48 Trotsky, 1975: 183–92.

> of the masses in so far as it was a condemnation of absolutism, aristocratic privilege, and the property qualification. But the longer it went on, the more it sent the consciousness to sleep, legalising poverty, slavery and degradation: for how could one revolt against slavery when every man has an equal right in determining the fate of the nation? . . . In the real conditions of life, in the economic process, in social relations, in their way of life, people became more and more unequal; dazzling luxury was accumulated at one pole, poverty and hopelessness at the other. But in the sphere of the legal edifice of the state, these glaring contradictions disappeared, and there penetrated only unsubstantial legal shadows (Trotsky, 1975: 60–1).

Besides defending the record of the Bolsheviks in detail, Trotsky made several illuminating remarks about the Marxist view of law and the state. These comments shed light not just on the particular problems confronting the Russian Revolution but also on the degree to which Trotsky and other Bolshevik leaders were acquainted with the debates over previous decades surrounding the Marxist analysis of law.

Trotsky accused Kautsky and the Austro-Marxism school of taking a mechanical view of the development of social relations. In essence, they argued that socialism could only arise gradually with the ripening of humanity's technological and productive capabilities and that socialists would have to wait for a democratic vote before assuming political power. In assessing the historical impact of their views, Trotsky drew upon a very different approach to Marx's base-superstructure analogy than that propagated by those who accuse Marxism of economic determinism. He identified a multiplying effect of legal and political factors on the economic base.

> If, beginning with the productive bases of society, we ascend the stages of the superstructure – classes, the state, laws, parties, and so on – it may be established that the weight of each additional part of the superstructure is not simply to be added to, but in many cases to be multiplied by, the weight of all the preceding stages. As a result, the political consciousness of groups that long imagined themselves to be among the most advanced, displays itself, at a moment of change, as a colossal obstacle in the path of historical development. Today it is quite beyond doubt that the parties of the Second International, standing at the head of the proletariat, which dared not, could not, and would not take power into their hands at the most critical moment of human history, and which led the proletariat along the road of mutual destruction in the interests of imperialism, proved a *decisive factor* of the counter-revolution. The great forces of production – that shock factor in historical development – were choked in those obsolete institutions of the superstructure (private property and the national state) in which they

> found themselves locked by all preceding development [italics in original] (Trotsky, 1975: 41).

Trotsky's argument was specifically directed against the leaders of the Second International, including Kautsky and the Austro-Marxism school, who had taken the side of their national governments in World War I, supporting the dispatch of millions of working people to kill each other in the trenches. His assessment incorporated his previously elaborated analysis that the war between the major colonial powers – Britain, France and Germany – over territories and world markets had expressed, in a fundamental sense, the irreconcilable conflict between the globalised development of economy and the nation-state system.[49]

Yet his approach has wider implications for the role assigned to superstructural factors, including law, in social change. Far from a mechanical determinist conception that economic changes would be automatically registered in politics and law, it is clear from Trotsky's view that questions of ideology, particularly political consciousness, could assume decisive importance at critical moments. This would follow, albeit perhaps to a lesser extent, for law (law being a lower 'stage' of the superstructure). Law, like other superstructural factors, could have a multiplied impact, either accelerating or retarding historical development. Thus, while law was shaped by economics, legal policies and problems could be critical under certain circumstances.

Trotsky related the need for the dictatorship of the proletariat in the transition to communism, to the political and economic tasks involved in overthrowing capitalism. He argued that genuine socialism and communism were impossible to achieve without the free and creative involvement of all people. The bureaucratic police state erected by Stalin was not only an affront to socialist democracy but also a suffocating barrier to the development of the productive and cultural capacities of society.

> The socialistic economy must be directed to ensuring the satisfaction of every possible human need. Such a problem it is impossible to solve by way of commands only. The greater the scale of the productive forces, the more involved the technique; the more complex the needs, then the more indispensable is a wide and free creative initiative of the organised producers and consumers. The socialist culture implies the utmost development of the human personality. Progress along this path is made possible not through a standardised cringing before irresponsible 'leaders', but only through a fully conscious and critical participation by all in a socialistic creative activity. The youthful generations stand in need of independence, which is wholly consistent with a firm leadership but rules out any

49 See Trotsky, 1971. See also Trotsky, 1977.

> police regimentation. Thus the bureaucratic system in crushing the Soviets and the party is coming ever more clearly into opposition with the basic needs of economic and cultural development (Trotsky, 1975: 9).

In line with Marx and Engels, Trotsky's emphasis was on the self-liberation of the entire population. This was the essence of communism, he insisted. Therefore, the task of the Soviet state was to encourage, not stifle, the maximum degree of conscious, well-informed and independent participation in political and administrative affairs.

Chapter 4

The dynamics of the Russian Revolution

> [W]ithout aid from the international world revolution, a victory of the proletarian revolution is impossible.[1]

Pashukanis' part in the legal debates and practices of Bolshevik-led Russia can only be assessed properly in the light of the nature, contradictions, trajectory and fate of the 1917 Revolution itself. This has four important aspects. The first is the mass character and social class composition of the Russian Revolution. The second is the revolution's strategic conception and historical content. The third concerns the roots of the degeneration under Stalin, and the fourth is the emergence of the Left Opposition from the end of 1923.

The mass character of the Russian Revolution

Trotsky, one of the leading participants in the three Russian Revolutions of 1905, February 1917 and October 1917, observed that 'the most indubitable feature of a revolution is the direct interference of the masses in historic events'.[2] During 1917, this intervention from below manifested itself, in the first instance, in the participation of masses of people in the stormy events of February 1917. The size of the crowds that gathered on the streets of Petrograd exceeded anything that had previously been seen, at least since the 1789 French Revolution.

Naturally, when millions of ordinary people participate in a great social revolution, they do not do so with a prepared plan. For instance, the basic unit of the Russian Revolution, the soviets or workers councils, pre-dated 1917 and were not established by the Bolsheviks. They initially emerged during the 1905 Revolution, semi-spontaneously, although they were similar to the communes envisaged by Marx in writing on the Paris Commune.[3] From April

1 Lenin, 1964, vol 32: 480.
2 Trotsky, 1977: 17.
3 Marx, 1948: 54–5.

1917, the Bolsheviks called for all power to the soviets, but it was not until late 1917 that the Bolsheviks won a majority in many of the soviets.

Some historians depict the Russian Revolution as an underground conspiracy organised by power-crazed intellectuals who lacked any substantial support among the masses.[4] Nevertheless, the evidence suggests that the revolution was deeply rooted and arose from protracted political experiences. For the present purposes, a relevant starting point is the Russian Revolution of 1905, although that tumultuous event was preceded by a rising tide of strikes, peasant disturbances and student unrest from the 1890s.[5] The 1905 Revolution began in St Petersburg in January that year when Tsarist troops fired on a crowd of workers, who, led by a priest, were marching to the Winter Palace to petition Nicholas II. This 'bloody Sunday' was followed in succeeding months by a series of strikes, riots, assassinations, naval mutinies, and peasant outbreaks. These disorders, coupled with the disaster of the Russo-Japanese War (1904–5), which revealed the corruption and incompetence of the Tsarist regime, forced the government to promise the establishment of a consultative duma, or assembly, elected by limited franchise. Nonetheless, unsatisfied popular demands provoked a general strike, and in a manifesto issued in October the Tsar granted civil liberties and a representative duma to be elected democratically.[6]

The manifesto split the groups that collectively had brought about the revolution. Those who were satisfied with the manifesto formed the Octobrist Party. The liberals who wanted more power for the duma consolidated in the Constitutional Democratic Party. The Social Democrats, who had organised a soviet, or workers' council, at St Petersburg, attempted to continue the strike movement and compel social reforms. The government arrested the soviet, then led by Trotsky, and put down a December 1905 workers' insurrection in Moscow.

When order was restored, the Tsar promulgated the Fundamental Laws, under which the power of the duma was limited. The Tsar's Prime Minister, Stolypin, made some attempt at economic reform but his efforts failed. The defeat of the 1905 Revolution resulted in a sharp decline in the numerical strength and political influence of the revolutionary organisations. In the years of revolutionary upsurge, between 1905 and 1907, both the Bolsheviks and Mensheviks, the two antagonistic factions of the Russian Social Democratic Labour Party (RSDLP), had grown by tens of thousands. After June 1907, their mass membership faded away and the impact of defeat produced widespread demoralisation. By 1910, according to Trotsky, Lenin's loyal and active contacts within Russia numbered about 10 people.

4 Pipes, 1993: 497.
5 Trotsky, 1977: Chapter 1.
6 See generally, Carr, 1978: 45–69.

Under Stolypin, the Tsarist regime enjoyed, after the close call of 1905, a revival of its political fortunes. However the assassination of Stolypin in 1911, which was the outcome of a plot organised by the secret police, removed the Tsar's most capable minister just as the workers movement entered into a new phase of radical activity. The outbreak of mass strikes in 1912 brought about a new political climate, which saw a rapid growth in Bolshevik influence. Throughout 1913 and 1914, the Bolsheviks won the leadership of major trade unions from the Mensheviks.[7] Another indication of the growth of the Bolsheviks' support at the expense of the Mensheviks comes from the respective sizes of their press circulation. The Menshevik newspaper, *Luch*, had a press run of about 16,000 per issue. But *Pravda*, the Bolshevik daily, had a press run of 40,000.

The 1917 Russian Revolution is commonly attributed to the acute social tensions produced by the Tsarist regime's disastrous engagement in World War I. But the actual course of development was different. By July 1914, on the eve of the war, the class struggle in the major industrial centres of Russia had already assumed revolutionary dimensions. Incidents of street fighting between workers and police were reported in St Petersburg. For the Tsarist regime, the war came at an opportune moment. While the barbarity of the war, and the terrible casualties suffered (nearly two million Russian soldiers perished) eventually led, over a period of three years, to an enormous intensification of social conflict, its initial impact was to douse the workers movement with nationalist fervour. The Bolsheviks, who had been operating under conditions of borderline legality, were again driven underground.

Trotsky was to write later that had it not been for the war, the eruption of revolution in late 1914 or 1915 would have meant a mass proletarian movement unfolding, from the beginning, under the leadership of the Bolsheviks. Instead, the revolution began in February 1917 under conditions that were far less favourable to the Bolsheviks than they had been in July 1914. First, their organisation was barely functioning in Russia. A great number of their working-class factory members had been drafted into the army and were dispersed along a wide front. The factories were now populated by far less politically experienced workers. Finally, the mass mobilisation of the peasantry inside the army meant that when the revolution erupted, the proletarian character of the social movement, at least in its initial stages, was far less pronounced than it had been in 1914. That is why the Socialist-Revolutionary Party, based largely on the peasantry, emerged out of the first weeks of the February Revolution as the largest political party.

However, despite their initial weakness, the Bolsheviks influenced the revolutionary events that brought about the collapse of the Tsarist regime in February–March 1917. As Trotsky explained, the uprising of February 1917

7 See generally, Bonnell, 1984.

was not purely 'spontaneous', without any trace of political leadership. Years of political agitation and education by the Social Democrats had left a Marxist residue on the consciousness of St Petersburg workers.[8]

Thus, the eruption of February 1917 led to the creation of soviets (workers councils) and assumed the form of a conscious political struggle against Tsarism, rather than of apolitical rioting and looting. The war had not entirely destroyed the underground organisation of the Bolsheviks, who were still in a position to impart a more militant consciousness to the mass uprising of February 1917. Contemporary historical research substantiates Trotsky's assertion that the February Revolution was led by 'conscious and tempered workers educated for the most part by the party of Lenin'.[9]

There were approximately 3.5 million workers in the factories and mines of Russia and another 1.25 million workers in transport and construction. The actual number of people who might be classified as wage workers comprised 10 per cent of the population, or about 18.5 million. Both St Petersburg and Moscow were great industrial centres and there were also concentrations of industrial workers in the Urals, the Ukraine, the Baltic region, Transcaucasia and Siberia. Relative to the size of the entire population, the working class was numerically small. However, it was highly concentrated. Over 70 per cent of the workers in Petrograd were employed in enterprises consisting of more than 1,000 workers. In Ukraine and the Urals, two-thirds of workers were in enterprises that employed more than 500.[10]

Scholars have unearthed considerable material about the scope and power of the mass working-class movement upon which the Bolshevik bid for power was based. One study has argued that Lenin's 'April Theses', in which Lenin reversed the policy of the Bolshevik Party, in order to call for the establishment of a government based on the soviets, had a direct impact on the consciousness of key sections of the Petrograd working class. For example, general assemblies of workers at the Puzyrev and Ekval factories passed the following resolution during the 'April Days', which saw the first large demonstrations against the Provisional Government, which assumed power after the February 1917 Revolution.

> The government cannot and does not want to represent the wishes of the whole toiling people, and so we demand its immediate abolition and the arrest of its members, in order to neutralise their assault on liberty. We recognise that power must belong only to the people itself, i.e., to the Soviet of Workers' and Soldiers' Deputies as the sole institution of authority enjoying the confidence of the people (Kaiser, 1987: 66).

8 Trotsky, 1977: 155–71.
9 Trotsky, 1977: 171.
10 Shukman, 1994: 22.

If anything, the Bolshevik Party spent much of the year trying to keep pace with a mass movement that possessed a dynamic momentum whose equal had not been seen since the 1789 French Revolution. At several key points, the Bolsheviks unsuccessfully attempted to hold back the movement from premature confrontations with the Tsarist regime.[11]

After the events of February, a form of dual power emerged, with working class bodies challenging the Provisional Government and employers for control over economic and political decision-making.[12] Legality was often cast aside. Factory committees evolved quickly into complex structures involved in virtually every aspect of daily life, reorganising society on anti-capitalist lines. They formed sub-committees that were responsible for the security of their factories, food supply, culture, health and safety, the improvement of working conditions, and the maintenance of labour discipline through the discouragement of drunkenness.

Soviet historian Z.V. Stepanov 'counted 4,266 acts by 124 factory committees in Petrograd between 1 March and 25 October and calculates that 1,141 acts related to workers control of production and distribution; 882 concerned organisation questions; 347 concerned political questions; 299 concerned wages; 241 concerned hiring and firing and the monitoring of conscription'.[13] By the late summer and autumn of 1917, the factory committees began to demand that the employers provide them with access to order books and financial accounts. By October, some form of workers control was in effect in 573 factories and mines, with a combined workforce of 1.4 million workers. Thus, well before the October Revolution, millions of workers were already challenging employer prerogatives, capitalist property rights in general and the legal power of the Provisional Government.

Throughout 1917, the Bolsheviks developed strength within the factory committees. Weeks before the Bolsheviks obtained a majority inside the Petrograd Soviet, they were in the leadership of the most important factory committees. A study of the resolutions passed by local assemblies shows that there was a broad-based response to the slogans and principal demands of the Bolshevik Party. In Moscow, which was less developed politically than Petrograd, the month of October 1917 saw more than 50,000 workers pass resolutions in support of the Bolshevik demand for the transfer of power to the soviets; and there is considerable evidence that the Bolshevik seizure of power was welcomed by a large majority of the working class.[14]

Between April and October, the Bolshevik Party experienced rapid growth. In April 1917 the Petrograd organisation of the Bolsheviks consisted of about 16,000 workers. By October its membership had risen to 43,000, of

11 Trotsky, 1977: 421–66, 515–72.
12 On dual power, see ibid: 223–32.
13 Shukman, 1994: 22.
14 Frankel, Frankel and Knei-paz, 1992: 160.

whom two-thirds were workers. In June 1917 the elections to the First All-Russian Congress of Soviets produced 283 Socialist-Revolutionary delegates, 248 Menshevik delegates and only 105 Bolshevik delegates. The elections to the Second All-Russian Congress, which assembled on the eve of the October Revolution four months later, produced a transformation: the Bolsheviks' share of the delegates rose to 390, the Socialist-Revolutionaries' share fell to 160 and the Mensheviks' to 72.

Workers generally moved to the left, as they became increasingly disgusted with the Provisional Government and the refusal of the moderate socialist parties to break with it. In the words of one historian:

> Economic crisis, the continuation of war, the acceleration of class conflict, and the Kornilov putsch transformed the vast majority of politically active workers into enemies of the Provisional Government in its various incarnations. . . . They came to see no essential distinction between the new government and the old Tsarist regime, except that the Provisional Government was now more clearly a 'bourgeois dictatorship' (McDaniel, 1988: 355).

Another historian summed up the results of his research into the causes of the Bolshevik victory as follows:

> [T]he Bolsheviks themselves did not create popular discontent or revolutionary feeling. This grew out of the masses' own experiences of complex economic and social upheavals and political events. The contribution of the Bolsheviks was rather to shape workers' understanding of the social dynamic of the revolution and to foster an awareness of how the urgent problems of daily life related to the broader social and political order. The Bolsheviks won support because their analysis and proposed solutions seemed to make sense (S. Smith in Kaiser, 1987: 77).

When the Bolsheviks ultimately seized power in October 1917, official resistance was short-lived. The Bolsheviks were not imposing a new political and economic structure from above. Rather, they were sitting astride a mass upheaval, which continued through the early years of the new order. This had definite implications for their approach to the old legal system, which was widely detested, discredited and paralysed.

The physiognomy of the Russian Revolution: permanent revolution

Equally important to an understanding of the legal experiences of the Russian Revolution are the dynamics, scope and character of the revolution. As discussed in the Introduction, the revolution embodied a great contradiction – the world's first socialist overturn occurred in a relatively backward country, rather than in the most advanced countries of Europe. The possibility of a socialist revolution first became apparent in the 1905 events, triggering major debates among Russian Marxists. According to Trotsky, the 1905 Revolution became:

> . . . not only 'the dress rehearsal of 1917' but also the laboratory from which emerged all the basic groupings of Russian political thought and where all the tendencies and shadings within Russian Marxism took shape or were outlined. The centre of the disputes and differences was naturally occupied by the question of the historical character of the Russian revolution and its future paths of development (Trotsky, 1945: 243).

Russian socialist thought advanced three possible and conflicting variants, one elaborated by Plekhanov, one by Lenin and the third by Trotsky. Plekhanov conceived of Russian social development in terms of a formal logical progression, in which a given level of economic development determined historical stages of development. As feudalism was replaced by capitalism, the latter would, in turn, give way to socialism when all the required conditions of economic development had been attained. This theoretical model assumed that Russian development would follow the historical pattern of Western Europe's bourgeois-democratic evolution. There existed no possibility that Russia might move in a socialist direction before the more advanced countries to its west. Russia, at the turn of the twentieth century, Plekhanov maintained, still had before it the task of achieving its bourgeois democratic revolution – by which he meant the overthrow of the Tsarist regime and the creation of the political and economic preconditions for a future, distant, social revolution. In all probability, Russia had before it many decades of bourgeois parliamentary development before its economic and social structure could sustain a socialist transformation. This organic conception of Russia's development constituted the accepted wisdom that prevailed among broad layers of the Russian social-democratic movement during the first years of the twentieth century. Plekhanov wrote in 1905:

> Marxists are absolutely convinced of the bourgeois character of the Russian revolution. What does this mean? This means that those democratic transformations which have become indispensable for Russia do not, in and of themselves, signify the undermining of capitalism, the undermining of bourgeois rule, but on the contrary they clear the soil, for the first time and in a real way, for a broad and swift, for a European and not an Asiatic development of capitalism. They will make possible for the first time the rule of the bourgeoisie as a class . . . We cannot leap

> over the bourgeois democratic framework of the Russian revolution but we can extend this framework to a colossal degree (Trotsky, 1945: 245).

The eruption of the first Russian Revolution in 1905 generated serious questions about the viability of Plekhanov's theorem. The most significant aspect of the Russian Revolution was the dominant political role played by the proletariat in the struggle against Tsarism. Against the background of general strikes and insurrection, the manoeuvrings of the political leaders of the Russian bourgeoisie appeared petty and treacherous.

Lenin accepted that the Russian Revolution was of a bourgeois-democratic character. But such a formal definition did not exhaust the problem of the class dynamics and balance of power in the revolution. Lenin said the task of the working class was to strive, through its independent organisation and efforts, for the most expansive and radical development of the bourgeois democratic revolution, that is, for an uncompromising struggle to demolish all economic, political and social vestiges of Tsarist feudalism; and thereby create the most favourable conditions for the establishment of a genuinely progressive constitutional-democratic framework for the flowering of the Russian workers movement. For Lenin, at the heart of this democratic revolution was the resolution of the 'agrarian question', by which he meant the destruction of all the economic and juridical remnants of feudalism. The vast landholdings of the nobility constituted an immense barrier to the democratisation of Russian life, as well as to the development of a modern capitalist economy.

Lenin drew the conclusion that the newly emerged and small Russian bourgeoisie was incapable of carrying through such tasks. The working class would have to wage the struggle for democracy independently of and, in fact, in opposition to the bourgeoisie. But due to its numerical weakness, the working class alone could not provide the mass basis of the democratic revolution. It had to advance the redistribution of the landed estates in order to mobilise behind it the multi-millioned Russian peasantry. The victory of the revolution, he wrote, required:

> [A] dictatorship because the accomplishment of transformations immediately and urgently needed by the proletariat and the peasantry will evoke the desperate resistance of the landlords, the big bourgeoisie and Czarism. Without the dictatorship it will be impossible to break the resistance, and repel the counter-revolutionary attempts. But this will of course be not a socialist but a democratic dictatorship. It will not be able to touch (without a whole series of transitional stages of revolutionary development) the foundations of capitalism. It will be able, in the best case, to realise a radical redivision of landed property in favour of the peasantry, introduce a consistent and full democratism up to instituting the republic, root out all Asiatic and feudal features not only from the

> day-to-day life of the village but also of the factory, put a beginning to a serious improvement of workers' conditions and raise their living standards and, last but not least, carry over the revolutionary conflagration to Europe (Trotsky, 1945: 247).

Lenin proposed that the new regime would be a 'democratic dictatorship of the proletariat and peasantry'. In effect, the two classes would share state power and jointly preside over the fullest possible realisation of the democratic revolution. Lenin offered no specifics as to the precise nature of the power-sharing arrangements that would prevail in such a regime, nor did he define or describe the state forms through which this two-class dictatorship would be exercised.

Trotsky's position differed markedly. Notwithstanding their different conclusions, both Plekhanov and Lenin based their perspectives on an estimate of the level of Russian economic development and the existing relations of social forces within the country. Trotsky's real point of departure was not the internal situation but rather the 'world-historical foundations' of Russia's belated democratic revolution.[15] Trotsky traced the historical trajectory of the bourgeois revolution, from its classical and youthful manifestation in the French Revolution of 1789 to its retreats in the 1848 European revolutions to the modern context of 1905. He concluded that the Russian proletariat would be able to limit itself to measures of a formally democratic character. The reality of class relations would compel the working class to exercise its political dictatorship against the economic interests of the bourgeoisie. In other words, the struggle of the working class would necessarily assume a socialist character. But given the backwardness of Russia, which was clearly not ready for socialism, the fate of the revolution would depend on its extension internationally. Trotsky noted that:

> [C]apitalism has converted the whole world into a single economic and political organism . . . This immediately gives the events now unfolding an international character, and opens up a wide horizon. The political emancipation of Russia led by the working class will raise that class to a height as yet unknown in history, will transfer to it colossal power and resources, and make it the initiator of the liquidation of world capitalism, for which history has created all the objective conditions (Trotsky, 1945: 240).

Trotsky's theory, known as permanent revolution, shifted the paradigm from which revolutionary processes were viewed. Prior to 1905, the development of revolutions was seen as a progression of national events, whose outcome

15 Trotsky, 1962: 161–254.

was determined by the logic of internal socio-economic structure and relations. Trotsky proposed another approach: to understand revolution, in the modern epoch, as essentially a world-historic process of social transition from class society, rooted politically in nation-states, to a classless society developing on the basis of a globally integrated economy and internationally unified mankind.[16]

Trotsky outlined the theory from his cell while awaiting trial for his participation in the Petersburg Soviet of 1905. The expression 'permanent revolution' was borrowed from Marx and Engels' 1850 'Address of the General Council to the Communist League'. Trotsky wrote:

> The permanent revolution, in the sense which Marx attached to this concept, means a revolution which makes no compromise with any single form of class rule, which does not stop at the democratic stage, which goes over to socialist measures and to war against reaction from without; that is, a revolution whose every successive stage is rooted in the preceding one and which can end only in complete liquidation (Trotsky, 1962: 6–7).

In 1939, Trotsky summed up his theory thus:

> The perspective of permanent revolution may be summarised in the following way: the complete victory of the democratic revolution in Russia is conceivable only in the form of the dictatorship of the proletariat, leaning on the peasantry. The dictatorship of the proletariat, which would inevitably place on the order of the day not only democratic but socialistic tasks as well, would at the same time give a powerful impetus to the international socialist revolution. Only the victory of the proletariat in the West could protect Russia from bourgeois restoration and assure it the possibility of completing the establishment of socialism (Trotsky, 1973: 72–3).

Trotsky had, as early as 1909, warned of the potential anti-revolutionary character of Lenin's formulation of the 'democratic dictatorship of the proletariat and peasantry', because it required the working class to limit itself to bourgeois tasks:

> The snag is that the Bolsheviks visualise the class struggle of the proletariat only until the moment of the revolution and its triumph, after which they see it temporarily dissolved in the democratic coalition, reappearing in its pure form, this time as a direct struggle for socialism only after the definitive establishment of a republican system . . . While

16 Deutscher, 1954: 145–63.

> the anti-revolutionary aspects of Menshevism have already become apparent, those of the Bolsheviks are likely to become a serious threat only in the event of victory (Trotsky, 1971b: 332).

This passage proved prescient in relation to the subsequent degeneration of the Soviet revolution. Trotsky warned that if the working class were held back from achieving socialist objectives by a 'proletariat in possession of state power', the result would be anti-revolutionary. This is what in fact happened after 1924, when Stalin's policy of 'socialism in one country' effectively renounced the objective of world socialism.

Lenin himself re-evaluated his political perspective during World War I and announced a new orientation on his return to Russia in April 1917. No doubt his study of world economy under the impact of the First World War gave him a deeper insight into the international dynamics of the world and Russian Revolution and led him to adopt, in essence, the perspective that had been associated with Trotsky for so many years. Lenin's *Imperialism*, written during the war, suggests such a process of reconsideration and can be read as a theoretical prologue to his 'April Theses'.[17]

Before Lenin's return to Russia in April 1917, the Bolshevik Party leadership in the capital had adopted a policy of giving conditional support to the bourgeois Provisional Government, including its continuation of the war against Germany and Austria-Hungary, on the grounds that the revolution could not leap over the bourgeois democratic stage of its development. Lenin opposed this policy, while he was still in Switzerland and unable to intervene directly in the deliberations of the party leadership. The editorial board of *Pravda*, which was led by Stalin, refused to publish statements by Lenin. Not until he returned was he able, in the course of several weeks of bitter factional struggle, to overcome the initial policy. Lenin was fighting to change a programmatic position that he himself had developed and then defended for many years. To the Old Bolsheviks whom he now attacked, Lenin's new line – calling for the preparation of the overthrow of the Provisional Government and the assumption of power by the working class – seemed a heretical capitulation to the theory of permanent revolution that had been propounded by Leon Trotsky, in opposition to the Bolsheviks, for a decade.

Lenin had come, by his own route, to the perspective with which Leon Trotsky had been so prominently identified. The experience of the World War, refracted through his own study of modern imperialism, had led Lenin to conclude that the Russian Revolution was the beginning of a world socialist revolution; that the international crisis of capitalism, interacting with the weakness of the Russian bourgeoisie and its subordination to international capital, left open no possibility of a progressive bourgeois democratic stage

17 Lenin, 1976.

of Russian development; and that the only class capable of breaking Russia's subordination to imperialism and carrying through the essential democratic tasks of the revolution was the proletariat. On this basis Lenin presented in the 'April Theses' the call for the transfer of state power to the workers soviet.

Central to both Trotsky's perspective of permanent revolution and the programmatic change introduced by Lenin in April 1917 was the link between the struggles of the Russian working class and the international, especially the European, proletariat. Neither Lenin nor Trotsky conceived of the October Revolution in primarily national terms. They understood and justified the overthrow of the Provisional Government as the beginning of an international resolution of the global capitalist contradictions that were exemplified by the First World War. As Lenin told the Third Congress of the Communist International in July 1921:

> It was clear to us that without aid from the international world revolution, a victory of the proletarian revolution is impossible. Even prior to the revolution, as well as after it, we thought that the revolution would also occur either immediately or at least very soon in other backward countries and in the more highly developed countries, otherwise we would perish. Notwithstanding this conviction, we did our utmost to preserve the Soviet system under any circumstances and at all costs, because we know that we are working not only for ourselves, but also for the international revolution (Lenin, 1964, vol 32: 480).

This perspective had nothing in common with the goal of establishing a self-sufficient socialist system within the boundaries of an economically backward Russia. It was not until the autumn of 1924, several months after Lenin's death, that Bukharin and Stalin introduced the idea that socialism could be established on a national basis, in one country. Before that time it was accepted as a basic premise of Marxism that the survival of the Bolshevik government, let alone the development of a socialist economy, depended upon the victory of socialist revolutions in Western Europe. It was believed that the conquest of power by the working class in the advanced capitalist countries would provide Soviet Russia with the political, financial, industrial and technological resources vital for its survival.

The roots of the degeneration

Understanding the strategic dimensions and contradictions of the Russian Revolution makes it possible to grasp the pressures on the Soviet government and the underlying factors in the betrayal of the revolution. The defeats suffered by the European working class in the aftermath of World War I, above all in Germany, were the primary cause of the political degeneration of the Soviet regime.

The isolation of Soviet Russia altered drastically the relation of class forces that had made possible the Bolshevik conquest of power. The principal social base of the October Revolution was a small but strategically positioned working class. The crisis of Bolshevism cannot be understood apart from the impact of the civil war of 1918–21, in which Japan, Britain, the US and other Western powers intervened behind the military opponents of the revolution, sending in more than half a million troops in an unsuccessful bid to overturn the revolution. Among them were some 10,000 US troops, who suffered considerable losses in Vladivostok and Siberia.[18]

In his writings on the objective causes of the degeneration of the Bolshevik Party, Trotsky referred to the physical and spiritual exhaustion of the working class by the end of the civil war. A number of historians have shed further light on the scale of the social catastrophe that confronted the Soviet government. One study cites statistical data on the shrinkage of the industrial working class in the course of the war.[19] At the time of the revolution, there were 3.5 million workers in factories employing more than 16 workers. That figure dropped to 2 million in 1918 and to 1.5 million by the end of 1920. The worst losses were in the big industrial centres of Petrograd, Moscow, the Donbass and the Urals, and the decline of the proletariat was part of a general process of urban depopulation. From a population of 2.5 million in 1917, only 722,000 people were left in Petrograd by 1920, the same number as had lived in the city in 1870. Moscow's population fell between February 1917 and late 1920 from 2 million to just over 1 million, somewhat less than the number recorded in the census of 1897. Kiev lost more than a quarter of its population between 1917 and 1920.

Many factors contributed to this disastrous process, of which disease and acute shortages of food and fuel were among the most important. Tens of thousands of people, already weakened by hunger, died during epidemics of cholera, influenza, typhus and diphtheria. The Moscow death rate rose from 23.7 per thousand in 1917 to 45.4 in 1919. Another major factor was the need of the Red Army for troops to fight the White armies. Mobilisations by the Red Army removed well over 600,000 workers from the factories between 1918 and 1920.

The impact was felt not only economically, but also politically. The Red Army depended for its successes, to a great extent, on the devotion and initiative of the most class-conscious workers. The depletion of the industrial proletariat involved the loss of those workers who had played important roles in the revolutionary struggles of 1917, in factory committees or in other party-led organisations. A significant section of workers who had, at the very least, voted for the Bolsheviks in elections to the soviets and then to the

18 Graves, 1931; Dobson and Miller, 1986.

19 Siegelbaum, 1992: 26–9.

Constituent Assembly were drawn away from the industrial locations by the demands of the civil war or by assignment to emerging soviet, party and trade union administrations.

It has been estimated that 200,000 out of 500,000 Communists who served in the Red Army were killed during the civil war.[20] The political implications of such mortality rates can be better appreciated by drawing attention to the influx of new members into the Communist Party, particularly after the military position of the Soviet government improved as a result of major victories in the autumn of 1919. Between August 1919 and March 1920, the membership of the party grew from 150,000 to 600,000.[21] But the calibre of this new intake was, in general, much lower than that of those who had been lost. The proportion of workers fell steadily, from 57 per cent at the beginning of 1918, to 44 per cent in 1920. The proportion of peasants, particularly young men who had entered the Red Army, and white-collar workers (the Western term for what the sources refer to as 'employees') rose. By January 1921, the party membership numbered 240,000 workers (41 per cent), 165,300 peasants (28.2 per cent), 138,800 'employees' (23.7 per cent) and 41,500 whose social origins were unknown (7.1 per cent).[22] Although precise statistics are not available, it is likely that a significant proportion of the white-collar 'employees' would be former Tsarist functionaries, given the limited access to education under the old regime.

Thus, by the end of the civil war, the social and political base of both the Soviet government and the ruling party had been profoundly reduced and altered. The percentage of Bolshevik Party members who described their social origin as white collar, as opposed to proletarian, had increased significantly. Within the administration of the soviets, the proportion was even higher. By 1920, 57 per cent of members of provincial executive committees were of white-collar background.[23] Siegelbaum draws attention to the growing importance of this 'lower middle strata' in the affairs of the party and state organisations:

> The lower middle strata thus successfully grafted themselves onto the workers' and peasants' revolution. The result was that the social composition of the revolutionary state was more heterogeneous and less proletarian than generally has been acknowledged. What impact these 'alien elements' had on the day-to-day functioning of the state, whether they possessed a specific psychology that was itself alien to the original revolutionary project, is not entirely clear (Siegelbaum, 1992: 62–3).

20 Siegelbaum, 1992: 29.
21 Ibid: 22.
22 Ibid: 22–3.
23 Ibid: 62.

The character of the Bolshevik Party was changed not only by the loss of seasoned working-class cadres and the influx of tens of thousands of inexperienced and politically questionable recruits. Among the older cadres that had survived the years of revolution and civil war, the 'professional demands of power' took an unforeseen but serious political toll. In a backward country where a vast portion of the population was illiterate and technical skills were in limited supply, party members were invariably dragged into management and administrative positions. The innumerable and ever expanding state agencies and party organisations vied with each other to obtain the services of cadres who possessed some sort of managerial skills. In this way a significant section of the party cadre was swept up in a process of bureaucratisation. At the same time, under conditions of economic chaos and desperate poverty, positions within the organisations and agencies of the state and party provided some small measure of personal security. Under the conditions that prevailed at the end of the civil war, the possibility of obtaining at least one passable meal a day at the workplace canteen constituted a not insignificant privilege. In all sorts of small but important ways, a bureaucratic caste, with specific social interests, gradually took shape. Trotsky summed up the social conditions for the victory of Stalin's bureaucratic caste as follows:

> The revolutionary vanguard of the proletariat was in part devoured by the administrative apparatus and gradually demoralised, in part annihilated in the civil war, and in part thrown out and crushed. The tired and disappointed masses were indifferent to what was happening on the summits (Trotsky, 1937: 105).

Another factor in the unfavourable economic conditions confronting the revolution was that the Soviet government was forced by the circumstances of the civil war, notably the armed resistance of business owners, to nationalise far wider sections of industry than had been intended originally. Given the low level of development of the Russian economy, the Bolshevik leadership initially planned to nationalise only the 'commanding heights' in the economic sphere, allowing private entrepreneurs to own or lease smaller and less essential undertakings.[24] The first decrees on nationalisation were confined to large industrial and financial enterprises. But the needs of the civil war compelled nationalisations of entire industries, even of small producers, which only led to widespread economic breakdown.[25]

One of the political indicators of the strains upon the Soviet economy and administration was the Kronstadt rebellion, which broke out in March 1921,

24 Lenin, 1964, vol 9: 282ff.
25 Schlesinger, 1945: 46–54.

soon after the eventual defeat of the White armies in the civil war. The sailors of the naval base near Petrograd (later Leningrad and now St Petersburg) mutinied against the Soviet regime, opposing many of the measures necessitated by the civil war. Although the rebellion did not attract wide support internally, it attracted prominent backing externally among opponents of the Russian Revolution.[26] Trotsky, who ordered the Red Army to put down the rebellion, always maintained that this response was a tragic necessity. The alternative was, he maintained, surrender of the October Revolution because, as he put it, 'a few dubious Anarchists and SRs [the peasant-based Social Revolutionaries] were sponsoring a handful of reactionary peasants and soldiers in rebellion'.[27]

The New Economic Policy (NEP), adopted during this period, was an effort to repair relations with the peasantry. The period of 'War Communism', in which economic life was completely subordinated to the needs of the civil war, gave way to the partial reintroduction of the market, which inevitably brought with it new problems of its own. Under these conditions, some of the Bolsheviks' other measures in the wake of Kronstadt, such as the banning of party factions in March 1921, a step that Trotsky also defended as a temporary necessity, contained within them serious dangers for party democracy. As the political and economic isolation of the Soviet state continued, the emerging bureaucracy under Stalin made use of the ban on factions to consolidate its grip on the party. It is possible that a different tactical course could have avoided the bloody confrontation at Kronstadt, and that the ban on factions, temporary at first, increased the dangers to the revolution by strengthening bureaucratic tendencies. Deutscher argued that the Bolshevik Party unintentionally condemned itself to exist by 'a process of permanent self-suppression'.[28] The underlying problem, however, was that the Soviet government faced tremendous odds as it fought to hold out against worldwide enemies. These pressures were, in turn, intensified by the material interests let loose by the NEP.

The NEP and the emergence of the Stalinist layer

Put briefly, the New Economic Policy was an attempt by the Soviet regime, born of necessity and desperation, to tolerate the revival of a capitalist market so as to restore the foundations of organised economic activity in Russia. By 1921, it was obvious that the post-war revolutionary tide had abated. The impoverished Soviet state faced a period of economic and political isolation.

Moreover, although the civil war was largely won, its economic, social and human costs were immense, adding to the devastation of the world war. In

26 Trotsky, 1938: 103–6.
27 Ibid: 104.
28 Deutscher, 1959: 17.

1920 the area of Russia under crops was 25 per cent less than in 1913. Agricultural production had fallen further: grain by 50 per cent, livestock by 40 per cent, flax by 35 per cent, sugar beet by 70 per cent. Droughts across the southern parts of the country worsened the situation; by the end of 1921, starvation had caused 23,227 deaths, according to official estimates.[29] By other accounts, 3 to 4 million people perished.[30]

Industries and cities were in no better shape. By the end of the civil war, Russia's national income was just one-third of her income in 1913; industry produced less than one-fifth of the pre-World War I total; coal mines turned out less than one-tenth; the iron foundries only one-fortieth. Lacking fuel and food from the countryside, people had fled the major cities – Moscow's population had fallen by half and Petrograd's by two-thirds.[31]

Facing economic collapse and a delay in the European revolution, Lenin and his co-thinkers were forced to make an economic retreat in the form of the NEP. To use Lenin's words, they sought to provide a 'stimulus, a jolt and a motivation'[32] to production by offering material incentives to peasants, cooperatives and manufacturers. In a concession to market forces, the wartime requisition of crops was replaced by taxation, and peasants were permitted to sell their surpluses for private gain. Nationalised industrial property was leased out to cooperatives or private owners and foreign capitalists were allowed to acquire mining and other interests.

Lenin admitted the NEP was a manoeuvre with far-reaching implications and possibly unforeseen consequences. Addressing the Moscow Soviet in November 1922, he warned: 'Where and how we must now restructure ourselves, reorganise ourselves, so that after the retreat we may begin a stubborn move forward, we still do not know.'[33] He advanced a revised notion of 'state capitalism', which would seek to re-establish the link (*smychka*) between town and country on the basis of market relations. Capitalist production and exchange would be permitted under state regulation. Small-scale manufacturing would be turned over to cooperatives and private investors, while foreign investors would be invited to help restore the fuel industries. No set blueprint was possible; instead, other measures to revive the economy would be worked out in practice.[34]

While the NEP may have been an unavoidable response to the ruinous economic situation, it accelerated the process of political degeneration within

29 Pogrebinskii, Motylev, Pazhitnova and Podkolzin, 1964: 96–7.

30 Siegelbaum, 1992: 89.

31 Deutscher, 1959: 4.

32 Lenin's report to the 10th Congress of the Russian Communist Party (Bolshevik), 15 March 1921, cited in Zile, 1970: 55–8.

33 'Speech at a Plenary Session of the Moscow Soviet, 20 November 1922', in Lenin, 1964, vol 45: 302.

34 On Lenin's revival and revision of the concept of 'state capitalism', see Bettelheim, 1976: 464–76.

the ruling party. Under conditions in which the proletarian base of both the state and the party had been drastically weakened, the impetus given by the NEP to the growth of capitalist tendencies within Soviet Russia was bound to have dangerous political consequences. Between 1921 and 1923, the NEP breathed new life into social elements who had opposed the Bolshevik Revolution. Businessmen and traders re-emerged, and by 1922 a stock exchange was once again functioning in Moscow.

The NEP also strengthened small proprietorship in the form of some 20 million household plots, while permitting the re-formation of the better-off land-holding kulak class in the countryside and a private entrepreneurial class, known as the NEPmen, in both the villages and the towns. Initially, it was hoped that commercial transactions could be limited to bartering or direct exchange of goods between peasants and city dwellers, with consumer cooperatives serving as conduits. By the spring of 1921, however, with the state possessing only a 'tiny supply of desirable consumer goods', and in the absence of controls over transport, 'a wave of private buying and selling had rolled into the void'.[35] As successive decrees loosened controls on prices and exchange, tens of thousands of private traders emerged. In many rural areas, the NEPmen were the only sellers of manufactured goods. Even the state-owned industries relied on them to obtain raw materials and sell their products, despite the official policy favouring cooperatives. Across the country, private businessmen handled over 75 per cent of all retail trade in 1922–23; in Moscow, they controlled over 80 per cent of retail, 50 per cent of mixed retail-wholesale and 14 per cent of wholesale trade. In more outlying areas, the proportions were higher still.[36]

Alongside this growth of privileged layers came a dramatic rise in unemployment among workers and peasants. According to the official and trade union labour exchanges, the jobless numbers rose from 160,000 on 1 January 1922 to 1,344,300 by 1 July 1924, or 18 per cent of all hired labour. Unemployed trade union members numbered 427,600 on 1 July 1923 and 676,000 on 1 July 1924, or 13.8 per cent of all union members.[37] The 1922–23 demobilisation of the army and the renewal of urban migration contributed to the soaring joblessness but it was also related to the rise of private employers and, in turn, increased the degree of social polarisation.

The social climate became more tolerant of inequality, and moods that reflected a certain moral and political decline found expression within the party membership, particularly those who were active in the upper echelons of the bureaucracy. There were also signs that the NEP revived nationalist sentiments. There were elements within the ruling party – especially the new recruits from the lower middle strata for whom the revolution had opened

35 Ball, 1987: 17; also Carr, 1978, vol 2: 330–4.
36 Nove, 1969: 103; Ball, 1987: 99, 104, 111–12, 191.
37 Siegelbaum, 1992: 104.

immense opportunities – who might be inclined to interpret the October Revolution as the beginning of a great national revival. Against the background of defeats of the European working class, the practical tasks of building the national Soviet economy appeared to these forces far more realistic than the vision of world socialist revolution.

No less important was a sharp reduction in the mass literacy and education campaigns in the villages and the Red Army, under Trotsky's leadership, during the civil war. The decline in state revenue that accompanied the revival of private trade meant a slashing of funds for cultural and educational institutions. By January 1923, only 3.8 per cent of the literary bases, 16.1 per cent of the reading rooms and 47.7 per cent of the libraries of two years earlier remained. The proportion of children aged 8–11 who attended school in the RSFSR shrank from 74.3 per cent in 1920–21 to 46.0 per cent in 1922–23. Lenin's wife Nadezhda Krupskaya, head of Glavpolitprosvet (Main Administration for Political Education) complained that the NEP had 'brought with it to the countryside an upsurge of darkness'.[38]

The social tendencies that began to predominate in 1922–23 were very different from those upon which the growth of Bolshevism was based in 1917 – which was a radicalisation of the working class in the major urban centres. The social forces which underlay the growth of the party in 1922 and 1923 were specifically from the lower middle classes in the urban areas for whom the revolution had opened up innumerable career opportunities, not to mention remnants of the old Tsarist bureaucracy. Lenin began to warn of this, and the emergence of a type of national Bolshevism, as early as 1922, and he became increasingly strident in his warnings about the growth of chauvinistic tendencies. In late 1922 and early 1923, those warnings were directed specifically against Stalin, whom Lenin referred to in his final writings as the individual who expressed the re-emergence of the Great Russian chauvinist bully.

Another important aspect of the crisis of Bolshevism was the deterioration in the quality of inner-party political life. From 1920 on, there were innumerable expressions by leading Bolsheviks of disquiet over the bureaucratisation of the state apparatus. Lenin referred to Soviet Russia as a 'workers state with a bureaucratic twist'. But despite the concerns, the process of bureaucratisation was nourished by deep-rooted objective tendencies related to the backwardness of Russia, and the party itself could not remain immune from the intrusion of bureaucracy into all spheres of social life. In the absence of a politically active working class, the methods of bureaucratic management and administration migrated rapidly into the affairs of the party. The most pronounced expression of this process was the growing influence of Stalin, whose principal responsibility as general secretary consisted of selecting the personnel required for the staffing of critical party and state positions. More

38 Siegelbaum, 1992: 93.

and more, the power of appointment, exercised ruthlessly by Stalin, invalidated and replaced the traditional forms of party democracy.

By the time that the Twelfth Congress convened in April 1923, Stalin, who became general secretary a year earlier, had assigned some 10,000 party members to various party and official positions and made another thousand or so senior appointments, including 42 gubkom secretaries. Supporters of Trotsky, together with the Workers Opposition and the Democratic Centralists, were dispersed and isolated. Within a few months, the Orgburo announced the regularisation of these procedures, marking the birth of the *nomenklatura* system of appointment.[39]

In March 1922, at the Eleventh Party Congress, Lenin warned that the party was in danger of being overwhelmed by the bureaucracy that administered the state. Shortly afterwards he was incapacitated by a stroke that removed him from political activity for several months. When he returned to work in the autumn of 1922, Lenin was stunned by the degree to which the situation within the party had deteriorated. He rapidly identified Stalin as the personification of the process of bureaucratic degeneration that threatened the party with destruction. It is clear from the notes and documents prepared by Lenin during the last months of his politically active life that he was preparing for a decisive confrontation with Stalin at the Twelfth Party Congress scheduled for April 1923. The testament written by Lenin calling for Stalin's removal from the post of general secretary, as well as the letter Lenin sent to Stalin threatening to break all personal relations with him, were part of a political dossier that Lenin intended to present to the party congress. The massive stroke suffered by Lenin in March 1923 saved Stalin's political career.

The Left Opposition

In the months that followed Lenin's final incapacitation, opposition grew to bureaucratic methods employed by the 'triumvirate' of Stalin, Zinoviev and Kamenev. The political tensions were exacerbated by deepening anxiety over the consequences of the NEP, expressed particularly, as Trotsky explained in the spring of 1923, in the worsening disparity between industrial and agricultural prices and the continuing deterioration in the conditions of the working class.

As it grew increasingly clear that Lenin would not recover and return to political activity, Trotsky came under mounting pressure from many of the most politically distinguished members of the Bolshevik Party to speak out against the party bureaucracy and fight for a far-reaching review and change in economic policy. On 8 October, Trotsky addressed a letter to the Central Committee that called attention to serious weaknesses in economic policy

39 Siegelbaum, 1992: 130.

and also criticised the bureaucratisation of party life. One week later, his criticisms were endorsed in a 'Platform' signed by 46 prominent party members, including Preobrazhensky, Antonov-Ovseenko, Piatakov, Sapronov and Osinsky. It indicted the 'progressive division of the party, no longer concealed by hardly anyone, into the secretarial hierarchy and the "laymen", into the professional party functionaries, selected from above, and the simple party masses, who do not participate in its group life'.[40]

These events marked the beginning of the political struggle of the Left Opposition. The Platform of the 46 warned that unless there was a radical change in the policies and methods of the leadership:

> [T]he economic crisis in Soviet Russia and the crisis of the factional dictatorship in the party will deal heavy blows at the workers' dictatorship in Russia and the Russian Communist Party. With such a load on its shoulders, the dictatorship of the proletariat in Russia and its leader the RCP cannot enter the phase of impending new worldwide disturbances except with the prospect of defeats on the whole front of the proletarian struggle (Trotsky, 1980: 400).

At first, the criticisms of Trotsky and the Platform of the 46 threw the triumvirate into disarray, and it offered a few insincere political concessions. But then it recovered its nerve, counter-attacked, and appealed to the social forces that, within the framework of NEP, had become the new constituency of the Soviet regime.

In order to counter the Left Opposition's charges of bureaucratism, while swamping the party with obedient recruits, the Politburo launched a mass enrolment campaign in December 1923 to admit 100,000 workers into the party. In the name of 'reproletarianising' the party, two recruitment drives were conducted in 1924 and 1925, which boosted the membership from 446,089 on 1 January 1924 to slightly over 1 million by 1 January 1926. This dramatic influx was orchestrated under the banner of the Lenin Levy, one of the earliest examples of Stalin invoking the name of the dead leader to strengthen his grip over the party.[41]

Stalin's unveiling in late 1924 of the theory of 'socialism in one country' appealed especially to the growing bureaucratic strata, which were tending with increasing consciousness to identify their own material interests with the development of the 'national' Soviet economy. Within broad layers of the working class a general political exhaustion expressed itself in a retreat from the internationalist aspirations of the October Revolution. Especially after the debacle suffered by the German Communist Party in October 1923, the

40 For the text of the Platform, see Trotsky, 1980: 400 and Carr, 1969: 374–80.

41 Siegelbaum, 1992: 181.

promise of a national solution to the crisis of Soviet society seemed to offer a new lifeline for the besieged revolution. Stalin suggested that the theory of 'socialism in one country' served the valuable function of offering the Soviet masses a reason to believe that the October Revolution had not been made in vain, and that those who denied the possibility of building socialism in Russia, regardless of the fate of the international revolutionary movement, were dampening the faith and enthusiasm of the working class. It was necessary to assure the workers that they were, through their own efforts, achieving socialism. To arguments of this sort Trotsky replied in 1928:

> The theory of socialism in one country inexorably leads to an underestimation of the difficulties which must be overcome and to an exaggeration of the achievements gained. One could not find a more anti-socialist and anti-revolutionary assertion than Stalin's statement to the effect that 'socialism has already been 90 per cent realised in the USSR.' . . . Harsh truth and not sugary falsehood is needed to fortify the worker, the agricultural laborer, and the poor peasant, who see that in the eleventh year of the revolution, poverty, misery, unemployment, bread lines, illiteracy, homeless children, drunkenness, and prostitution have not abated around them. Instead of telling them fibs about having realised 90 per cent socialism, we must say to them that our economic level, our social and cultural conditions, approximate today much closer to capitalism, and a backward and uncultured capitalism at that, than to socialism. We must tell them that we will enter on the path of real socialist construction only when the proletariat of the most advanced countries will have captured power; that it is necessary to work unremittingly for this, using both levers – the short lever of our internal economic efforts and the long lever of the international proletarian struggle (Trotsky, 1970: 66).

Trotsky's insistence on the dependence of the Soviet Union upon the development of world socialist revolution and, conversely, the impossibility of constructing socialism in a single country, constituted the theoretical and political foundation of the struggle that he and the Left Opposition waged against the Stalinist bureaucracy. The central elements of the programme of the Left Opposition – such as the re-establishment of party democracy, the development of planning, the strengthening of industry – flowed from this conception.

The 'triumvirate' accused the Left Opposition of violating the party's 1921 ban on factions. Trotsky retained strong support among educated youth and within the army, but refused to appeal to the military to move against the emerging Stalinist regime, insisting that such an intervention, far from overcoming the deep-seated political, economic and cultural roots of the bureaucratisation, would endanger the very social and political base of the workers' state itself. Historians, including those sympathetic to Trotsky,[42] are inclined to see in his commitment to world revolution the weakest element of his overall programme. This criticism underestimates the revolutionary potential that existed in the international workers movement of the 1920s and 1930s, and fails to appreciate the impact of Stalinism on the development of world revolution. The political destruction of the Comintern by the Stalinists – that is, its transformation into an appendage of the Soviet bureaucracy – was the major cause of the calamitous defeats suffered by the working class, above all in Germany in 1923, Britain in 1926, China in 1926–27, Germany again in 1933 and Spain in 1936–37. These defeats, in turn, profoundly affected the course of developments within the Soviet Union. Trotsky noted that two dates were especially significant in this historic process.

> In the second half of 1923, the attention of the Soviet workers was passionately fixed upon Germany, where the proletariat, it seemed, had stretched out its hand to power. The panicky retreat of the German Communist Party was the heaviest possible disappointment to the working masses of the Soviet Union. The Soviet bureaucracy straightaway opened a campaign against the theory of 'permanent revolution' and dealt the Left Opposition its first cruel blow. During the years 1926 and 1927 the population of the Soviet Union experienced a new tide of hope. All eyes were now directed to the East where the drama of the Chinese revolution was unfolding. The Left Opposition had recovered from the previous blows and was recruiting a phalanx of new adherents. At the end of 1927 the Chinese revolution was massacred by the hangman, Chiang-kai-shek, into whose hands the Communist International had literally betrayed the Chinese workers and peasants. A cold wave of disappointment swept over the masses of the Soviet Union. After an unbridled baiting in the press and at meetings, the bureaucracy finally, in 1928, ventured upon mass arrests among the Left Opposition (Trotsky, 1937: 91).

If the revolution had spread to the advanced countries of Western Europe, starting with the German revolutionary upsurges of 1918–23, and the many-millioned countries of the East, beginning with the Chinese revolution of 1926–27, the history of the USSR and the world would almost certainly have been very different.

The Soviet bureaucracy's consolidation of power was accompanied by the discrediting, criminalisation and physical destruction of its political opponents. Trotsky was forcibly exiled in 1928, expelled from the Soviet Union in 1929 and assassinated by a GPU agent in Mexico in 1940. The

42 For example, Deutscher, 1954 and 1959; Carr, 1971.

process of physical destruction was supplemented by a campaign of historical falsification that sought to obliterate from the consciousness of the Soviet and international working class all traces of the Marxist alternative to Stalinism advanced by Trotsky and other leaders of the Left Opposition, such as Rakovsky, Preobrazhensky, Piatakov, Joffe, Sosnovsky, Eltsin, Ter-Vaganian, Boguslavsky, Vilensky and Voronsky. But in many fields, including law, these figures contributed to the immense political and intellectual life of the early years of the Russian Revolution.

Chapter 5

Bolshevik 'law' in practice

> The reversal of the initial hostility of the revolution towards law was one of the most striking symptoms of the change in the climate of opinion.[1]

Despite being quite abstract in its approach, Pashukanis' *General Theory* cannot be assessed without some knowledge of how Marxist legal theory looked in practice in the early years of Soviet Russia. Another question also arises: Why was Pashukanis, writing in 1924, the first Soviet scholar to attempt to outline a general theory of law for the Soviet state that had been inaugurated seven years earlier?

In its initial phases, the Russian Revolution saw far-reaching efforts to end the old legal order based on private property, de-legalise all aspects of family and social life and pave the way for a self-governing society without a separate legal apparatus of lawyers, judges, police and prisons. These were unprecedented endeavours at the time, and remain unparalleled to this day. We need to examine these policies and experiences in order to evaluate the intense legal debates throughout the first decade of Soviet Russia, from 1917 to 1927, and the rise and fall of Pashukanis. This book can only provide a brief outline of the main periods of legal activity.

Lagging behind events

In examining early Bolshevik legal policy, one factor must not be overlooked, flowing from the mass character of the October 1917 Revolution. Well before the Soviet government was formed, and decreed the abolition of the Tsarist courts, in key areas the working people themselves had already swept aside the authority of the old police agencies and courts. Immediately after the February Revolution, in Kronstadt and the Vyborg side of Petrograd, for example, the workers had ignored the Tsarist courts and begun to set up their

1 Carr, 1971, vol 5: 88.

own revolutionary courts.[2] Trotsky records that on 1 March, the Provisional Government had issued an order for the arrest of all police officials, public, secret and political, but the gesture was 'purely platonic in character, for the police were already being arrested and the jails were their only refuge from massacre'.[3] By April 1917, Trotsky records, under the pressure of the masses, 'the soviets were becoming organs of administration', interfering in all aspects of government, 'even in the courts of justice'. In Tiflis, for example, the local soviet 'confiscated a private printing establishment for its own uses, made arrests, took charge of investigations and trials for political offences, established a bread ration, and fixed the prices of food and the necessaries of life'.[4]

After seizing power in October 1917, the Bolsheviks initially lagged someway behind the events concerning the courts. Judges continued to act in the name of the overthrown Provisional Government. Writing in *Pravda* in November 1917, Stuchka, the first Soviet Commissar of Justice, stated: 'We must concede that the Russian Revolution acts very slowly with respect to the old apparatus of power; except for the commanding heights, all the old apparatus is intact.'[5] Under the headline 'A Class Court or a Democratic Court?' he complained that judges were continuing to preside over cases, even though they were not yet subjected to democratic election and recall. As an interim measure, Stuchka proposed to transfer the following cases from the courts: agrarian cases (to land committees), apartment disputes (to apartment house mediation committees) and all other civil cases (to special workers' institutions). He observed that the overall volume of cases would also diminish significantly with the removal of such obsolete institutions as tribal property and predetermined inheritance, the abolition of political and religious crimes and the simplification of the penal system.

Stuchka proposed the election of all judges, the equalisation of all judicial salaries and the earliest possible replacement of the old legal institutions with revolutionary courts. But there were heated discussions among the Bolsheviks about how to proceed. One faction urged the retention of the pre-revolutionary courts during the period of socialist transition. Another faction insisted that all existing legal institutions and law should be abolished because they were incompatible with socialism.[6] Lenin effected a compromise with the enactment of Decree No. 1 on the courts on 24 November 1917. First, it abolished most of the old legal system, including the district courts, military and naval courts, commercial courts, court chambers, the departments of the Ruling Senate, the Procuracy and justices of the peace. Second,

2 Sharlet, Maggs and Beirne, 1988: 3.
3 Trotsky, 1977: 200.
4 Ibid: 371–2.
5 Sharlet, Maggs and Beirne, 1988: 7.
6 Ibid: 4.

it declared that all laws were invalid if they contradicted the decrees of the Central Executive Committee or the minimum programmes of the two parties in the ruling coalition – the Russian Social Democrats (Bolsheviks) and the Left Social Revolutionaries. Third, it instituted a system of local (later people's) courts and revolutionary tribunals. The former were to hear civil cases and minor criminal trials; the latter were to consider offences of a counter-revolutionary character. Both were to be democratically elected, and their members were to be guided by revolutionary consciousness.[7]

According to Stuchka, Lenin supported Stuchka's first draft of the decree and worked on it personally, adding a note to Article 5. The original draft stated:

> Local workers and peasants revolutionary courts are approved, guided in their decisions and sentences not by the written laws of the overthrown governments, but by the decrees of the Council of People's Commissars, revolutionary conscience and revolutionary legal consciousness (Sharlet, Maggs and Beirne, 1988: 90).

Concerned that insufficient decrees existed and that the terms 'revolutionary conscience' and 'revolutionary legal consciousness' were too abstract and vague, and facing opposition from the Social Revolutionaries and among the Bolsheviks to the sweeping nature of the proposal, Lenin added a note specifying that all laws would be regarded as repealed that contradicted the Soviet government's decrees or the minimum programmes of the ruling coalition partners (the Bolsheviks and Left Social Revolutionaries). Lenin also delayed the measure by two days and asked Lunacharsky to write a *Pravda* article in support of the decree.[8] Thus from the first days of the revolution, lively and considered debates erupted over legal policy.

Educative decrees

Another, related, factor must be considered. Many of the early decrees and declarations were intended to be educative and normative, setting out the aspirations of the new government, lifting the expectations of the working and peasant masses and indicating the standards by which the new order wished to be judged by citizens. Lenin and other Bolshevik leaders did not primarily conceive of their proclamations, such as the January 1918 'Declaration of Rights of the Working and Exploited People' as legal codes; rather as statements of intent and exhortation.

Soviet labour legislation afforded the right to labour to 'all able-bodied

7 Sharlet, Maggs and Beirne, 1988: 4.
8 Ibid: 220.

citizens', regardless of gender, and protected women from discriminatory dismissal, rights that were unheard of elsewhere.[9] There were similar proclamations in labour protection (e.g. the eight-hour day), social welfare (e.g. social insurance) and housing (e.g. rent controls and rent-free public housing).[10] A leading Soviet jurist of the time, A.G. Goikhbarg, stated that the labour code was more of a hope than a reality in 1918, given widespread unemployment and economic crisis.[11] Nevertheless, the vast array of declarations issued by the Soviet government in the early 'honeymoon' period of the revolution, that is before the invasion of the White armies and the onset of the civil war, were important statements of principle.

According to one study, the two formal organs of the Soviet government – the All-Russia Central Executive Committee of the Soviets and the Council of People's Commissars – issued no less than 950 decrees and other enactments in the first nine months after October 1917. The measures were by no means confined to declarations of law; they were sweeping in their character, covering every aspect of economic, social and political life.[12] The Soviet leaders 'made the principles of their policy known to millions of ordinary workers and peasants by mass publication of all decrees and decisions'.[13] Within two days of their adoption, decrees had to be published in the central government newspapers – *Izvestia* and *Gazeta Vremennogo Rabochego i Krestyanskogo* – and in the 'Collection of Laws and Ordinances of the Workers and Peasants Government'. From January 1918, the Council of People's Commissars required the official newspapers to also publish reports of the Council's proceedings.[14]

Another scholar divided the early decrees into four main categories. The first had no legal meaning at all. They were political proclamations or directives, such as the Decree on Peace of 8 November 1917, renouncing the war against Germany and appealing for peace negotiations. The second group contained legal provisions but could not be implemented due to the circumstances of civil war and 'War Communism' or were not intended to be implemented. They were also issued mainly for propaganda purposes, including the November 1917 Decree on Workers Control. A third category 'legalised arbitrariness and terror', notably the establishment of the Cheka. The fourth group consisted of 'normative acts which were aimed at a gradual building up of a new system of law in the ordinary sense of the term', such as decrees dealing with the judiciary, crime, family, property and labour

9 Quigley, 1988: 139.
10 Ibid: 141–51.
11 Cited in P. Maggs, 'Choice and Compulsion in Soviet Labor Law: Labor Conscription 1917–21', in Butler, Maggs and Quigley, 1988: 38.
12 Akhapin, 1970: 11–16.
13 Ibid: 11.
14 Akhapin, 1970: 14–15.

relations.[15] This classification has merit in drawing attention to the wider, consciousness-raising role of many early Soviet measures, as well as the variety of aims and purposes behind the decrees generally. Only after the adoption of the NEP in 1921, however, could it be said that 'a new system of law' was erected.

Six periods stand out in the approach to law between 1917 and Pashukanis' execution in 1937:

(1) The establishment of Soviet power (October 1917–mid-1918)
(2) The civil war and intervention by foreign armies – 'War Communism' (1918–21)
(3) The New Economic Policy (1921–26)
(4) The defeat of the Left Opposition (1927–29)
(5) Stalin's 'Third Period' and forced collectivisation (1929–35)
(6) The Popular Front and the great purges (1935–39).

The establishment of Soviet power

Neither the first months of the 1917 Revolution nor the civil war period allowed for a great deal of theoretical elaboration. As Goikhbarg noted in 1923 (by which time the NEP had dramatically changed the legal outlook): 'Prior to the revolution, no one had thought of drawing up (whether in detail or in a general form) the legal relations to be established and adjusted during the transition from the proletarian revolution to the consolidation of socialism and communism . . . At present, therefore, research in this area is like plowing virgin soil . . .'[16]

Nevertheless the assumption underpinning the actions of the new government remained, as the historian E.H. Carr concluded, 'that law was a temporary expedient, borrowed for specific purposes from the defunct bourgeois order of society, and destined to die away as soon as socialism became a reality'.[17]

In accord with the notion that the state would immediately begin to wither away, the Bolshevik leaders urged the working-class masses to take all decision-making power, and even the power of arrest, into their own hands. A few days after the October Revolution, Lenin drafted his appeal 'To the Populace':

> Comrade workers! Remember that *you yourselves* now administer the state. Nobody will help you if you yourselves do not unite and fail to take

15 Lapenna, 1968: 43–5.
16 Zile, 1970: 50.
17 Carr, 1971, vol 5: 67.

> *all the affairs* of the state into *your own* hands. *Your* Soviets are henceforth the organs of state power, plenipotentiary organs of decision-making . . . Arrest and bring before revolutionary tribunals anybody who dares to harm the people's cause, whether such harm take the form of sabotage (spoiling, wrecking, injuring), or concealment of supplies of grain or other foodstuffs, or interference with the operations of the railroad, postal, telegraph and telephone systems, or any kind of opposition to the great cause of peace, the task of transferring the land to the peasants, and the task of securing the workers' control over the production and distribution of goods (Zile, 1970: 12).

This was not an invitation to mob rule but an appeal for the ordinary people to actively involve themselves, through the soviets and revolutionary tribunals, in fully wresting economic and political power out of privileged hands. As discussed earlier, the soviets, or workers' councils, had pre-dated the Bolshevik Revolution of October 1917. They first emerged as a mass phenomenon during the February 1917 Revolution, which overthrew the Tsarist dictatorship.

By the end of 1917, the Soviets had become official forms of government. There were 30 provincial, 121 city, 286 county and 6,088 township soviets. If district and regional soviets were added, there were 7,550 bodies of local administration with more than 100,000 working people participating in their operation.[18] Between their periodically convened congresses, elected executive committees ran the soviets. One year after the October Revolution, 6,550 such committees existed – 6,111 at the volost level, 286 uezd, 121 city, 30 provincial and two regional.[19] All over the age of 18 could vote in Soviet elections, regardless of sex, creed, nationality or residential qualifications, except for those who 'employ others for profit'.[20]

Among the earliest decrees of the new central government were those abolishing ownership of land and inheritance without any compensation, subject to the protection of individual homes, the sustenance of the poor and the right of those who tilled the land to use it.[21] Thus, the revolution set out to replace private ownership of the means of production, including land, with social ownership. It also sought to eliminate, or at least greatly restrict, employment for wages and market relations based on exchange of commodities. These fundamental changes to the economy and the very conception of property had vast implications for the role of law, not just radically altering

18 'Forty Years of Soviet Law 1917–57', in Zile, 1970: 12.

19 Siegelbaum, 1992: 16.

20 'Constitution (Fundamental Law) of the Russian Socialist Federative Republic (1918)', in Zile, 1970: 13.

21 See Zile, 1970: 14–15, 25.

economic and social relationships, but recasting core concepts such as property and employment. They also laid the basis for beginning to de-legalise society, to the extent that much law, both civil and criminal, is either directly or indirectly predicated upon the protection of private property interests, or arises from the socio-economic and personal conflicts generated by private ownership and social inequality.[22]

The Bolsheviks sought to abolish the traditional apparatus of legal and state power and set in motion processes leading to a self-regulating society. The initial judicial decree of November 1917[23] set up local people's courts, elected or nominated by soviets, with two rotating lay assessors to sit with each judge. Not only were the previous courts dissolved, but the legal profession lost its monopoly on representation, enabling any citizen of good character to appear as a prosecutor or defence counsel. The practice of law was opened to 'all who enjoy civil rights'. Later, a body of salaried legal representatives was established, appointed by the local soviets, with any clients' fees to be collected by the state treasury.[24]

Distrust of judges, dating from the days of the Tsarist dictatorship, influenced the introduction of one of the unique features of Soviet justice, the people's assessors. Their creation by Article 2 of the decree recognised a form of justice that had already arisen semi-spontaneously in the immediate aftermath of the October Revolution. In various centres, local revolutionary authorities had established new courts in order to replace the hated judiciary and the complex, slothful judicial procedures, which were still based on the Tsarist-period principle of treating citizens unequally according to their legal status. Local justices of the peace functioned as chairmen of the courts, accompanied by elected assessors representing different sections of the community. Based on this experience, Article 2 provided for the assessors to be provisionally nominated by the local soviets, with the prospect of eventual democratic elections.[25]

The November 1917 decree also established elected revolutionary tribunals with rotating assessors to deal with counter-revolutionary activity, as well as pillaging, plundering and sabotage, including that conducted by officials. This marked the beginning of a separate system to deal with those seeking to overturn the revolution.[26] Nevertheless, the first regulation governing the tribunals

22 This proposition has been much contested. Fuller, 1949, for example, as previously noted in the Introduction, asserts that human nature makes legality essential. Berman, 1963: 48–65, concludes that the Bolshevik efforts to de-legalise life ultimately foundered on lack of popular support for Marxist-Leninist internationalism, and the restoration of strong bonds of traditional Russian family life – legal, economic and spiritual – together with the 'age-old' questions of personal claims and interests.

23 Zile, 1970: 35–7.

24 Berman, 1963: 31.

25 Schlesinger, 1951: 62–3.

26 Carr, 1971, vol 5: 68.

contained certain democratic safeguards, including public hearings, the right to defence counsel and the restriction of punishments to imprisonment and banishment.[27]

Subsequent decrees modified the new judicial order in certain respects. A February 1918 decree 'On the Judiciary' established elected circuit courts, provided for a right to representation in criminal cases and created a 'college of advocates' to appear in them. In order to stabilise and legitimise the emerging legal system, the decree was adopted as the Statute on the Courts, although it was commonly referred to as the 'second decree'.[28] It preserved the civil and criminal procedures of the 1864 Judicial Code, in so far as they were not abrogated by the revolution and contradicted 'socialist conceptions of justice'. In civil cases, considerations of 'justice, not formal law' should prevail over rules of limitations and other formal objections.[29]

Article 29 of the February statute strengthened the role of the people's assessors in acting as a check on the court presidents, who were likely to be lawyers. The assessors could remove the president from his post at any stage of the proceedings and reduce any sentence as much as they thought just, even to acquittal. On the other hand, there were guarantees against 'revolutionary' arbitrariness. Under Article 8, a court, if deviating from existing procedure as 'obsolete and bourgeois' had to state its reasons for so doing, so that its decision could be reviewed on appeal. Article 6 established a Supreme Judicial Control, comprising delegates from the local courts elected for no more than a year, unless their electors or local soviet recalled them previously.[30] Article 6 provided for the Supreme Judicial Control to set down guiding decisions for local courts and to propose legislative amendments. Interestingly, the scheme incorporated a certain separation of powers, by insisting that only the legislative organ – the national Soviet assembly – not the Council of People's Commissars, could overturn Supreme Judicial Control rulings:

> If observing distortions of the law or contradictions in the interpretation of the law by various Courts of Appeal, the Supreme Judicial Control has to carry a principal decision which serves the courts as a rule. . . If the Supreme Judicial Control should be confronted by an insurmountable contradiction between the existing law and the revolutionary sense of justice, it will suggest to the legislative organ the necessity of amending the law. Only the legislative organ is allowed to overrule decisions of the Supreme Judicial Control (Schlesinger, 1951: 67).

27 Zile, 1970: 42–8.
28 Schlesinger, 1951: 64.
29 Zile, 1970: 37–8; Schlesinger, 1951: 64–5.
30 Schlesinger, 1951: 66.

One consideration must be mentioned here. From December 1917 until March 1918, the Bolsheviks were in coalition with the Left Social Revolutionaries, from whose leadership I.N. Shteinberg was appointed Commissar of Justice. The Left SRs opposed the complete abolition of the old judicial system, backed the reintroduction of circuit courts and proposed basing criminal law on a reformed Tsarist code. After the Left SRs quit the government over the signing of the Brest-Litovsk treaty with Germany, Shteinberg was replaced by Stuchka, who introduced decrees of July and September 1918 to return to the single level of people's courts.[31] But the underlying conception of supervising the local courts through a combination of assessors, judicial self-government and an elected appellate body was preserved in the Law of Procedure of War Communism, the Statute on the People's Courts of November 1918, which is outlined below.

As quoted earlier,[32] the first Constitution of the Russian Republic, adopted in 1918, stated that its task was to help create the conditions for 'socialism, under which there will be neither division into classes nor state authority'.[33] Thus, the purpose of, and need for, the proletarian dictatorship was clearly defined: it was to overcome the violent physical and economic opposition of the propertied elites, so as to pave the way for ending economic exploitation, the prerequisite for the state to begin to wither away. This conception envisaged an initial strengthening of the state, but for temporary and definite purposes. In 1920, Trotsky outlined the prospective 'withering away of the state' as follows: 'The whole population of the country will be drawn into the general Soviet system of economic arrangement and self-government. The Soviets themselves, at present the organs of government, will gradually melt into purely economic organisations.'[34] As Trotsky was to later explain in *The Revolution Betrayed*, the Bolsheviks hoped for an early victory of the socialist revolution in Western Europe, which would make possible a relatively short transition to genuine communism.

'War Communism'

These hopes and initiatives were overtaken by the invasion of Soviet Russia by foreign armies and the onset of the civil war. In June 1918, under conditions of armed resistance to the revolution, Stuchka, newly appointed as People's Commissar of Justice, allowed the revolutionary tribunals to impose the death penalty. At the same time, the tribunals were given the sole power to pass death sentences, displacing the Cheka.

31 Juviler, 1976: 20–1.
32 Chapter 1.
33 Berman, 1963: 30–1.
34 Trotsky, 1961: 47.

In November 1918, after months of fighting against the White armies backed by military contingents dispatched by the various Western powers and Japan, the Sixth All-Russian Extraordinary Congress of Soviets adopted a decree 'On the Strict Observance of Laws'.[35] It frankly sought to legitimise, but also limit, emergency measures taken 'because of the continued extraordinary plots and the war which was forced on the peasants and workers of Russia by the imperialists'. The decree stated that measures that deviated from or exceeded the limits of the law had to be justified by 'extraordinary circumstances of the civil war' and reported to the Council of People's Commissars. Over the same months, Trotsky, as People's Commissar for Military and Naval Affairs, forged the Red Army which ultimately, after four years of severe fighting, prevailed in the civil war.[36]

A further decree of November 1918 established a central People's Court within the Russian Socialist Federated Soviet Republic (RSFSR) and another decree of October 1920 specified qualifications for people's judges and defence counsel. In addition to being entitled to vote, a judge was required to either have experience in the political work of the party, trade unions, cooperatives, factory committees or soviets, or have theoretical or practical preparation for the duties of a judge.[37]

Under Article 1 of the November decree, the people's courts held three kinds of sessions. The president sitting alone could make non-controversial decisions, such as granting a divorce or ordering an arrest. The president with two people's assessors could hear the bulk of civil and criminal cases. Accompanied by six assessors, the president could judge crimes against life, grave bodily injury, rape, forgery, bribery or speculation in goods contrary to a state monopoly. Under Articles 15, 17 and 18, the assessors were chosen by lot from lists prepared by local soviets. Like juries in other countries, the assessors were obliged to perform this civic duty, except that they participated in six consecutive sessions of the court, not just a single hearing.[38]

Another characteristic feature of early Soviet criminal justice was a strict separation between investigation, preliminary inquiry and final verdict in a public trial. An Investigating Commission of six judges had to conduct a preliminary investigation in order to decide whether sufficient grounds existed for a public trial. Defence was organised by a College of Advocates, chosen by the executive committee of the local soviet. Defence counsel was obligatory in the serious cases to be heard by the president and six assessors, and in all other cases where prosecuting counsel was admitted.[39]

35 Zile, 1970: 51.

36 See Trotsky, 1979.

37 Zile, 1970: 38–41.

38 Schlesinger, 1951: 67–8.

39 Ibid: 68.

The November decree contained clauses that reflected and perhaps influenced the early legal debates over the role of 'law' in the transition to communism. Article 22 specified that the only written laws to be applied were decrees of the Soviet government. If no relevant decree existed, 'the Socialist consciousness of Justice' had to be applied. A footnote to this article prohibited reference, in giving judgment, to laws or judicial decisions of the pre-revolutionary regime. Stuchka later concluded from this that law was formally lacking from 1917 to 1922.[40]

While these courts dispensed justice according to 'revolutionary conscience', the statistics suggest that they approached cases leniently and with an open mind. A 1919 analysis prepared by Kursky, then the Justice Commissar, reported that of 61,128 criminal cases, 43 per cent resulted in acquittal, 35 per cent in imprisonment (four fifths with probation), 8 per cent in socially necessary work, 4 per cent in fines and 10 per cent in other determinations, usually admonitions. Even the Supreme Revolutionary Council, which dealt only with cases of treason or with former leading agents of the Tsarist Ochrana secret police, passed fewer sentences of death than of imprisonment, and then commuted most of the death sentences by way of amnesty.[41]

During 1920, the people's courts tried 881,933 people, of whom nearly 300,000 were exonerated. Among those convicted, 34 per cent were sentenced to confinement, 30 per cent were fined and 23 per cent had to perform compulsory labour. Revolutionary tribunals, which heard more serious cases and consisted of six assessors and a judge, handled far fewer cases – 26,738 – but had a higher conviction rate (85 per cent, compared to 66 per cent) and imposed heavier penalties. Among those convicted, 16,107 (70.7 per cent) were sentenced to confinement and 766 (3.4 per cent) were shot.[42]

There was official resistance to local Soviet interference in people's court decisions. A Moscow general meeting of people's court judges on 30 March 1918 adopted a resolution moved by Pashukanis, then a people's court judge, demanding complete autonomy for the courts, after a borough soviet set aside a people's court decision.[43] A 1921 decree gave the People's Commissariat of Justice the responsibility to supervise and train the judicial bodies and also to invalidate their decisions, albeit in defined circumstances. These were enumerated as: (a) a clear violation of the laws of the Soviet government; (b) acting outside jurisdiction; and (c) a clear conflict with the guiding principles of Soviet legislation and general government policies.[44]

Stuchka was the author of the first attempt by the Soviet authorities to define law in general and Soviet law in particular. The 'Guiding Principle of

40 Schlesinger, 1951: 68, 79.
41 Ibid: 72.
42 Juviler, 1976: 20, 26; also Huskey, 1986: 39–79.
43 Juviler, 1976: 21–2.
44 Zile, 1970: 41.

Criminal Law of the RSFSR' (1919)[45] defined law as: 'A system (order) of social relations which corresponds to the interests of the ruling class and which protects the ruling class by means of its organised force, in other words, state.' This definition, Stuchka argued, sought to apply the Marxist understanding of law as essentially an instrument of class rule, enforced by a coercive state apparatus. (The merits of this definition and its criticism by Pashukanis are discussed in Chapters 6–9.)

Thus in the first period of 'war communism' the Bolshevik leaders were preoccupied with physically defending the revolution while providing basic democratic guarantees. Their approach to law was characterised by efforts to encourage mass participation in decision-making, explain the ideological basis for law and hasten the demise of purely legal measures. By 1921, the direct military threats to Soviet Russia had been repelled, but expectations of victorious social revolutions elsewhere in Eastern and Western Europe were dashed.

The New Economic Policy

Designed to buy time for the isolated Soviet state, the adoption of the NEP in 1921 led to a marked shift in the role assigned to law. Exchange on the market was only possible if the buyers and sellers were assured of legally protected property rights. Lenin warned of the dangers of creating a new economic elite. He told the Bolshevik Party's Tenth Congress:

> Freedom of market is freedom of trade, and freedom of trade means a return to capitalism. Freedom of market and freedom of trade mean the exchange of commodities between small individual operators. All of us who have studied the ABC of Marxism realise that such [freedom of] market and freedom of trade inevitably cause the producers to break into two elements: the owners of capital and the owners of two toiling hands, that is, into the capitalists and the hired laborers. This is the revival of the capitalist slavery of hire (Zile, 1970: 51).

In a resolution, the party congress declared that 'the exchange of commodities is recognised as the basic moving force of the New Economic Policy' and 'enterprise and local initiative must be given manifold support and developed at all cost'.[46]

The next congress, just seven months later in December 1921, adopted a resolution 'On the Current Tasks of the Party in Connection with Restoration of the Economy' that drew the following conclusion in relation to law: 'the

45 Zile, 1970: 50.
46 Ibid: 65.

immediate task is to introduce strict principles of revolutionary legality into all areas of life.'[47] This notion of 'revolutionary legality' was, however, a far cry from the 'socialist legality' later proclaimed by Stalin to be inherently associated with the achievement of socialism. For Lenin it was an unavoidable concession made to private property relations in order to revive the economy. The Eleventh Congress resolution stated:

> The new types of relations established both during the course of the revolution and as a result of the government's economic policy must now find their expression in the law and must be protected by the courts. Firm rules of civil law must be laid down for the resolution of all kinds of conflicts in the area of property relations. Citizens and corporations entering into contractual relations with state organs should receive an assurance that their rights will be protected. The judicial institutions of the Soviet republic should be elevated to appropriate heights (Zile, 1970: 51).

The Soviet government was conscious of the fact that investors demanded certainty before parting with their capital. 'To end doubts as regards the sincerity of the new course of economic policies', a 1921 decree specified that only courts were permitted to annul contracts and that, in the future, nationalisation of any enterprise was allowed only by special enactment.[48] With the restoration of the market under the NEP came the acknowledged necessity of restoring bourgeois law. The Bolsheviks therefore instructed jurists to study the pre-revolutionary Russian codes, as well as the German, Swiss and French codes, and adapt them to the new Soviet conditions. In 1922 and 1923 there appeared a Judiciary Act, a Civil Code, Code of Civil Procedure, Criminal Code, Code of Criminal Procedure, Land Code and Labour Code. The Judiciary Act established a traditional hierarchy of courts, with a system of appeals, but retained some innovative features. Among them were people's assessors, chosen from the general population for periods of 10 days. Two assessors sat alongside each judge.

The Civil Code dealt in traditional terms with legal capacity, persons, corporations, legal transactions, a statute of limitations, property, mortgages, landlord and tenant relations, contract and tort, unjust enrichment and inheritance. At the same time, the codes contained provisions to protect the economically weak and uphold the public interest. Under the Civil Code, any transaction 'directed to the obvious prejudice of the state' was invalid and any profits accrued from such a transaction were to be forfeited to the state as 'unjust enrichment'[49] [Article 1]. Thus, the absolute character of private

47 Zile, 1970: 66–7.
48 Schlesinger, 1951: 87.
49 Berman, 1963: 35–6.

rights was tempered by public policy, giving rise to what Berman describes as 'the dualism of private rights and public policy'.[50]

With regard to civil liability for personal injury, as in criminal law, the concept of fault was minimised, if not eliminated. 'Our code does not view the fault of the person causing the injury as essential for the imposition of liability,' stated Goikhbarg, the principal author of the Civil Code. 'Compensation for injury is, generally speaking, an institution beneficial to the workers' and therefore 'it is necessary to give extensive interpretation to the liability of the person causing the injury (except where the liability of the state is involved) and a narrow construction to rules permitting the defendant to escape liability'.[51]

Similar considerations underpinned the code provision that 'where a person, under the pressure of distress, concludes a transaction clearly unprofitable to him, the court, on the petition of the damaged party, or on the petition of a proper government agency or social organisation, may either declare the transaction invalid or preclude its operation in the future'.[52] In both tort and contract law, the focus was upon preventing financial distress and redressing social injustice, rather than assigning individual fault.

Likewise, the 1922 Civil Code afforded legal protection to private commercial transactions and associated individual liberties, subject to regulatory decrees. Article 5 included the following:

> Every citizen of the RSFSR and the union of soviet republics has the right to move about freely and to settle down within the territory of the RSFSR, to choose any occupation and profession not prohibited by law, to acquire and alienate property within the limitations established by law, to enter into legal transactions and to incur obligations, and to organise industrial and commercial enterprises in compliance with all decrees regulating industrial and commercial activities and protecting hired labor (Zile, 1970: 69).

Article 6 stated: 'No one may be deprived of civil-law rights or limited in rights except in the cases and in the manner prescribed by the law.'[53] Much discussion in Soviet legal circles centred on Article 1, which sought to clarify the relationship between the recognition of civil-law rights and the needs of socialism. It subordinated these rights to the requirements of production: 'Civil-law rights shall be protected by law, except in those instances when they are exercised in contradiction to their socio-economic purpose.'[54]

50 Berman, 1963: 36.
51 Ibid: 36.
52 Ibid: 37. See also Gsovski, 1948, vol 1: 415ff, 485ff.
53 Zile, 1970: 69.
54 Ibid: 84.

While these provisions established a prime facie protection of individual and commercial rights, they allowed these rights to be overridden where they were utilised in a socially harmful or wasteful way. Writing on Article 1 in the *Weekly of Soviet Justice*, Asknazil said that these rights were secured not so much to satisfy personal interests as to achieve certain economic ends. He gave the example of an idle enterprise being taken temporarily from its owner and transferred to other operators so that the enterprise could serve its productive function. The owner would be compensated according to the normal profitability of such an enterprise. Asknazil argued that the public interest should always prevail over private interests, but that it was also in the public interest for individual property rights to be assured in order to promote the growth of commodity trade. The author argued for this purpose to be more clearly defined in the Civil Code, to prevent Article 1 being excessively invoked against owners.[55]

The Land Code adopted in 1922 formally declared all land the property of the state and prohibited its sale or purchase but permitted households to hold, cultivate and, under certain circumstances, lease land. These arrangements arguably codified nineteenth-century peasant legal custom, developed under serfdom, which maintained that land belonged 'to nobody'. Important decisions, including on the extent to which peasant holdings could be partitioned, were left largely in the hands of communal assemblies.[56]

Lenin advocated definite administrative and political measures to guard against the growth of a privileged bureaucracy within the state. The rise of the NEPmen threatened to become the social and material basis for an emerging elite. Lenin's campaign against bureaucratism was translated into measures to try to prevent state power from being usurped by apparatchiks, in line with the party programme of 1919:

> Conducting the most resolute struggle against bureaucratism, the Russian Communist Party advocates for the complete overcoming of this evil the following measures:
>
> (1) an obligatory call on every member of the Soviet for the fulfillment of a definite task in the administration of the state;
> (2) a systematic variation in these tasks in order that they may gradually cover all branches of the administration;
> (3) a gradual drawing of the whole working population into work in the administration of the state.
>
> The full and universal application of all these measures, which represents a further step on the road trodden by the Paris Commune, and the

55 Zile, 1970: 87–9.
56 Siegelbaum, 1992: 92; Lewin, 1985: 86.

> simplification of the functions of administration accompanied by a rise in the cultural level of the workers will lead to the abolition of state power (Carr, 1971, vol 1: 248).[57]

With Lenin largely incapacitated by illness, however, from the time of his first stroke in 1923, the NEPmen and bureaucrats found a champion in Stalin. By autumn 1924, less than a year after the defeat of the October 1923 German revolution and eight months after Lenin's death, Stalin had unveiled the new doctrine of 'socialism in one country'. This new nationalist programme appealed to a mood of exhaustion in the country, abandoning the struggle for international socialism and instead concentrating on constructing a strong national state. It became the ideological and material underpinning of the bureaucrats who assumed the role of presiding over terrible scarcity and inequality, all the while declaring these social conditions to be necessary for the forging of socialism. According to the historian E.H. Carr, the consolidation of a corresponding legal regime was one of the signs of the emergence of the elite layer and its nationalist doctrine:

> The reversal of the initial hostility of the revolution towards law was one of the most striking symptoms of the change in the climate of opinion which paved the way for the doctrine of socialism in one country (Carr, 1971, vol 5: 88).

This suggestion provides a key for analysing the early Soviet debates about law. The reversal of earlier aspirations of a transition to a classless, stateless society led to the consolidation of state authority, which in turn was bound up with the emergence of a nationalist outlook. Contained in this were the seeds of the later reversals of the early legal experiments and accomplishments.

Over the ensuing decade, Stalin's nationalist doctrine of building socialism in just one country became intertwined with the development of a totalitarian order and the reversal of the early legal initiatives. It reversed the Marxist conception that the transition to communism required overcoming scarcity, instead holding out the prospect of gradually building socialism, even on an impoverished basis. For this, Stalin and his supporters, who initially included Bukharin, insisted that the state apparatus had to be strengthened and stabilised, rather than reduced. Trotsky explained:

> The 'theory' of socialism in one country – a 'theory' never expounded, by the way, or given any foundation, by Stalin himself – comes down to the sufficiently sterile and unhistoric notion that, thanks to the natural riches of the country, a socialist society can be built within the geographic

57 For Lenin's last article on this struggle, see 'Better Fewer, But Better', Lenin, 1964, vol 33: 487.

confines of the Soviet Union. With the same success you might affirm that socialism could triumph if the population of the earth were a twelfth of what it is. In reality, however, the purpose of this new theory was to introduce into the social consciousness a far more concrete system of ideas, namely: the revolution is wholly completed; social contradictions will steadily soften; the kulak will gradually grow into socialism; the development as a whole, regardless of events in the external world, will preserve a peaceful and planned character. Bukharin, in attempting to give some foundation to the theory, declared it unshakably proven that 'we shall not perish owing to class differences within our country and our technical backwardness, that we can build socialism even on this pauper technical basis, that this growth of socialism will be many times slower, that we will crawl with a tortoise tempo, and that nevertheless we are building this socialism, and we will build it.'

We remark the formula: 'Build socialism even on a pauper technical basis,' and we recall once more the genial intuition of the young Marx: with a low technical basis 'only want will be generalized, and with want the struggle for necessities begins again, and all the old crap must revive' . . . The juridical and political standards set up by the revolution exercised a progressive action upon the backward economy, but upon the other hand they themselves felt the lowering influence of that backwardness. The longer the Soviet Union remains in a capitalist environment, the deeper runs the degeneration of the social fabric (Trotsky, 1937: 295, 300).

Stalinist 'legality'

After 1924, from enlightened legislation and vibrant legal debates, the climate shifted dramatically to repressive laws and mindless diatribes.[58] One of the central features of that reversal was the adoption of what the regime called 'socialist legality'. Ironically, as the regime became increasingly lawless in practice – seen, for example, in the show trials of 1934–37 – it proclaimed the erection of a new permanent legal system, overturning the previous emphasis on moving towards the disappearance of the state and law.

By 1936, the Stalinist regime had not only trampled over, but formally repudiated the basic Marxist conception of the withering away of the state. While claiming to have created socialism and dissolved antagonistic social classes, the regime denied that the legal institutions and state apparatus would disappear, even in the final stage of communism. This abandonment of Marxist precepts flowed organically from the doctrine of 'socialism in one country' adopted by Stalin in 1924. The formal reason given for the new

58 See further, Chapter 7.

policy of 'socialist legality' was the existence of socialism in one country, encircled by capitalist powers, making it essential to strengthen the state power.

In the midst of the Great Purges of 1936–37, directed against all socialist opposition, Stalin emphasised the need for stability, orthodoxy and legality to consolidate power. 'We need stability of laws now more than ever,' he said in his Report on the Draft Constitution in 1936.[59] Over the following two years, every surviving feature of Bolshevik jurisprudence was overturned. 'Crime' and 'punishment' were restored, as were the sanctity of marriage and contracts, individual fault as the chief criterion of personal injury liability and 'judicial authority'.[60] Correspondingly, Soviet legal theory became reduced to self-serving and platitudinous gibberish. In a series of articles and a book on Soviet public law published in 1938, Procurator-General Vyshinsky denounced Pashukanis and Stuchka and their insistence that genuine socialism would mean the end of law.

> History demonstrates that under socialism, on the contrary, law is raised to the highest level of development . . . Our laws are the expression of the will of our people as it directs and creates history under the leadership of the working class. The will of the people with us is fused with the will of the whole people (Berman, 1963: 55).

As Western legal observers have readily concluded, these banalities cannot compare to the theoretical work of Pashukanis, let alone provide a coherent conception of law. 'Such generalities hardly constitute a theory of law,' comments Berman.[61] Berman also points to the relationship between the lawless despotism of the Stalinist regime, its annihilation of the Bolshevik Party and its increasing need for the political prop of 'socialist legality':

> Stalin deintellectualised the Party; he purged it of the men who were in love with revolutionary ideas. The revolutionary ideas themselves became liturgical rather than rational in Soviet Russia. Marxism was chanted. Not reason as such but loyalty, patriotism, discipline, responsibility, were now stressed. It was in this context that law was restored, not only as legality but also as a system of justice. Without a legal system and a legal order – without Law with a capital L – the Stalinist regime could neither control the social relations of the people nor keep the economy going nor command the political forces in the country as a whole (Berman, 1963: 64).

59 Zile, 1970: 53.
60 Ibid: 57.
61 Ibid: 55.

While Marxism was chanted, however, the Stalinist doctrine was the antithesis of Marxism. As Trotsky observed in *The Revolution Betrayed*, the evolution of the Soviet state into an ever more totalitarian regime under Stalin could not be reconciled with the classical Marxist conception of the withering away of the state. Referring to the 1918 programme adopted by the Bolshevik Party, he wrote:

> The state as a bureaucratic apparatus begins to die away the first day of the proletarian dictatorship. Such is the voice of the party program – not voided to this day. Strange: it sounds like a spectral voice from the mausoleum. However you may interpret the nature of the present Soviet state, one thing is indubitable: at the end of its second decade of existence, it has not only not died away, but not begun to 'wither away'. Worse than that, it has grown into a hitherto unheard of apparatus of compulsion . . . While continuing to publish the works of Lenin (to be sure, with excerpts and distortions by the censor), the present leaders of the Soviet Union and their ideological representatives do not even raise the question of the causes of such a crying divergence between program and reality (Trotsky, 1937: 51–2).

In other words, 'Stalinist legality' was a terrible demonstration of the truth of the Marxist analysis of law as a defender and facilitator of privilege, inequality and private property interests.

Chapter 6

The passionate legal debates of early Soviet Russia: 1917–24

> When we speak of a proletarian law, we have in mind law of the transition period . . . law in a completely new meaning of the term.[1]

Numbers of scholars have acknowledged the richness of the legal debates that emerged during the first years of the Soviet revolution, from 1917 to 1924. It was a period of wide-ranging discussion and intellectual output. The audacity of the contributions is all the more striking when contrasted with the stultified regurgitation of Stalinist orthodoxy that increasingly predominated after 1927. Beirne and Sharlet, the editors of a valuable collection of Pashukanis' writings, noted:

> Pashukanis was merely one of a dozen authors in the Soviet Union to publish on the Marxist theory of law and state during the years 1923 to 1925. In fact, he was one of the less well-known authors whose works appeared during this early flowering of Soviet legal philosophy. It was a crowded and distinguished field which included the Marxist philosopher Adoratsky; the pupil of Petrazhitsky, M. A. Reisner; the jurist and civil war hero Nikolai Krylenko; and of course Piotr Stuchka, an Old Bolshevik and the Soviet Russian founder of Marxist legal philosophy (Beirne and Sharlet, 1980: 37).

The same authors commented that the language and vocabulary of the legal discourse of the 1920s was 'rich, open-ended and diverse, and varied tremendously with the personal preferences of the individual author'. By the 1930s, however, this gave way to 'a standardised and simplified style of prose devoid of nuance and ambiguity, and which was very much in keeping with the new theoretical content which comprised official textbooks on the theory of state and law'.[2]

1 Stuchka, 'Proletarian law', in Jaworskyj, 1967: 72–3.
2 Beirne and Sharlet, 1980: 274.

Likewise, Jaworskyj, who compiled an important anthology of the debates, described the 'revolutionary twenties' as 'a dynamic and prolific period in the history of Soviet legal thought', characterised by 'intellectual ferment, optimism and impatience'.

> The literature of this period – produced by political and legal theorists, economists, philosophers, historians, and ideologists – is diverse, original, and full of cognitive content; and the range of both theoretical and practical problems discussed is indeed impressive. Soviet social thinkers in the twenties took these problems seriously, much more so than did their Western counterparts, for they were engaged in a new type of social engineering. They considered themselves to be the builders of a new, 'rational' social order founded on principles presumably never before applied (Jaworskyj, 1967: v, 4).

Jaworskyj pointed to some of the central features of the discussion: its ferment, diversity and connection to pressing, uncharted, practical problems. Ironically, he attributed the intensity of the debates to the alleged inconsistencies of Marxism, arguing that its vagaries produced scope for a variety of contending interpretations. Lenin's writings, in particular, were said to be 'too far removed from existing reality and hence could not contribute much to the solution of the immediate problems'.[3] This contention is not only questionable;[4] it denies that the contributions made by the early Soviet theorists arose from the intellectual tradition that inspired them, that of Marxism. The kernel of Jaworskyj's argument is as follows:

> Unable to find the answers in the 'classics' of Marx and Engels, Soviet writers began to study Western literature on this subject. Originally, they intended to subject various Western theories of law to a Marxist analysis, hoping that in the process they would develop a systematic Marxist theory of law. This attempt, however, proved abortive. Its outcome was a split among Soviet writers into various schools of thought roughly corresponding to those in the West (Jaworskyj, 1967: 50).

Schlesinger advanced a similar scenario:

> Marxism recognises the existence of purely legal ideologies, and even their influence on the real development of Law. But it certainly rejects the explanation of Law by the development of legal or supposedly general ideologies. Anyone desiring purely legal theories had to look round the

3 Jaworskyj, 1967: 47.
4 See Chapter 2.

> existing ones elaborated by bourgeois jurists, and choose those he found most compatible with a Marxist approach to sociology and politics. All the classical bourgeois theories, based on certain assumed fundamental rights, were excluded by their evident function as idealisations of the foundations of capitalist society. So Duguit's functional approach became popular among Soviet jurists. By its influence on Goikhbarg, who shaped the Civil Code, it certainly influenced the latter's formulation (Schlesinger, 1949: 148).

The material reviewed in this chapter suggests that these propositions are flawed. The extraordinarily rich legal debates provoked by the October Revolution were far from a simple reworking of concepts borrowed from Western authors. The early Soviet theorists regarded their tasks as (1) developing, or contributing towards an overall Marxist theory of law, something that Marx and Engels had been unable to complete, and (2) clarifying the immediate and long-term approaches and policies that were needed to effect the transition to a genuine communist society.

Rubinshtein, a Ukrainian contributor to the debates, addressed this issue in his 1924 article, 'New Ideas in Bourgeois Jurisprudence and the Marxist Theory of Law'. After reviewing some similarities between the Marxist theory of law and recent trends in bourgeois jurisprudence, he concluded:

> What differentiates the Marxist theory of law from its bourgeois counterparts is its philosophical depth, consistency and completeness, but the main difference is its class principle, which is not always adhered to by bourgeois jurists. At the same time, however, the corresponding trends in bourgeois jurisprudence remain of interest to us; they reveal a deep, almost insoluble crisis in jurisprudence (not only of bourgeois jurisprudence), a crisis that is developing under the direct influence of Marxism (Jaworskyj, 1967: 153).

A review will show that while the Soviet theorists naturally studied Western writers and were influenced by them – some Soviet writers more than others – it is unhelpful and even misleading to regard them as adherents of Western schools of jurisprudence. In the main, they remained firm, yet perceptive and profound, critics of Western scholars. Two of the theorists – Reisner and Goikhbarg – were established pre-revolutionary scholars who sought to develop aspects of previous jurisprudence. Reisner was a student of Petrazhitsky and his psychological theory of law, while Goikhbarg drew on the social function analysis of the French writer Duguit.[5] But both regarded

5 Schlesinger, 1949: 147–8.

themselves as Marxists, solidarised with the October Revolution and sought to utilise the theories of their respective schools to shed light upon and deepen Marxist analysis.

Jaworskyj groups the Soviet writers into four schools: sociological, psychological, social function and normative. He begins with the *sociological* school, describing it as the strongest and most popular. He names Stuchka, Pashukanis, A.K. Stalgevich, N.V. Krylenko, A. Piontkovsky, S. Kechekyan, M.M. Isaev, N.N. Polyanlenko, N. Totsky, F. Ksenofontov, A. Trainin, L. Uspensky, F.D. Kornilov, M. Dotsenko and I. Razumovsky.

The *psychological* school consisted of M. Reisner, I. Ilinsky, E. Engel, M. Cheltsov-Bebutov, D. Dembsky, Ya. Berman, M. Rezunov and A. Popov. The *social function* school comprised A. Goikhbarg, S. Raevich, E. Kelman and S. Asknazy. The smallest group, the *normativist* school, was represented by D. Magerovsky, I. Podvolotsky, I. Voitinsky and V. Veger.

The views exchanged in the early legal debates were more diverse than Jaworskyj's matrix suggests, and changed over time, according to the shifting economic and political climate. There were important differences between contributors assigned to the same school. For example, Stuchka's views differed from Pashukanis' and diverged at different points between 1924 and 1932, yet Jaworskyj includes them both in the sociological school. Moreover, it is not clear that Jaworskyj has correctly classified each scholar. For example, Ilinsky drew quite different conclusions from Reisner, but Jaworskyj includes Ilinsky in the psychological school. In addition, Jaworskyj's list is not exhaustive. Others who participated in the early debates included Krestinsky (initially one of Trotsky's supporters), Lunacharsky (an early Bolshevik leader), I. Naumov, M. Kozlovsky, A.S. Rubinshtein and S. Volfson, who was associated with the Left Opposition.

More importantly, the suggested classification obscures more critical issues in the debates. The early Soviet writers were in dispute over three main questions, which were bound up with the trajectory of Soviet Russia: (1) the class character and function of the Soviet state and Soviet laws, (2) whether and how quickly the state would wither away in the transition to communism, and (3) the underlying role of law in socialist and communist society. Wherever possible, this chapter examines each contribution to the debates from the standpoint of these three issues.

From 1924, a pivotal year which saw the launching of the political war against 'Trotskyism' and also the publication of Pashukanis' *General Theory of Law and Marxism*, new alignments emerged. Most notably, the group of jurists working with Pashukanis in the Communist Academy became known as the commodity exchange school of law, which was identified as the official Marxist theory of law for the remainder of the decade. A number of commentators have pointed to a division of that school into two wings after 1927 – a radical branch led by Pashukanis and a moderate one led by

Stuchka.[6] Essentially, as we will see in the next chapter, Stuchka argued that Pashukanis over-extended the commodity exchange concept of law and insufficiently emphasised the class content of law.

Before examining the evolution of these debates chronologically, it is worth noting that the number of Soviet writers listed suggests broad involvement in the debates. It also indicates that neither Pashukanis nor Stuchka, nor anyone else, enjoyed or exercised unchallenged authority in the scholarly exchanges that took place. Jaworskyj concludes that the fact that early Soviet writers offered conflicting theories showed that during the twenties, they 'were free to determine the meaning of "the Marxist method" in their own way, without political interference'.[7] Certainly, in reading the legal theorists' articles, one is struck by the open and democratic spirit in which they conducted their polemics. No one was above reproach or critique, and there appeared to be no attempt to lay down a 'party line'. But that is not to say that the disputes were unrelated to the political challenges confronting the Soviet government, or the political conflicts that developed within the Soviet leadership.

1917–21: From revolution to civil war

One of the earliest contributions came from Lunacharsky, one of the foremost Bolshevik leaders. As Commissar of Education, he wrote a December 1917 article for *Pravda* on 'Revolution and the Court', stating the case for the abolition of the old court system and its replacement by people's courts. Lunacharsky's article sought to answer two factions within the Bolshevik Party. One, the more conservative, favoured the retention of the pre-revolutionary courts; the other opposed all courts on the grounds that they were incompatible with the aims of the revolution.

Lunacharsky observed that it was hardly realistic to expect workers and peasants, having taken power, to tolerate the old judges and laws that had served the Tsarist autocracy. 'The revolution itself is a fact of counterposing a new law to the old one, an act of a popular mass trial over the hated system of privilege.'[8] On the other hand, while outlining the foundations of new people's courts, the revolution had to proceed gradually and cautiously, because 'there is no precedent in history for a proletarian law'.

> Since under capitalism the proletariat was deprived of the opportunity to develop its legal creativity, it has no choice now but to learn how to adjudicate pragmatically and create its own customary law, deducing it from the sources of the same spiritual movement that led the proletariat

6 Beirne and Sharlet, 1980: 20; Schlesinger, 1949: 153–6.
7 Jaworskyj, 1967: 51.
8 Jaworskyj, 1967: 53.

> to the victorious revolution and that reflects its class characters, its growth, and its significance in the social life (Jaworskyj, 1967: 54).

Some may find Lunacharsky's references to 'customary law' and 'spiritual movement' suggestive of an appeal to a natural law conception that ascribes law to inner human instincts or deeply rooted historical customs. But the context of the October Revolution points to a more democratic and class-oriented conception of forming popular institutions to fashion new social norms that would reflect the interests and aspirations of the majority of previously downtrodden people. Like other Bolshevik leaders, Lunacharsky was familiar with traditional social and legal theory, as well as with the writings of Marx and Engels. He referred to various Western and pre-revolutionary Russian legal theorists to justify the introduction of new revolutionary norms. Among the scholars he cited were Fritz Berolzheimer, Anton Menger, Georg Jellinek and L. Petrazhitsky. The latter was known across Europe for his psychological approach to legality. Lunacharsky referred to Petrazhitsky's emphasis on the need for 'positive' (written) law to correspond to the 'intuitive' law, or sense of justice, of the mass of the population, or be swept aside through social revolution.

While Jaworskyj suggests that the early Soviet writers turned to Western theorists because they found no answers in Marxist literature, Lunacharsky's references to Petrazhitsky were of a different character altogether. Lunacharsky was arguing for a Marxist approach. He quoted Petrazhitsky, a respected liberal figure within traditional Russian ruling circles, in order to turn some perceptive observations of a well-regarded participant in the old order against the former political and legal establishment itself. Lunacharsky noted that Petrazhitsky was regarded by official Russian science as 'one of the greatest authorities in Europe', before quoting a prophetic passage from Petrazhitsky, published in 1909, four years after the first Russian Revolution of 1905:

> The simultaneous existence and functioning of the positive (written) law with the intuitive law (with the ideal of the new classes) is possible only if there is general agreement between them; if the discord reaches a certain degree, then the disintegration of the positive law becomes inescapable; in a case of opposition, the disintegration is brought about through a social revolution (Jaworskyj, 1967: 55–6).[9]

Lunacharsky continued:

> Petrazhitsky describes in detail how the new ideal grows among the lower classes . . . under the influence of changing conditions. He states that the

9 The quote is from Petrazhitsky, 1909.

> sense of justice becomes even more offended when it encounters opposition, then, 'it reaches a fanatical hatred of the existing order with its laws, and ultimately it arouses an explosion – the Revolution' (Jaworskyj, 1967: 56).

Lunacharsky may have adopted Petrazhitsky's concept of 'intuitive law', but he gave it a new content, treating it as a reflection of the objective class interests of the working people. Lunacharsky concluded as follows:

> The people engender a new intuitive law, which calls, first of all, for the destruction of all organs of the old law that are perceived by them as complete injustices. This intuitive law (reflecting class interests of the masses, and corresponding to the new rising social structure) can be distinctly formulated only in the process of direct, revolutionary legal creativity (Jaworskyj, 1967: 56).

Lunacharsky's observations about the 'complete injustices' perceived by the mass of people can only be understood in relation to the considerable rejection of the old legal system that had already taken place among broad layers of the population. At the same time, his utilisation of concepts developed by an eminent non-Marxist theoretician to elucidate the significance of these developments was entirely in line with the overall Marxist approach to previous political and social philosophy. Rather than discarding the achievements of bourgeois theory, Marx and Engels emphasised the need to recognise its strengths (and weaknesses) as insights into underlying historical processes.

Another early contributor was Goikhbarg, a professor who was influenced by the social function view advanced by Duguit. Goikhbarg said the revolution could not limit itself to the 'mere negative activity of issuing decrees'. It had to completely change the conditions of human existence in order to regenerate social psychology so that legal coercion would no longer be needed as an instrument of social control. Essentially, he argued that only by fundamentally uplifting social conditions could human relations be improved.

> Completely changed conditions of human existence will bring about such a regeneration of social psychology that the individual arbitrariness, which disturbs the harmony of humanity's life, will become such an infrequent anomaly that it can either be discarded or eliminated by means other than the contemporary legal guarantees (Jaworskyj, 1967: 58).

Writing in 1918, Goikhbarg pointed to the profoundly different role of social regulation under capitalism and socialism. Comparing the French Revolution of 1789 with the Russian Revolution of October 1917, he laid the basis for drawing a distinction between bourgeois *law* and socialist *regulation*:

> Decrees – which in brief but harsh statements have abolished survivals of the past, have untied old fetters that bound men and hindered their activity, and thus have given to individuals a complete freedom of action, while assuming or hypocritically pretending that the clash of egos would produce general well-being – were appropriate and have attained their goal in the period of the exemplary French *bourgeois* Revolution, which aimed at creating a system of *anarchistic individualism* in the sphere of economic relations. But the proletarian revolution, which pursues entirely different goals and which faces the task of constructing and consolidating a diametrically opposed system of *regulated collectivism*, cannot, obviously, limit itself to the mere negative activity of issuing decrees [emphasis in original] (Jaworskyj, 1967: 58).

Goikhbarg gave the following example of bourgeois law versus a socialist programme of work and education:

> The bourgeois law declares: 'You, subjects of bourgeois law, may or should build houses with such and such legal limitations.' Such an order is issued with one stroke of the pen. On the other hand, the social, general will proclaims: 'We will build accommodations for everyone.' The latter law is no longer an order but a program of work (Jaworskyj, 1967: 61).

This process, Goikhbarg described as 'the transition from legislation to administration'. That is, law would be superseded by social improvements, giving rise to higher social norms. Decrees would 'merely furnish the stimuli that accelerate movement in this direction'.[10] His approach was clearly reflected in the later work of Pashukanis, who sought to develop the distinction between capitalist legal form and socialist social regulation.

Likewise, in an early article, Kozlovsky, a former legal advocate who joined the Justice Commissariat, wrote of proletarian 'law' in quotation marks, throwing a question mark over the very conception of law under socialism:

> With the final suppression of the bourgeois, the function of proletarian 'law' will gradually diminish and be replaced by the organisation rules of economic life – production, distribution and consumption. The organs of law will be transformed into economic, administrative organs. Judges will be replaced increasingly by workers, overseers and bookkeepers (Jaworskyj, 1967: 70).

Kozlovsky criticised proponents of the sociological school of law, such as Menger, for agreeing that the legal order would be transformed gradually into

10 Jaworskyj, 1967: 68.

an economic organisation, but refusing to accept that law would disappear completely. He disputed the view that crime would continue because of the 'basic instincts of man's nature'. In the first place, the source of most crime lay in the anarchy, personal insecurity and class antagonisms produced by capitalism. These gave rise to 'excesses, extremism and crime, indeed, most atrocious crimes. Exploitation of the masses produces want, misery, ignorance, savagery and vice.'

Moreover, because offenders were products of the social milieu, it would be absurd to resort to retribution or seek to 'reform' individuals through punishment. Instead, the state of society had to be improved. Punishment should be confined to preventing danger to society. 'In conformity with our view of the causes underlying criminality, the only aim of the imposed punishment should be self-defence or the protection of society against encroachments.'[11]

Amid the difficulties of the civil war, from mid-1918 to 1921, the first period of discussion was truncated and limited. For almost three years, the survival of Soviet Russia hung in the balance and the harsh conditions were hardly conducive to theoretical contemplation. But these early contributions displayed considerable knowledge, as well as hopes for effecting a reasonably short transition to socialism.

1921–24: The impact of the NEP

The advent of the NEP brought a more complex view. One theme that emerged, which warrants further examination, was a discussion of the relationship between socialism and individual rights. As the civil war drew to a close and the NEP emerged, Soviet legal theorists insisted on a strict protection of individual as well as economic rights. 'It is slanderous to maintain that the working class does not want to safeguard the interests of the individual,' wrote Slavin in an officially published 1922 article on the 'The Judiciary and the New Economic Policy'. He went on:

> On the contrary, the working class, as the class of the majority, is interested in giving the broadest and the most complete guarantees of the rights of the individual. Consequently, when the present objective conditions evoked by the civil war change, the courts of Soviet Russia will be free to defend the rights of the individual in the near future . . . (Zile, 1970: 76).

There is much to be said for the view that socialism guarantees genuine individual freedom, by liberating people from the dictates of market forces. But a proper treatment of the relationship between individual and collective

11 Jaworskyj, 1967: 70–1.

rights in the transition to communism would involve an historical assessment of the rise of individualism and its actual content under capitalism.

Magerovsky was another legal theorist to reflect the changed economic climate and requirements. His 1922 article 'Soviet Law and Methods of Its Study' observed that law was necessitated not only by the inner class contradictions of a society but also by society's relation to nature and to other antagonistic societies. In other words, the transition to socialism could take longer than previously acknowledged because of external pressures on Soviet Russia and also deep historical legacies. His view expressed, in part at least, the ongoing capitalist encirclement of the Soviet state and its inability to immediately overcome the primitivism and backwardness inherited from Tsarism. Magerovsky, regarded as a normativist who was influenced by sociological jurisprudence, drew attention to the 'dual' nature of Soviet law:

> On the one hand, it is still directed toward the past, toward bourgeois society; it still comprises elements of bourgeois law. On the other hand, it is directed toward the future, toward a socialist society, and, owing to this, it comprises elements of socialist law (Jaworskyj, 1967: 95).

Stuchka later criticised this view[12] but it is in accord with Lenin's warning, in *The State and Revolution*, about the bourgeois nature of law in the first stages of socialism. Interestingly, Magerovsky also commented that after the revolution, the Bolsheviks had brilliantly exploited the organisational force of legal norms. Here was an assertion that legality and legally sanctioned force had a role to play in the struggle to consolidate the revolution.

Another sign of the shifting debate came with the 1923 publication of Podvolotsky's *The Marxist Theory of Law*, with an Introduction by Bukharin. Bukharin and his supporters were at this stage on the 'left' of the Bolshevik Party, initially critical of the NEP's concessions to market relations, but their views were rapidly evolving. Podvolotsky criticised Stuchka for defining law purely in terms of social relationships and for presenting law as simply the juridic expression of economic relations. He posed the question: if law equals social relationships, why speak of law at all? Law, he argued, was a coercive norm established by the dominant class for the purpose of sanctioning existing relationships. In other words, law was, and would remain, an active instrument of class rule. Quoting Marx and Engels, he also pointed out that law could have a reciprocal influence on economic development, including under socialism.[13]

From these premises, he maintained that in the transition to communism,

12 Sharlet, Maggs and Beirne, 1988: 45.
13 Jaworskyj, 1967: 107.

law could be proletarian as well as 'bourgeois'. By placing 'bourgeois' in quotation marks, he sought to show that law, as a form, could serve the proletariat despite being 'bourgeois'. He cited only half of Lenin's previously quoted comment in *The State and Revolution*,[14] leaving out Lenin's reference to the continued existence of a bourgeois state in the transitional period. Podvolotsky misleadingly asserted that Lenin declared there could be no bourgeois law in a proletarian state. Podvolotsky further asserted a permanent need for law under socialism. 'But does the proletariat need law in general?' Podvolotsky asked. 'Yes, beyond any doubt,' he answered.[15]

As a supporter of Bukharin, Podvolotsky's views could be expected to be aligned with Bukharin's emerging right-wing faction in the party. Known for being ultra left-wing in the early years after the revolution, Bukharin shifted ground by the mid-1920s to become a champion of making major concessions to the peasantry and other small property holders and proceeding towards socialism at a 'snail's pace'. Bukharin's followers aligned themselves with Stalin's faction against the Left and United Oppositions in 1924–27, only to have Stalin move against them in 1929, during the forced collectivisation of the peasantry.[16]

Podvolotsky's arguments did not go unchallenged. In 1924 Goikhbarg published his *Foundations of Private Property Law*, which began with a stinging attack on all law as 'even more poisoning and stupefying opium for the people' (borrowing Marx's phrase about religion). He referred to the dangers of a 'new mythology' of law, quoting Marx's warning in *The Eighteenth Brumaire* that 'the traditions of the deceased generations haunt the minds of the living like a nightmare'.[17]

Jaworskyj classifies Goikhbarg as belonging to the 'social function' school, as did some of Goikhbarg's protagonists in the legal debates, but Goikhbarg's writings, at least his early publications, do not correspond entirely to that categorisation. He argued strenuously against the conception that law has a natural or indispensable social function to perform. Drawing on Marx's *Critique of the Gotha Program*, Goikhbarg emphasised that all law is an expression of inequality. Proletarian legislation should not present itself as 'any presumed, eternally existing concept of law' but should instead refer to the expediency of measures to meet certain goals, notably the development of the productive forces.[18]

Importantly, Goikhbarg drew attention to the dependence of the economically backward Soviet state on the victory of revolutions in more advanced

14 Chapter 3.
15 Jaworskyj, 1967: 113.
16 See Chapter 10.
17 Jaworskyj, 1967: 121.
18 Ibid: 130–2.

countries, notably Germany. Such a victory would enable a more rapid reduction in the 'unavoidable concessions' to bourgeois legal conceptions:

> Our revolution took place earlier than in other countries, and hence under less mature conditions. In addition, it was accomplished in a most economically backward country. The forthcoming revolution in Germany will take place not only later but also under more mature economic conditions than those existing in our country six years ago. It will do away with the survivors of the bourgeois system in a more radical manner (Jaworskyj, 1967: 134).

These hopes of early support from a socialist Germany were dashed by the defeat of the bungled German revolution in October 1923, one of the events that precipitated the emergence of the Left Opposition and the subsequent Stalinist campaign against 'Trotskyism'. Goikhbarg's very mention of the international environment and its impact on the Soviet state contradicted Stalin's theory of 'socialism in one country'.

Krylenko, an early Bolshevik, produced, in his 1924 *Discourse on Law and State*, a passionate call for action to combat the degeneration of the Soviet state apparatus, and a recognition of the mounting obstacles facing the country. Krylenko had been a supporter of Bukharin and an opponent of Trotsky but his intervention seemed to reflect Lenin's concerns. Krylenko invoked Lenin's comment of March 1923 that: 'The conditions in our state apparatus are to such a degree grievous, if not shocking, that we must begin to think all over again of how to struggle against its deficiencies.'[19]

Krylenko decried the impetus given to material inequality by the NEP and blamed it for the revival of privilege. 'We have re-established bureaucracy as a special cadre of man, have made it directly dependent upon the "ruling hierarchs", and consequently have made it again independent of the masses.' Displaying a sense of urgency, he asked what should be done at 'this very minute, to come at least a little bit closer to at least the first phase of the communist society outlined by Lenin and Marx?' Before answering that question, he stated the following:

> Objectively, it is not our fault that the proletarian revolution in Russia stumbled over two objective obstacles that it could not overcome by itself, single-handed. These two obstacles were the following: (1) the belatedness in the coming of the proletarian revolution in the West; (2) the economic structure of our own country (Jaworskyj, 1967: 177–8).

19 Jaworskyj, 1967: 162. Lenin's comment is from 'Better Fewer, But Better', Lenin, 1964, vol 33: 487.

Krylenko said the objective prerequisites did not exist to achieve Lenin's egalitarian and participatory principles but:

> We undoubtedly should be capable of reforming our state apparatus so as to liquidate its negative features, which have been so vividly manifest in recent times and which we were incapable of paralysing in years past. These features are: separation from the masses, bureaucratisation, red tape, bureaucratic attitudes towards work, and the colossal inequality in the material position of workers and public functionaries (Jaworskyj, 1967: 177–8).

Krylenko's ability to issue such a broadside is testimony to the fact that political opposition to the emerging Stalinist apparatus was still possible in 1924. It was not long, however, before that debate was suppressed in law, as in other fields.

Volfson wrote a 1924 article, 'Contemporary Critics of Marxism', offering a critique of Hans Kelsen's *Socialism and the State*, as well as Karl Kautsky, Max Adler and various 'pseudo-Marxists'. Answering Kelsen's normative view of law, Volfson pointed to some of the underlying issues in the early Soviet legal debates. He emphasised that 'Marxists erect their concept of the state not on the principle of juridical normativism but on the basis of a living, dynamic, sociological approach to society':

> According to Marx, society and the state are by no means categories in opposition to each other. The state is nothing but a form of existence of society, a form determined by economic relationships; it is 'a product of society at a given stage of development,' as Engels stated. At a certain stage in the development of human society, the economy forced society to assume the form of a state, whereas at succeeding stages of development the economy will force society to get rid of the state. The great merit of Marx and Engels lies precisely in the fact that they ceased to regard the state as a certain eternal norm; they converted the state from a logical into a historical category (Jaworskyj, 1967: 183–4).

It seems that behind Volfson's treatment of Kelsen and Kautsky was an underlying agenda – that of defending the classical Marxist perspective of the withering away of the state.[20]

One sign of the shifting climate was Veger's 1924 volume, *Law and the State in the Transition Period*. Verger was regarded as a normativist. On the one hand, he specifically referred to Lenin's often disregarded warning, in

20 Volfson's contribution is considered further in Chapter 10, which examines the alternative analysis advanced by the Left Opposition.

The State and Revolution, that the new state established by a social revolution would remain a capitalist state, albeit without a bourgeoisie, during the transition to communism. Veger noted that while the new state was organised on transformed economic, moral and intellectual foundations, it still bore 'the imprint of the old society in whose womb it originated'. He also reiterated the Marxist thesis that 'in the higher stage of communism, there will be no need for the apparatus of an organised coercion'.[21]

On the other hand, Veger emphasised that the transition would 'constitute a long process', including the 'creation of a new psychology' for solving conflicts without state force and that 'such organisation now is hardly conceivable'.[22] This could be seen as foreshadowing the later insistence on the protracted nature of the transition to communism and the need for a strengthened state apparatus in the meantime.

The year 1924 saw the adoption of the Fundamental Law (Constitution) of the USSR, setting out the Union's legislative, administrative and judicial bodies. 'In order to maintain revolutionary legality', Clause 43 established a Supreme Court, attached to the Central Executive Committee of the USSR.[23] As is apparent from the latter clause, the constitution contained no strict separation of the judiciary from the executive. In an accompanying article, Turubiner maintained that the judicial power could not be set apart from the country's political and social structure. He cited Marx's reference in *The Civil War in France* to the lack of independence of judges from the ruling elite. Marx poured scorn on the myth that the supposed separation of powers provided protection against arbitrary, class-biased decision-making. To substantiate Marx's observation, Turubiner quoted a work on congressional government by United States President Woodrow Wilson, in which Wilson traced out the changing political complexion of the US Supreme Court under different governments and in various historical periods.[24] This is an important issue that goes beyond the scope of this volume. The separation of powers doctrine, developed in England and France during the struggle against feudal absolutism, may have a place in socialist legal theory in facilitating the withering away of the state. Yet a full discussion of this question would require a detailed historical examination of the doctrine and its possible relationship to the transition to genuine communism.

Stuchka and Pashukanis

Before examining the 1924–27 period, we need to briefly outline the views of the first pre-eminent Soviet legal theorist, Stuchka, and his relation to

21 Jaworskyj, 1967: 192–3.
22 Ibid: 192.
23 Zile, 1970: 72.
24 Ibid: 73–4.

Pashukanis. It was in the economic and social context of the NEP that both began to more systematically enunciate a theory of Soviet law. Pashukanis' efforts are examined in Chapters 8 and 9. But it is helpful at this stage to relate their roles in the evolving legal debates.

Latvian-born Bolshevik Piotr Ivanovich Stuchka (1865–1932) was probably, apart from Lenin, one of the most pivotal participants in the early development of legal practice and theory following the October 1917 Revolution. An early Bolshevik, Stuchka was one of 14 candidates for the Presidium at the Congress of Soviets of October 1917, with Stuchka representing the Lettish Bolsheviks.[25] In the first Soviet government, he was named Commissar of Justice and was actively involved in drafting the first revolutionary decrees, including those on the abolition of the old Tsarist courts.

Stuchka returned to the Baltic region in late 1918 as the political situation developed there. Shortly after, the German army was finally driven out and he became the first prime minister of the Latvian Soviet Republic. However, in January 1920 his government was overthrown in the course of the Russian Civil War, through the foreign military intervention against the Russian Revolution. Stuchka then returned to Moscow and resumed his legal work. In various roles, as a party leader, Commissar of Justice, text writer, judge and academic, he remained a central figure in the realm of legal policy throughout the period of the New Economic Policy after 1921, the defeat of the Left and United Oppositions between 1923 and 1927, and the consolidation of Stalin's grip on power from 1927.

In 1921, he was appointed a commissar in the Justice Commissariat, from where he guided the programmes of re-legalisation and recodification necessitated by the 'retreat' to the limited, state-regulated capitalism of the NEP. At the request of the party leadership, he wrote *The Revolutionary Role of Law and State: A General Doctrine of Law* in just four months during 1921, making the first attempt to outline a Soviet theory of law. In January 1923, at the age of 58, Stuchka became Chairman of the Supreme Court of the Russian Republic and a member of the Control Commission of the Communist International. As a leading figure in the Communist Academy, Stuchka organised its section on the general theory of law, which became the leading authority on Marxist jurisprudence. He was also a Professor of Law at Moscow State University, a law lecturer in the Institute of Red Professors, and the first Director of the Moscow Institute of Soviet Law.[26]

In these capacities, Stuchka initiated many of the policies and statutes of the Soviet government and was actively engaged in the lively legal debates

25 Trotsky, 1977: 1149–50.
26 Sharlet, Maggs and Beirne, 1988: xvi.

of 1917–24, often serving as a reference point for the contending schools of thought. While never brilliant, and often turgid in his attempts to apply the writings of Marx, Engels and Lenin, Stuchka was clearly earnest, dedicated and principled. Having been a revolutionary socialist all his adult life, a leader of the Marxist movement in Latvia and an early supporter of Lenin and the Bolsheviks following the 1903 split with the Mensheviks, he loyally served the Soviet government throughout times of enormous turmoil and hardship. Moreover, until his death (of natural causes) he defended the basic tenets of classical Marxist jurisprudence: the purely transitional character of the dictatorship of the proletariat; the withering away of the state; the possibility of organising human society without formal legal forms; the vision of communism as a classless and stateless society.

Nevertheless, he sided with the emerging Stalinist regime against the Marxist Opposition after 1923, adopted Stalin's doctrine of building socialism in one country and increasingly adapted his views to those of the ruling layer. Indeed, both in his prestige and his writings, he provided a veneer of orthodoxy to the bureaucratic caste that formed Stalin's power base, justifying the concentration of power in its hands under the banner of 'socialist legality'.

His relationship with the much younger Pashukanis (26 years his junior) was somewhat complex and symptomatic of the broader rise and degeneration of political and legal discussion in the early years of the Russian Revolution. Stuchka was initially a mentor and vigorous defender of Pashukanis, welcoming the latter's probing of the commodity-related form of law as an important contribution to Marxist theory in dealing with the contradictions posed by the NEP. By 1927, in aligning himself with Stalin and Bukharin against the United Opposition of Trotsky, Zinoviev and Kamenev, Stuchka began to differentiate himself from Pashukanis, making substantial criticisms of Pashukanis' theories. While Stuchka's critique had merit, it also assisted the Stalinist machine by attacking Pashukanis' insistence that in the transition from socialism to communism, law and the state itself necessarily retained vestiges of capitalist social and economic relations. By 1931, following Stalin's blunt assertion of the necessity for a protracted historical period of a strengthened dictatorial state apparatus, both Stuchka and Pashukanis retracted aspects of their writings and became reduced to accusing each other of undermining the Soviet order.

Initially, Stuchka eschewed the very notion of a written proletarian code. In 1919, he dismissed the term 'proletarian law' because 'the goal of the socialist revolution is to abolish law and to replace it with a new socialist order'. He said the expression 'proletarian law' could only be used in a special sense: 'When we speak of a proletarian law, we have in mind *law of the transition period*, law in the period of the dictatorship of the proletariat, or law of a socialist society, law in a completely new meaning of the term.' [Emphasis in original.] To illustrate his point, he quoted Voltaire, the

French Enlightenment figure: 'Law and right are inherited like an eternal disease.'[27]

Stuchka modified these views with the advent of the NEP. He later related that on 31 January 1921 – on the eve of the launching of the NEP – the Organising Bureau of the Central Committee of the Russian Communist Party (Bolsheviks) commissioned him to write a textbook on the Theory and Practice of Soviet Law. He took Lenin's *The State and Revolution* as his principal guide, besides drawing on the practical experience of the revolution, manifested in the early judicial decrees.[28]

Nevertheless, Stuchka still regarded the process of the state and law withering away as having already commenced. The fifth edition of his *The Theory of the Proletariat's and Peasant's State and Its Constitution*, published in 1926, included the following strong assertion:

> All our People's Commissariats are divided into two groups: economic organs (production and distribution) and organs of coercion (military, internal affairs, and judiciary) . . . It is quite apparent that the latter are gradually withering away and that they undergo atrophy, while the former, directing the economic orchestra, are growing. This development may ultimately result even in an 'orchestra without a conductor,' but this is a matter of the distant future. One thing remains indisputable: *the state, as well as the law in its class meaning, evaporates, i.e., withers away, together with the organs of coercion* [emphasis in original] (Jaworskyj, 1967: 243).

In 1927, in his *Introduction to The Theory of Civil Law*, Stuchka explicitly related Soviet civil law to the NEP. 'The Soviet code of civil law is the economic policy of our transition period, or more precisely the NEP, put into the form of articles of law.'[29] In an echo of Lenin's warning in *The State and Revolution* of the continuation of bourgeois law in the transition to communism, Stuchka wrote that during the first phase, socialism, 'bourgeois law' was not abrogated in full, but only in relation to the socialisation of the means of production. 'Bourgeois law' remained in the determination of the distribution of production and the allotment of labour among members of society. By joining Podvolotsky in placing inverted commas around 'bourgeois law' Stuchka was already, as Podvolotsky had proposed, softening Lenin's sharp characterisation of the contradiction facing the workers' state. Nonetheless, Stuchka adhered to the Marxist conception of the withering away of law, insisting that Soviet law was not eternal.[30]

27 Jaworskyj, 1967: 72–3.

28 Zile, 1970: 229.

29 Ibid: 211.

30 Ibid: 211–15.

In the meantime, Pashukanis had published his 1924 work, *The General Theory of Law and Marxism*. His essential proposition was that all law was inherently related to the commodity exchange relationship that reaches its highest point under capitalism. The very form of law was derived from the acquisition by individuals of private property interests, which inevitably gave rise to conflicts.

> It is only with the advent of bourgeois-capitalist society that all the necessary conditions are created for the juridical factor to attain complete distinctness in social relations . . . A basic prerequisite for legal regulation is the conflict of private interests. This is both the logical premise of the legal form and the actual origin of the development of the legal superstructure. Human conduct can be regulated by the most complex regulations, but the juridical factor in this regulation arises at the point when differentiation and opposition of interests begin (Beirne and Sharlet, 1980: 58 and 81).

Pashukanis argued that law was an inherently bourgeois phenomenon because it reflected commodity exchange. There could never be proletarian or socialist law. Pashukanis conceived of the transition to communism not as the utilisation of new legal forms, but as the gradual extinction of the legal form in general. He argued that the Soviet Union had two forms of law: administrative/technical rules that regulated the general economic plan and social life, and the civil and commercial codes that governed the commodity exchange underpinning the NEP. Pashukanis characterised the law of the NEP, including the new criminal code, as bourgeois law.

To law, Pashukanis counterposed the use of technical regulation to achieve common purposes. He gave the examples of the technical rules for the operation of a railway system and for medical treatment. These rules would be devised and revised by technical and scientific experts, not jurists. Any element of official coercion would be determined by technical expedience, and would only become a legal issue in the realm of conflicting individual interests, such as those between a doctor and patient.[31]

Pashukanis criticised the demand for a new theory of 'proletarian law'. This tendency, he commented, appeared to be 'revolutionary par excellence' but was thoroughly flawed.

> In reality this tendency proclaims the immortality of the legal form, in that it strives to wrench this form from the particular historical conditions which had helped bring it to full fruition, and to present it as capable of permanent renewal. The withering away of certain categories

31 Zile, 1970: 215–19.

> of bourgeois law (the categories as such, not this or that precept) in no way implies their replacement by new categories of proletarian law (Beirne and Sharlet, 1980: 61).

Pashukanis' argument contradicted one of the central aspects of Stuchka's theory of law, namely that law is a class phenomenon. At several points in his *General Theory*, Pashukanis explicitly criticised Stuchka's definition of law and his failure to examine the historical and economic roots of the legal form. Nevertheless, in the preface to the third edition of *Revolutionary Role of Law and State*, published in 1924, Stuchka noted the number of new works on the Marxist theory of state and law and identified Pashukanis' work as the most outstanding. With a few reservations, he praised Pashukanis' book as a 'valuable contribution to our Marxist theoretical literature on law' that 'directly supplements my work, which provides only an incomplete and generally inadequate general doctrine of law'. In this way, Stuchka helped elevate Pashukanis from academic obscurity.

Several scholars, including Sharlet, Maggs and Beirne, have characterised Stuchka and Pashukanis as representing the moderate and radical wing, respectively, of the commodity exchange faction of Soviet jurists.[32] There is no doubt that Stuchka and Pashukanis both adhered to this school, at least to the extent that it provided a framework for reconciling the requirements of the NEP with the withering away of law. Stuchka proposed to restrict the application of Soviet civil law to the regulation of surviving private property relations. Within this realm, Stuchka recognised the principle of equivalence, based on commodity exchange. However, the internal relations of the socialist sector of the economy were to be excluded, as not requiring judicial regulation.[33]

Thus, Stuchka and Pashukanis agreed on distinguishing 'law', which applied to commodity exchange, from Soviet regulation. But from that point of agreement, their views diverged. A closer examination of their differences in the context of the Stalinist suppression of the Left and United Oppositions between 1924 and 1927 suggests a more complex dynamic in their relationship. Initially, it seems that Stuchka welcomed and fostered Pashukanis' theoretical work, in so far as it made a seemingly coherent and sophisticated contribution to Marxist legal theory and helped to explain the dichotomy between the reinstatement of legal forms during the NEP and the ultimate withering away of law. But the onset of the battle with the Opposition highlighted defects and perceived excesses in Pashukanis' analysis.

32 Sharlet, Maggs and Beirne, 1988: xviii.
33 Schlesinger, 1949: 154.

Chapter 7

From debates to diatribes: 1924–37

> We are for the withering away of the state, and at the same time, we stand for the strengthening of the dictatorship of the proletariat.[1]

1924–27: The final period of genuine debate

The Left Opposition's struggle against the emerging Stalinist bureaucracy commenced at the end of 1923. This had a polarising impact on intellectual, as well as political life, with Stalin's faction seeking to slander and intimidate political opponents. It was not possible, however, for the ruling layers to immediately shut down the legal debates.

Ilinsky

In a 1925 article, Ilinsky, a supporter of the psychological school, said the interpretations of various laws generated 'hot discussions' among legal practitioners and theorists alike.[2] Yet his article also evinced a new sharpness in the debates, stridently demanding recognition of 'proletarian law'. He identified the main axis of disagreement as follows:

> We are issuing laws every day . . . and juridical publishing houses print voluminous commentaries on them . . . the Supreme Court quite frequently delivers lengthy theories of principal juridical concepts . . . Does this mean that we have law? Indeed, we do. One could claim, as A. K. Goikhbarg and others do, that our law is merely a system of socio-technical norms, or one could invent other euphonious formulas, but the essence of things is not changed thereby. It is obvious that, in the communist society, law as a coercive social order will not exist. But, *in a class*

1 Stalin (1930) in Sharlet, Maggs and Beirne, 1988: 229.
2 Jaworskyj, 1967: 203.

> *society, even in the transition period, the existence of law is inevitable* [emphasis in original] (Jaworskyj, 1967: 203).

Ilinsky lightly dismissed the argument of Goikhbarg and others that Soviet 'law' should have an entirely different character, akin to, or at least pointing in the direction of, collective regulation. Moreover, his emphatic tone and use of italics suggest that a less tolerant atmosphere was beginning to emerge. Ilinsky went on to mock and scold his opponents.

> Furthermore, private property is recognized in our country by law, and legal punishments are provided for violation of property . . . Our law is class law, a proletarian law, but nevertheless a law; it is neither an instruction to military units concerning the shoeing of horses nor a recipe for making cold or hot soup . . . Those who participate in building up socialism ought to know the nature and qualities of the law that is used as an instrument in constructing socialism (Jaworskyj, 1967: 203–4).

Even so, Ilinsky's writings displayed a continuing readiness to engage in lively exchanges, pay attention to the history of legal theory and make considered use of non-Marxist thought. In his 1925 *An Introduction to the Study of Soviet Law*, he wrote:

> The supremacy of domination of law is not simply an innocent juridical speculation or an adornment of bourgeois constitutions. One can speak ironically of the idolatry of law, but it would be absurd to deny that respect for the law, cultivated among the masses, is one of the most powerful means for bringing about mass conduct in the interest of the ruling class. Jurists and historians, who carefully study the influence of positive law upon social life, know this quite well. For example, P. B. Vinogradov stated: 'The decisive moment in the existence of law is not so much its coerciveness as the psychological habit of recognising the bindingness of norms created by social authority and of subordinating one's self to these norms' (Jaworskyj, 1967: 217).[3]

There is an evident tension in this passage. On the one hand, Ilinsky argued the need for the Soviet government not to rely solely upon formal legal measures, but to command the respect of the population. On the other hand, he cited a pre-revolutionary legal scholar – one influenced by Petrazhitsky's psychological theories – to call for the inculcation of 'respect for the law'.

3 Ilinsky's citation is from Vinogradov, 1915: 32.

Kornilov

In 1925, Kornilov, a supporter of the sociological school, published *Juridical Dogmatism and Dialectical Materialism*. He sought to survey and critique the development of Soviet theories of law. He said the debates saw three contending schools: one identifying law with social relationships, the second taking a normative approach and the third approaching law as an ideological question.

Kornilov criticised Stuchka, said to be the main representative of the first approach, for defining law as 'a system of social relationships corresponding to the interests of the ruling class and protected by its organised power'. Citing Engels' *Ludwig Feuerbach and the End of Classical German Philosophy*, Kornilov insisted that law is merely the formal reflection of economic and social relationships. He concluded that 'law is not a system of social relationships but a form of these relationships – a form that finds its concrete expression in the juridical norm'.[4]

Kornilov stated that Pashukanis represented the second, normativist, trend. Turning to the ideological camp, Kornilov focused his attention on Goikhbarg, describing him as the most consistent representative of the 'social function' school, a 'still fashionable' theory that had exerted the greatest influence upon Soviet civil legislation. Kornilov accused Goikhbarg of sanctifying private property by referring to it as a social function, placed in the hands of a person for use in the interests of society. This indictment was based on Goikhbarg's comment that:

> Private property is looked upon as a certain good placed in the hands of a person for safekeeping in the interests of society; and, therefore, the person holding private property has positive obligations toward society . . . This view permeates also the construction of the institution of property in our civil code (Jaworskyj, 1967: 210).

According to Kornilov, Goikhbarg's views were derived from Duguit, who was 'an ideologist of finance capital'. Kornilov quoted Duguit:

> With regard to property, it is no longer treated in modern law as an inalienable right . . . It simply exists and must exist. It constitutes an indispensable prerequisite for the growth of society, whereas all collectivist doctrines are tantamount to a return to barbarism. However, property is not a right; property is a social function. The proprietor, or to put it differently, the owner of wealth, shall, because he owns this wealth, fulfill a social function (Jaworskyj, 1967: 211).

4 Jaworskyj, 1967: 208–10.

Kornilov attributed Duguit's theory to the development of the finance bourgeoisie, as the ownership of the means of production became increasingly concentrated in the hands of trusts, cartels and joint-stock companies. But while Goikhbarg may have utilised Duguit's concepts in an attempt to elucidate the contradiction inherent in the restoration of limited property rights and market relations under the NEP, Kornilov's attempt to label Goikhbarg a defender of finance capital was one-sided and far-fetched. Goikhbarg appears to have been grappling with the real problems of defining, delineating the use of, and providing a rationale for the state regulation of revived private property rights.

Kornilov dealt with two other 'ideologists' in similar fashion. The first was Razumovsky, a philosopher who had written a 1923 article entitled 'Marx's and Engels' Conception of Law' and delivered a lecture at the Socialist Academy, subsequently published in 1924 under the title *Sociology and Law*.[5] Kornilov asserted that the two works present mutually contradictory views. Razumovsky's article treated law as an ideology, whereas the lecture was based on the concept of 'relationship'. Nevertheless, Kornilov suggested, the latter work gave the impression that law was not a reflection of social and economic reality but a product of the ideological activity of legal theorists.

Kornilov criticised the following sentence from Razumovsky's article: 'Law ceases to be an ideology and becomes an undisguised expression of the class domination of the proletariat; it becomes a theory of this class domination.'[6] Kornilov declared this formulation to be completely contradictory to the views of Marx and Engels, cited by Razumovsky, because it implied that law did not exist in bourgeois society, but would exist in proletarian society. Kornilov's assertion was drawing extravagant conclusions from a single sentence, taken out of context. As discussed below, Razumovsky was pointing to the ideological role of capitalist law in contributing to the camouflage of the social relations of wage labour and commodity production, which Marx termed 'commodity fetishism'.[7] This mystifying function ceased under socialism, with 'law' being presented openly as an instrument of proletarian rule, subject to the limitations and problems of making the transition to genuine communism.

Displaying a somewhat mechanical approach, Kornilov denied that law was a form of social consciousness, insisting that it was simply a formal reflection of the relationships of production. Rejecting Razumovsky's suggestion that law is 'a peculiar reflection of a definite aggregate of economic relationships *within the human consciousness*', Kornilov stated: '*Law is not a form of social consciousness but a form of social relationships*.'[8] This position ignores the ideological role of law.

5 Jaworskyj, 1967: 213.

6 Ibid: 214.

7 See Chapter 2.

8 Jaworskyj, 1967: 214. Both sets of emphasis appear to be Kornilov's.

Kornilov was even more dismissive of the work of Reisner, the most prominent Soviet follower of Petrazhitsky, who had earlier been criticised by Lunacharsky. Kornilov accused Reisner of uncritically following Petrazhitsky's psychological theory of law. Kornilov sought to ridicule Reisner's attempt to trace a connection between economic life and subconscious psychological emotions. Reisner wrote that Petrazhitsky dwelt on the individual psychic aspects of man's emotional life 'which characterise his activities – primarily his economic activities'. According to Kornilov, this amounted to seeking the lever of economic relationships in man's psyche and 'one could hardly outdo this psychological fanaticism'.[9] As a matter of fact, Reisner's statement does not make that contention; it merely points to a psychological element in how economic relations are experienced and perceived. Reisner himself claimed that his work refashioned Petrazhitsky's doctrine concerning intuitive law, placing it upon a Marxist foundation. Whatever the merits of that claim, it deserved more serious treatment than it received at Kornilov's hands.

Reisner

Reisner's contributions to the legal debates raised important questions. Reisner had first outlined his views in his 1908 volume *The Theory of Petrazhitsky: Marxism and Social Ideology*. He restated his theory in a modified form in his 1925 book *Law, Our Law, Foreign Law, General Law*. Pashukanis devoted pages of his writings to answering Reisner's approach, which argued for an ideological role for law to continue under socialism and communism.

Reisner was impressed by Petrazhitsky's view that law consisted of normative ideas existing as psychological reality in the mind of humanity, not identical with the law of the state and sometimes directed against it. This 'intuitive law', he wrote in 1908, differed according to social groups, including families, social circles and classes. 'And to the extent that it embraces ever broader and broader circles intuitive law becomes *pro tanto* both powerful and dominant in a given milieu.'[10]

Long before the October Revolution, Reisner had sought to enrich the concept of intuitive law with the Marxist understanding of the class struggle and the revolutionary upheavals produced by the economic and social impasse produced by capitalism.

> When the production forces outgrow a particular means of production, and when the latter turns into a brake pressing upon them and fetters confining them, then intuitive law is born under the veil of the existing

9 Jaworskyj, 1967: 215.
10 Reisner, *The Theory of Petrazhitsky: Marxism and Social Ideology*, in Hazard, 1951: 82.

> traditional law. Sometimes it grows for a long time in the unconscious stillness. Finally – as a real law existing and operative, defining the psyche of a given class – it collides with positive law (and in particular with official law) and on this basis of the struggle of the two laws, the tragedy of insurrection and suppression, of revolution and a turn backward, is played. Each class takes its stand under the banner of its own law: the oppressing class clings to the authority of traditional symbols, ideas and state practice; while the insurgent class relies on the demands of a 'justice' whose foundation is in philosophy and morality and history, and not on considerations of historical necessity or on the laws of sociology (Hazard, 1951: 86).

He substantially maintained this analysis of intuitive law in 1925. 'It needs no force in order that it may exist . . . the norms of intuitive law . . . are an exalted standard and criterion for the appraisal of positive norms [law of the state] and for disapproving them if their content is incongruous.'[11] Moreover, he claimed that this conception had guided the initial decrees and measures of the October Revolution.

> I refashioned Petrazhitsky's doctrine concerning intuitive law in the sense that I put it upon a Marxist foundation, and thereby obtained not intuitive law in general (which could here and there furnish individual forms adapted to certain social conditions) but the most genuine class law which was worked out in the form of intuitive law (in the ranks of the oppressed and exploited mass) independently of any official framework whatsoever; and it is for this reason alone that we were able to utilize 'the revolutionary legal consciousness of the proletariat' as the foundation of the activity of our revolutionary justice, which at the beginning was without any positive norms whatsoever (Hazard, 1951: 85).

As a purely factual claim, Reisner's account of the initial measures of the revolution was one-sided. It will be recalled that Lenin intervened in the drafting of the first decree on the courts to insist that some objective, ascertainable standards, based on the minimum programmes of the Bolsheviks and the Social Revolutionaries, had to be included to guide or limit the interpretation of 'revolutionary legal consciousness'. Nonetheless, there is no doubt that Reisner's approach was influential in the early period.

In mounting this argument, however, Reisner had a further agenda. He contended that law could not be identified with capitalist law per se and that law would continue to have a role in communist society. Even more, he argued that law could perform a valuable ideological role under socialism and

11 Reisner, *Law, Our Law, Foreign Law, General Law*, in Hazard, 1951: 84.

communism in legitimising the demands and authority of the working people. He had originally outlined this thesis in 1908, criticising those Marxists who adopted a 'lawless ideal' with 'extraordinary practical disadvantages':

> The claims of the proletariat, asserted as the basis of new social conditions, are thus bereft of all the vigour of legal demands and sink to the position of economic and political importunities. They lose all the force of an ideal robed in legal vestments and all the authority of a categorical legal demand admitting of no objections. They are positively weakened by reason of the unsteady ideology of economic expediency, even though it be founded on the inevitability of the social process . . . Only when the worker class shall be conscious of its fundamental demands in law, when the legal ideology shall become a part of the social ideal of that class and when law shall have been transferred as an organized element by that class into its future society freed from constraint of every sort – only then will the mighty struggle for economic freedom attain its culmination, and only then will the new law triumphantly take the place of the official constraint of the present time (Hazard, 1951: 72).

Reisner modified his conception in 1925, stating that he had 'exaggerated the significance of the legal element' in insisting that the 'revolutionary masses must have their own class intuitive law which must lie at the foundation of its future dominance'.[12] Defending himself against those who criticised him for taking an idealist approach, he also sought to relate his theory to the materialist interpretation of history.

> That the basis of law in class society is economic is beyond doubt; for each class here builds its law on the basis of its position in production and exchange, and the general legal order reflects in itself the features of that form of production which in its turn defines the class order. We must make the same observation also with regard to the future communist society whereof the modern Soviet and socialist order is the precursor: law is here built in conformity with its collective economy and with the part played by the proletariat in production. The association between law and economy thus provides us with the first point of our definition: law is the result of economic relationships – and in particular of production relationships (Hazard, 1951: 97).

Nevertheless, Reisner adhered to his view that law would continue to exist under communism, where it would serve an ideological purpose. He criticised Soviet scholars for denying or underestimating the ideological character of

12 Hazard, 1951: 89.

law. 'The fundamental teaching of Marxism concerning law – its teaching as to the ideological character of law – is, with negligible exceptions, either ignored or perverted.'[13] Reisner argued that legal ideology was not changed by being dependent upon an economic basis.[14]

Referring to Marx's statement, in his *Critique of the Gotha Program*, that 'the narrow horizon of bourgeois law' would be overcome in the communist society of the future, Reisner asked 'Does this mean that when the narrow horizon of bourgeois law is abandoned every sort of law will disappear as well?' His answer was:

> This problem is not so simply decided, inasmuch as the excerpt taken from Marx contains a proposition which – pointing out the contrast between factual inequality and juridic equality – says that 'in order to eliminate all these evils, law must be unequal, instead of being equal'. From this it may be supposed that law can continue to exist in communist society in the form of a juridic ideology which, however, will inscribe on its banner the formula of the higher justice to be found only in communist society – that is to say, the law which says: 'From each according to his ability, to each according to his needs' (Hazard, 1951: 107).

However, Reisner's final answer was that this communist 'law' would not be law, at least not in the sense understood by capitalist legal theory. 'Law', as ideology, would no longer exist under communism. His conclusion appears to be at odds with his earlier call for law to remain an ideological tool in the struggle for socialism. But his somewhat strained line of reasoning drew on his consistently maintained insistence that law is an ideological form.

> Law and legal ideology are by no means a merely objective (we would say, a merely technical) formulation of existing production relationships. Then it would cease to be an ideology and would become merely a scientific and technical expression of the given relationships without the slightest addition of any subjectivism, refraction, or perversion of any character whatsoever. It must not be forgotten that law is an 'ideological form,' and so always bears within itself the seed of a similar perversion and is capable (with the aid of the formal method of presentation) of being isolated from reckoning with reality (Hazard, 1951: 108).

13 Hazard, 1951: 95.
14 Ibid: 103.

Razumovsky

In another 1925 work, *Problems of the Marxist Theory of Law*, Razumovsky strongly defended the necessity to recognise the ideological role of law. Jaworskyj classifies Razumovsky in the sociological school, yet his analysis had similarities to Reisner's psychological approach. Razumovsky quoted some of the key passages from Engels' letters to Conrad Schmidt (27 October 1890) and Franz Mehring (14 July 1893), where Engels emphasises the need to take into account the ideological peculiarities of jurisprudence, as he and Marx had done in *The German Ideology*.[15] Moreover, he correctly pointed out that Marx and Engels commenced their studies with the ideological forms in which law was presented, and, while they had been concerned to trace the socio-economic roots of these forms, had never denied the need to take into account their influence:

> The problem of ideology and, in particular, the problem of law, were for Marx and Engels the *starting points* in the development of their historical view. A critical re-examination of Hegel's philosophy of law . . . led them to the material conditions of life in which legal relationships are rooted [emphasis in original] (Jaworskyj, 1967: 220).

Razumovsky summed up the conclusions drawn by Marx and Engels as follows:

> Marx and Engels quite frequently asserted that reflection of the real economic process takes place in an 'inverted way', by means of 'placing it on its head'. They used these expressions in order to demonstrate that, in the process of the objectivisation of the thought material, *the real relationship between this process and the social reality reflected in it is inverted*: it is not the economic process which gives rise to the corresponding forms of consciousness but the other way around; the thought appears as the real source of social actions (Jaworskyj, 1967: 222).

Razumovsky did not deny that economic processes ultimately determine social consciousness; but he pointed out they that do not do so directly. On the contrary, because of the 'inverted' appearances generated by the commodification of economic and social relationships, thought itself appears to shape human consciousness. In a passage that echoes some of the analysis made by Plekhanov, Razumovsky elaborated on the 'inverted' process involved:

15 All cited in Chapter 2.

> The reflections of fundamental economic relationships in social consciousness (that is, reflections that historically separate themselves from economic relationships and that are regarded as 'free ideas') become the point of departure of a further thought process; they become a 'condensing lens' and thus give to the new, more particular reflections of social reality an appearance of deductions made from the fundamental guiding 'principles' (Jaworskyj, 1967: 222).[16]

Developing his argument further, Razumovsky pointed out that ideological concepts, properly understood, could serve as essential analytical tools, contributing to more concrete understanding of underlying economic and social relations:

> As stated by Engels, ideological notions are not the ultimate *foundation*. They do not enter into the economic process, into the development of material social relations, as a causal element, but they do serve as a medium for the expression and representation of those of man's activities which constitute this process. Hence, they are an indispensable condition for the development of social relationships . . . Only such a truly dialectical understanding of the nature of ideology will make it possible to see in it an 'inverted reflection' and at the same time an inevitable side of the social process, that is, a form of social relationships. Only then shall we understand why ideology, because of inner contradictions, *abstracts itself* from social relationships and at the same time contributes toward their concretisation [emphasis in original] (Jaworskyj, 1967: 224–5).

It is not clear how far Razumovsky intended this analysis to apply to law in the transition to communism. Certainly, the Soviet leaders recognised that 'legality' continued to play both legitimising and normative roles in their administration. But Razumovsky appears to have been arguing for an ongoing, or even inevitable, role for ideological 'inversion' under socialism. It also seems that he identified himself with Bukharin, whom he cited as an authority for his analysis. Nevertheless, his views were a serious contribution to the legal debates.

Rights

The 1925–27 period produced an interesting discussion on the nature of 'rights' under socialism. Uspensky's 1925 article 'Law and Socialism' argued for a collectivist approach to rights based somewhat on Duguit's social

16 For Plekhanov, see Chapter 3.

function theory. Uspensky examined three basic economic rights: to work, to the full product of one's labour and to sustenance (existence). On the first, he argued that capitalism was incapable of providing the right to work, yet the right was unnecessary under socialism, in which work became a public obligation. With regard to the second, the demand for the right to the produce of one's labour was a justified reaction of the exploited, dissatisfied with the unequal distribution of society's produce under capitalism. But it had validity under socialism only in the negative sense that unearned income was unjust. As Marx had explained in his *Critique of the Gotha Program*, distribution according to labour remained unequal in relation to social needs.

On the third basic right, to the indispensable conditions for existence, Uspensky argued against Novgorodtsev, who based the right on an individualistic conception of a human personality and its dignity. Uspensky preferred Pokrovsky's argument that the complete realisation of the right could only be attained through the socialisation of all means of production. He drew from this some important observations on the nature and role of law under socialism:

> The socialist system of law is distinct from a capitalist system, not because it expands the concept of subjective rights, but because it advances a new principle of juridical regulation. It is well known that the very idea of subjective right – as a right presumably prior to and independent of objective legal norms – has the character of natural-law individualism. This idea came into being as a protest against police-state absolutism and found its expression in the theory of the innate and inalienable rights of man. Indeed, the idea of subjective rights is connected with the goods-producing society. And, if this idea were indispensable to the creation of law, then Pashukanis would be quite right in connecting all legal regulation to the relationships of goods producers in a capitalist society. But is it really so? (Jaworskyj, 1967: 230)

To answer this question, Uspensky examined Duguit's social function theory. While Duguit was not a socialist and his construct presupposed private property, nevertheless 'property, in his opinion, ceases to be a right of the individual and is transformed into a social function'.[17] Uspensky suggested that Duguit's view reflected the shift in capitalist economy from independent producers to finance capital and state capitalism. This shift, Uspensky implied, undermined Pashukanis' commodity exchange analysis.

Uspensky argued, in agreement with Goikhbarg, that the Soviet civil code had adopted social function theory to a certain extent. Where Article 1 of the code stated, 'Civil rights are protected by law, with the exception of when

17 Jaworskyj, 1967: 231.

they are used in conflict with their socio-economic purpose,' it indicated that the scope of rights was determined by collective, not individual, interests.

> The rights that we grant are not the innate rights of man; they are rights granted by the state for the purpose of attaining the goals that are indispensable to collective preservation. Such a fundamental goal is the development of the productive forces of the country . . . The theory of law as a social function is entirely opposed to the concept of law as a system of subjective rights (Jaworskyj, 1967: 232).

In reaching his conclusions, Uspensky sought to unify aspects of Marxist and capitalist legal theory. He presented the collectivist approach as the logical end-product of a shift in the concept of property made under finance capitalism. He presented his thesis as the ultimate realisation, in a socialist form, of the transition pointed to not only by Duguit but also by Comte:

> The problem of the socialist system of law implies the replacement of juridical regulation, based on the principle of subjective rights, by the regulation grounded upon the principle of objective law. The juridical system, conceived as a system of subjective rights, did not regulate all aspects of life; it halted before a subject with his rights as an inviolable sanctuary. On the other hand, regulation in conformity with the principle of objective law implied a thorough mastery of social reality, a complete victory of law over life. Following the translation of such a regulation into practice, the idea of rights and the idea of obligations will blend together. Then, August Comte's precept will be fulfilled: 'In the positive state each has duties toward everyone, but no one has any rights . . . To put it differently, no one has a right other than the right to fulfill his duty' (Jaworskyj, 1967: 232–3).

Although he did not cite Lenin, some support for this view could be derived from Lenin's analysis of finance capitalism in *Imperialism, the Highest Stage of Capitalism*. Writing in 1916, Lenin observed that the rise of giant monopolistic corporations, the dominance of finance capital via the banks and other institutions, the 'interlocking' of ownership of the means of production via the stock exchange and the intricate planning of production and distribution on a global scale by rival conglomerates had transformed social relations. In Lenin's words:

> It becomes evident that we have socialisation of production, and not mere 'interlocking'; that private economic and private property relations constitute a shell which no longer fits its contents, a shell which must inevitably decay if its removal is artificially delayed (Lenin, 1976: 178–9).

However, Uspensky's reference to a 'complete victory of law over life' and his uncritical comparison to Comte's model of 'the positive state' under capitalism indicate a tendency to entrench legality as a means of enforcing new Soviet social relations. This approach was at odds with the classic Marxist view of the withering away of law and the state.

Naumov voiced basic opposition to the 'social function' school in a 1926 article entitled 'The Role and Significance of Legal Forms in the Transition Period'. Naumov emphasised Marx's insistence, in the *Critique of the Gotha Program*, that law protects economic inequality. Under socialism, in the transition to communism, inequality would remain and that was why Marx designated the law operating in this first stage of communist society as bourgeois law. Naumov concluded:

> Since law, which at the first stage of communist society has a bourgeois character, will disappear completely under full-scale communism, it is inadmissible to speak of communist law, communist property, etc. First, this would be a logical fallacy, *contradictio in adjecto*. Second, this would be a false methodological approach, pregnant with unfortunate consequences concerning the meaning of law, and its significance in man's social life (Jaworskyj, 1967: 237).

Naumov rejected the 'very popular view' that human society was inconceivable without law. It was true that law occupied a very significant place in social life and was not artificially invented. It was equally true that legal life changed with social life. But it was not true that law was an inescapable attribute of human society at all stages of its development. 'In a developed communist society – in which not antagonism but cooperation and economic collaboration will be the motivating forces – there will be no law and no legal norms.'[18]

Naumov addressed the apparent contradiction involved in regarding Soviet law as bourgeois when it sought to promote the development of communism. His views can be seen as an attempted bridge between the classical Marxist view and the developing Stalinist insistence upon the existence and sanctity of 'proletarian law'. Naumov observed that capitalist law protected the interests of the bourgeoisie as a class, not necessarily the interests of individual members of that class, and sought to draw an analogous class role for bourgeois law under socialism. In the course of his exposition, he poured scorn on the social function school.

> We say that, judging by its principles, contemporary Soviet law is bourgeois law; and at the same time, we assert that it is proletarian law. There

18 Jaworskyj, 1967: 238.

> seems to be a contradiction. We are told that only one of these assertions can be true . . . These objections call for an explanation. First of all, we do not assert that contemporary Soviet law is, *on the one hand*, a bourgeois law and, *on the other hand*, a proletarian law. We reject eclecticism unconditionally. Bourgeois legal codes comprise norms that protect the interests of the working class, for example, the norms limiting the working day. But, with the exception of hopeless Philistines, no one would assert that bourgeois law therefore begins to lose its class character and becomes gradually 'socialised'. The same is true of our civil code. It comprises norms that protect even the interests of private owners. This, however, does not mean that our law is losing its proletarian class character. We assert that our Soviet law is at one and the same time both proletarian and bourgeois [emphasis in original] (Jaworskyj, 1967: 245).

Naumov acknowledged Lenin's warning that in the transition period, the state would remain 'a bourgeois state without the bourgeoisie'. But he suggested that just as the bourgeois state protected the interests of the ruling class as a whole, so it did under socialism.

> Being a bourgeois law in its principle, it protects the interests of the proletariat as a class, whose ultimate objectives are *the destruction of all classes, all law, all states, and the creation of a classless society without law and without a state* [emphasis in original] (Jaworskyj, 1967: 246).

These mental gymnastics ignored the material circumstances confronting the Soviet state. The contradiction between the bourgeois character of the state and the interests of the working masses was a real one. It reflected the continued recourse to capitalist property rights and norms of distribution, which entrenched inequality and therefore threatened the interests of ordinary people.

As Trotsky observed at around the same time – in November 1925 – in the English foreword to *Towards Socialism or Capitalism*, the Soviet government was quite aware that the NEP brought with it the dangers of renewed class polarisation, particularly in the rural areas between wealthy, employer peasant farmers and pauperised hired labourers. In a prescient warning of the future evolution of the Soviet Union, Trotsky wrote:

> As far as there is struggle between the capitalistic and socialistic tendencies in our economic life – it is the cooperation and competition between them which actually constitutes the essence of the New Economic Policy – the issue of the struggle depends on the rate of development of the two tendencies. In other words, should State industry develop more *slowly* than agriculture and should the latter *with increasing speed* produce the two opposite poles we have spoken of – the capitalistic farmers at the top,

> the proletarians at the bottom – this would, of course, lead to a restoration of capitalism [emphasis in original] (Trotsky, 1976: 6).

While praising Pashukanis and Stuchka for their contributions to Marxist legal theory, Naumov criticised Stuchka for insufficiently taking up the cudgels against 'legal nihilism', which Naumov identified with Goikhbarg. This 'nihilism', Naumov argued, was an echo of earlier 'militant communism' and had its roots in nihilist tendencies that emerged in the struggle against Tsarism in the 1860s, protesting against all forms of oppressive law. According to Naumov, in combating the 'normativists', Stuchka had underlined the fact that law was a social relationship, but had failed to 'see the connection between law and other social phenomena'.[19]

Naumov condemned Goikhbarg for restating in his 1924 *Foundations of the Private Property Law*, that law was a 'stupefying opium of the people'. As Naumov noted, Goikhbarg denied that Soviet rules and regulations were 'law'. Naumov declared that, to be consistent, Goikhbarg would have to advocate anti-state propaganda.

> He proposes to struggle against all law in general. He proposes to conduct anti-law propaganda in the same way as anti-religious propaganda is being conducted. In his opinion, legal regulation of social relationships has no place in the transition period: 'That which we call Soviet law is not a law *but rules established by the Soviet authorities, correct norms, expedient rules, rules realising the goals for which they have been created* ... To be consistent, A. G. Goikhbarg should also advocate anti-state propaganda' [emphasis in original] (Jaworskyj, 1967: 249).

Naumov asserted that the principal defect in Goikhbarg's views lay in an underestimation of the significance of legal forms in the history of a commodity-producing society. By depicting law as a bourgeois invention for deceiving and exploiting the masses, Goikhbarg had jumped to the conclusion that all law could simply be abolished following a socialist revolution, regardless of the continuation of commodity–money relationships. This approach, Naumov declared, smacked of the views of the French socialist Proudhon, whom Marx had criticised. For all the vehemence of this rhetoric, Goikhbarg's insistence that Soviet regulatory measures were not 'law' in the same sense as bourgeois law has merit and accords with Lenin's view that the state would begin withering away, in the sense of taking on a qualitatively different character, immediately following the seizure of power.

19 Jaworskyj, 1967: 247.

'Soviet Law'

While these debates went on, another jurisprudential enterprise embodied the shifting political and theoretical climate. From 1925 to 1927, Stuchka initiated and undertook a major project, *The Encyclopedia of State and Law*. He edited the three-volume undertaking and wrote many of its key entries. Sharlet, Maggs and Beirne characterise his entries as 'in retrospect, pedestrian, repetitive and unenterprising' and attribute these defects to 'the lack of serious Marxist analysis both of legal history and of the history of ideas'.[20] Their first observation seems fair but not the second. Rather, the increasingly turgid tone and content of Stuchka's contributions relate to their underlying thrust, which is to justify, as a more or less permanent requirement, the use of state repression. Stuchka declared that the dictatorship of the proletariat was likely to be 'extremely long'.

In his entry on 'Soviet Law', written in 1927, just as the struggle against the Left Opposition was at its height, Stuchka reiterated his rejection of the view that Soviet law was in any way a remnant of bourgeois law, retained as a temporary measure until the withering away of the state and law. In doing so, he quickly glossed over the well-known passage in *The State and Revolution*, where Lenin, quoting Marx, warned that post-revolutionary law would still be bourgeois law, enforced moreover by a bourgeois state, until it faded away. Sharlet, Maggs and Beirne conclude:

> Thus, while the Encyclopedia entries are often cryptic and dogmatic, they served the important purpose of providing a theory of law that could support the Soviet legal system not for the brief transition period envisioned by the more radical communists, but for decades, indeed for the indefinite future. Their logic in fact suggests the abandonment of the idea of the withering away of the state (Beirne and Sharlet, 1980: 63).

Stuchka's entry on 'bourgeois law' explicitly repudiated Marx's comment, in his *Critique of the Gotha Program*, that bourgeois law would continue into the first phase of communism. Stuchka argued that the unexpected length of the transition period required a qualitative reappraisal of Marx's prognosis. At the same time, suggesting the theoretical mess he found himself in, Stuchka conceded that Soviet law included 'elements of bourgeois law':

> We see that life, in our revolution, has somewhat departed from Marx's latter view, because under the extreme length of the transitional period, there has naturally been formed a special *Soviet* law for the transitional period. This obviously contains elements of bourgeois law, but in essence

20 Beirne and Sharlet, 1980: 61.

it introduces profound changes in principle into all social relations, including law [emphasis in original] (Beirne and Sharlet, 1980: 97).

1927–37: From debates to diatribes

Even though Pashukanis lined up against the Left Opposition, he came under criticism as early as 1927, which was the year before Trotsky and other leaders of the Left Opposition were sent into exile. Stuchka made a critique of Pashukanis' treatise in a report reprinted in the journal *Revolution of Law*.

Stuchka, through the Communist Academy, had launched the journal earlier that year. Ostensibly directed against foreign bourgeois jurists, the periodical served the struggle against the Left and United Oppositions. Stuchka's article 'State and Law in the Period of Socialist Construction', which appeared in the journal's second edition, denounced the United Opposition, accusing it of sowing discord.[21] Stuchka made only a fleeting, unclear and unsubstantiated reference to the Opposition, attributing to it the position that the state was a dual class formation – worker and peasant – and should become a two-party government. No details or quotations were offered to support these allegations.

Stuchka's 1927 article marked an adjustment of his earlier views. It justified a lengthy period of socialist transition, during which Soviet law would have a positive and even creative function, rather than being regarded as a residual product of the poverty and capitalist encirclement of the Soviet state. The article reflected the line adopted at that year's Fifteenth Party Congress. The congress met in the wake of the defeats of the British general strike of 1926 and the Chinese revolution of 1926–27, both of which had huge global implications. These routs intensified the isolation of the Soviet state and hence helped pave the way for the removal of Trotsky and other Opposition leaders. The congress attempted to belittle the impact of the defeats and advance a seemingly optimistic orientation. It called for the end of the NEP's period of strategic defeat, the accelerated construction of socialism and a 'cultural revolution' throughout Soviet society. Under these conditions, while still praising the originality of Pashukanis' theses, Stuchka made serious criticisms of them.

First, he argued that Pashukanis wrongly identified the origin of law solely in commodity exchange. Law arose out of the appropriation of land and in the class struggles in the processes of production. Law reflected not simply the exchange of commodities but the authority and power of the dominant class.

Second, Stuchka argued that while Pashukanis had identified the connection between commodity fetishism, as analysed by Marx, and legal fetishism

21 Beirne and Sharlet, 1980: 176.

under capitalism, he had erred in extending this critique to law in general. Law pre-dated capitalism and even commodity exchange, and real differences existed between feudal, capitalist and Soviet law.

Third, Pashukanis had based his theory on simply commodity exchange in the formative period of capitalism, whereas advanced capitalism involved production for capital accumulation, not exchange, and saw the advent of imperialism, featuring capitalist monopolies, trusts and syndicates, operating with state support.

Fourth, because Pashukanis had falsely equated bourgeois law with law in general, he committed the utopian error of seeing the withering away of law involving a direct transition from bourgeois law to non-law.

Finally, flowing from the above, Soviet law could and should have a creative role in the period of socialist construction. 'Soviet law must be the political economy of the transitional period, the economic policy of Soviet power laid out in paragraphs.'[22] Although Soviet law was 'in general a reprint of bourgeois law', it existed without a bourgeoisie. Soviet law was a necessary, relatively temporary feature of the proletarian dictatorship, whose object was socialist planning and whose Soviet character was guaranteed by the class nature of the workers' state.

These criticisms underscore the fact that by 1927 the role of law was being entrenched, as a special category called 'Soviet law'. Its transitory character as an inevitable but risky and contradictory consequence of the continuation of unequal market relations was being downplayed. This process took a new turn after Stalin, in his political report to the Sixteenth Party Congress in 1930, effectively repudiated Lenin's insistence on the inherent and immediately commencing withering away of the state. Stalin now labelled that as Bukharin's position.

> We are for the withering away of the state, and at the same time, we stand for the strengthening of the dictatorship of the proletariat, which represents the mightiest and most powerful authority of all forms of state that have ever existed. The highest development of the state power for the purpose of preparing conditions for the withering away of the state power, . . . this is the Marxist formula. Is this 'contradictory'? Yes, it is 'contradictory'. But this contradiction springs from life itself and reflects completely the Marxian dialectic (Beirne and Sharlet, 1980: 229).

Stuchka felt compelled to 'correct' his earlier stance on the withering away of the state in a 1931 article 'My Journey and My Errors'. He drew a distinction between 'proletarian law', which existed in the transition to socialism, and a

22 Beirne and Sharlet, 1980: 186.

new sense of law – 'the law of the socialist society' that would last beyond the elimination of the state as an organ of class oppression.[23] Pashukanis followed suit in his 1932 article 'Theory of State and Law', which mirrored Stalin's pronouncement.

> The achievement of the practical construction of socialism must be accompanied by a growth of the might of the state, both externally and internally. This does not in the least contradict the theory of Marx and Lenin concerning the withering away of the state during the higher phase of communism (Beirne and Sharlet, 1980: 234).

Such recantations did not save Stuchka, Pashukanis and others. The crowning glory of the Stalinist regime's repudiation of Marxism came at the Seventh Congress of the Communist International in August 1935. It declared that with the nationalisation of industry, the collectivisation of agriculture and the liquidation of the kulaks as a class, 'the final and irrevocable triumph of socialism and the all-sided reinforcement of the state of the proletarian dictatorship, is achieved in the Soviet Union'.[24] Trotsky pointed out that this resolution was entirely self-contradictory.

> If socialism has 'finally and irrevocably' triumphed, not as a principle but as a living social regime, then a renewed 'reinforcement' of the dictatorship is obvious nonsense. And on the contrary, if the reinforcement of the dictatorship is evoked by the real needs of the regime, that means that the triumph of socialism is still remote. Not only a Marxist, but any realistic political thinker, ought to understand that the very necessity of 'reinforcing' the dictatorship – that is, governmental repression – testifies not to the triumph of a classless harmony, but to the growth of new social antagonisms (Trotsky, 1937: 62).

The publication of the draft of a new constitution in June 1936 formalised the corresponding shift in official legal policy. It established a constitutional right of ownership of personal property and, together with the provisions of the first all-USSR civil and criminal codes, signalled the reinforcement rather than the withering away of law. Article 14 of the constitution asserted that the jurisdiction of the USSR covered, among other things, 'Legislation on the judicial system and judicial procedure; criminal and civil codes'. Stalin's remark later that year that 'stability of the laws is necessary for us now more than ever' and the promulgation of the new constitution a few weeks later, in December 1936, pronounced a new stage in the Stalinist

23 Beirne and Sharlet, 1980: 233.
24 Trotsky, 1937: 62.

reversal of Soviet legal theory. Pashukanis was arrested and disappeared in January 1937.[25]

Stuchka died before the great purges of 1936–37, but there is every reason to believe that he would have been executed along with Pashukanis. By 1938 Stalin's judicial henchman, A. Vyshinsky had made the improbable discovery that the entire jurisprudential leadership of the Soviet Union had for years been enemies of the state. Vyshinsky, the chief prosecutor of the Moscow Trials, denounced the 'Trotsky-Bukharin band headed by Pashukanis, Krylenko and a number of other traitors'.

> Over the course of years an almost monopolistic position in legal science has been enjoyed by a group of persons who have turned out to be provocateurs and traitors – people who actually knew how to contrive the work of betraying our science, our state and our fatherland under the mask of defending Marxism-Leninism (Zile, 1970: 258–9).

Vyshinsky's diatribe drew a connection between the new doctrine of 'socialist legality' and the programme of 'socialism in one country'. He railed against anti-Soviet 'runt-theories' such as 'the impossibility of constructing socialism in the USSR' and 'the provocateur theory of Pashukanis and others concerning Soviet law as bourgeois law, as law withering away'. Vyshinsky gave a number of examples of the need for law, interestingly all of which concerned the protection of private property interests. 'To reduce law to policy would be to ignore such tasks confronting law as that of the legal defence of personal, property, family and inheritance rights and interests, and the like.'[26]

Law was portrayed not as a product of particular social and production relations but simply as a set of normative prescriptions to be enforced by whatever regime was in power. Vyshinsky's doctrine was little more than a crude neo-positivist schema for legitimising the rule of the Kremlin elite in the name of constructing socialism within national confines. Its purpose was to instill and police discipline and order: 'Why is stability of statutes essential? Because it reinforces the stability of the state order and of the state discipline, and multiples tenfold the powers of socialism.'[27]

Beirne and Sharlet summed up the shift from Pashukanis to Vyshinsky, and from early Soviet to Stalinist jurisprudence, as follows:

> The legal culture of NEP along with the statutory legislation of the intervening years, so long castigated as bourgeois, was redefined as a

25 For further detail, see Sharlet, 1977: 161–2.

26 Zile, 1970: 258–9.

27 Vyshinsky, 1948: 75.

> socialist legal culture. The need to systematize the legal culture, so long obstructed as inconsistent with its withering away, became the new agenda for the legal profession. Jurists, driven from the law schools, the research institutes, and the legal press by the revolution of the law, reappeared as participants in the reconstruction of legal education and research. Disciplines banished from the law curriculum by the radical jurists were reintroduced beginning in the spring term of 1937. New course syllabi and textbooks for every branch of law, especially those eliminated or suppressed by the legal transfer cultures, began to appear with great rapidity. New editions of earlier texts were purged of Pashukanis' influence and quickly re-issued. Carrying out the mandate of Article 14 of the Stalin Constitution, numerous jurists were mobilised to prepare drafts for the all-union civil and criminal codes. Finally, a vulgar neo-positivist jurisprudence, based on 'class relations' and largely derived from the Stalin Constitution . . . replaced the tradition of revolutionary legal theory epitomized by Pashukanis (Beirne and Sharlet, 1980: 33–4).

This summary conveys some sense of the magnitude of the abandonment of the early ideals of the Soviet revolution, even if it somewhat uncritically identifies those principles with Pashukanis. As will be further explored in the next chapter, Pashukanis himself played a definite part in the process of degeneration that began in 1923–24. In a sense, Pashukanis ultimately helped dig his own grave, providing theoretical cover, both in some of his original theses and his subsequent 'corrections' for the needs of Stalin's bureaucracy. Nevertheless, his removal and replacement by Vyshinsky marked a new stage in the repudiation of the entire Marxist understanding of the role of law and the state.

Conclusion

Certain conclusions can be drawn from the evolution of the legal debates. There is a marked contrast between the post-1917 discussion and the post–1923 degeneration. The period after the revolution was characterised by genuine jurisprudential dialogue and efforts to minimise legal formality, replacing state coercion with mass involvement.

The adoption of the NEP in 1921 caused a shift back to legalism, particularly concerning the protection of private property rights. After 1923, with the ascendancy of Stalin and the doctrine of 'socialism in one country', a new atmosphere of 'corrections' and diatribes set in, accompanied by a strengthening of the repressive state apparatus. The classical Marxist perspective of the withering away of the state and law was ditched in favour of the entrenchment of a legal edifice, erected in the name of 'socialist legality'. In this sphere, as in others, Stalinism was a repudiation of Marxism, not a continuation of it.

Chapter 8

Evgeny Pashukanis and Stalinism: the rise and fall of a Soviet jurist

> Pashukanis superimposed the Stalinist concept of the state in Soviet socio-economic development onto the remnants of his original theory of law.[1]

Having examined the context of Pashukanis' work, we can return to the first enigma: How and why did Evgeny Pashukanis emerge as one of the most influential Soviet jurists from 1924 to 1930, come under only moderate criticism from 1930 to 1936 and then be denounced and executed in 1937 as a 'Trotskyite saboteur'?

Until 1937, he led the Institute for Soviet construction of the Communist Academy and became publisher of its legal theory journal. From 1935, he worked on drafting Stalin's 1936 constitution and in 1936 became deputy Commissar for Justice. Within a year, however, according to official statements, he became, together with Krylenko, a 'counter-revolutionary Trotskyist -Bukharinite parasite' and 'fascist agent' (Vyshinsky). The NKVD shot him without a trial.

Of course, Pashukanis was not alone. Virtually every leading figure associated with the October 1917 Russian Revolution and the early years of the Soviet Union fell victim to Stalin's purges by 1937, from Trotsky, Zinoviev, Kamenev and Bukharin to thousands of less-known socialists.[2] Krushchev's famous secret report to the Twentieth Congress of the Communist Party of the Soviet Union in 1956 revealed that of the 1,966 delegates to the party's seventeenth congress in 1934, 1,108, or more than half, were later arrested on charges of anti-revolutionary crimes. Of the 139 Central Committee members and candidates elected at the seventeenth congress, 98, or 70 per cent, were arrested and shot, mostly in the show trials and purges of 1937–38.[3]

Yet there are some particularly revealing aspects in the case of Pashukanis that have not been probed adequately by most Western or Soviet writers. His

1 Beirne and Sharlet, 1980: 28–9.
2 See Rogovin, 1998.
3 *Moscow Trials Anthology*, 1967: 21.

rise to leadership of Soviet legal work in 1924, at the relatively young age of 33, with the publication of his book *The General Theory of Law and Marxism*, coincided with Stalin's initial victory over the Left Opposition and the enunciation of Stalin's programme of seeking to build 'socialism in one country'.

His early prominence was particularly remarkable because initially Pashukanis saw his book as only the starting point for Marxist jurisprudence. He described it as a 'sketch', 'a first draft of a Marxist critique of the fundamental juridical concepts'.[4] He saw this project as one of clarification of a theory already existent, although not rigorously formulated, in Marx and Engels. 'The basic thesis,' he claimed, 'namely that the legal subject of juridical theories is very closely related to the commodity owner, did not, after Marx, require any further substantiation.'[5] Beirne and Sharlet commented:

> When the General Theory first appeared it is doubtful that anyone, least of all Pashukanis himself, could have foreseen its immediate success and the meteoric rise of its author within Marxist legal philosophy and the Soviet legal profession (Beirne and Sharlet, 1980: 37).

But the authors did not relate Pashukanis' unexpected emergence from obscurity to the fact that he publicly lined up against the Left Opposition as early as 1925. Pashukanis joined in the concerted drive that was launched to discredit Trotsky for his alleged 'Menshevism', based on his differences with Lenin at the time of the split between the Bolsheviks and Mensheviks in 1903. In 1903, at the Second Congress of the Russian Social Democratic Labour Party, Trotsky had opposed the resolute manner in which Lenin conducted the split within the Russian Social Democratic Party. However, Trotsky had reconsidered and retracted that view by 1917.

In order to understand Pashukanis' comments on 'Menshevism' and their political significance, we need to briefly review the issues at stake in the 1903 split and Trotsky's subsequent reforging of an alliance with Lenin during the course of 1917. Lenin insisted that the divisions over party rules of membership contained underlying differences of political outlook. He argued that those who opposed a requirement for members to work under party discipline were adapting to the pressure of political opportunism, that is, to abandon the perspective of socialist revolution in favour of seeking social reform from a capitalist government. Later, between 1908 and 1914, Trotsky unsuccessfully attempted to achieve a reunification between the Bolshevik and Menshevik wings of the party, neither of which he had aligned himself with. Ultimately, in early 1917, following the February Revolution, he fused his organisation with the Bolsheviks on the basis of Lenin's shift in position on

4 Pashukanis, 1978: 36.
5 Ibid: 39.

the strategic character of the Russian Revolution, as discussed in Chapter 4. At the same time, Trotsky acknowledged that Lenin had been correct in 1903 to recognise that the split over party rules was rooted in a fundamental divergence in political perspective.[6]

Yet in his 1925 article on 'Lenin and Problems of Law', Pashukanis drew a crude parallel between the 1903 split and the charges of bureaucratism levelled against Stalin's faction by the Left Opposition.

> When after the Second Congress [in 1903], Lenin's opponents had conducted a struggle against 'bureaucratic formalism', they constructed their argument on a deeper and, it seemed, more Marxist understanding of the course of historical development. Lenin, of course, did not think of concealing the fact that his organisational plan had a more definite political significance: to protect the Party from opportunism. Against this, his opponents from the Menshevik camp put forth the following weighty objection. 'Opportunism', they said, 'is caused by more complex and deeper causes than some paragraph of a charter' (Beirne and Sharlet, 1980: 152).

In the context of the official campaign against 'Trotskyism', it is impossible to read this passage as anything else but an endorsement of Stalin, who was, by implication, continuing the course charted by Lenin, against Trotsky the 'opportunist' who was making groundless accusations of bureaucratism. To reinforce the point, Pashukanis went on to quote Lenin's charge that 'Trotsky speaks again as an opportunist'.[7] He concluded by accusing Trotsky of lining up with 'liquidators' and of lacking a 'dialectical approach' to politics:

> How can one fail to compare Trotsky's abstract opinions after the Second Congress – on the theme of the inevitability of dissidence – with his concrete statement in 1908–1914 for 'unity' with those liquidators who had placed themselves both ideologically and organisationally outside the Party? To popularise the harmfulness of formal unity, after *Iskra* [Lenin's newspaper] had laid the basis in a 3-year struggle for both programmatic and tactical unity, and to raise a cry against dissidence and dissent when a whole political chasm had opened between the parties and the liquidators – this is a rare and, one may say, classical example of the complete absence of a dialectical approach to the question (Beirne and Sharlet, 1980: 156).

This denunciation of Trotsky appeared to be inserted in Pashukanis' article, published by Stuchka's *Revolution of Law* journal, solely for the purpose of

6 For an examination of these issues, see Deutscher, 1954: 254–60.
7 Beirne and Sharlet, 1980: 152.

identifying Pashukanis, and Stuchka and their associates, firmly with the Stalin faction's campaign to discredit and oust Trotsky and other Left Oppositionists from the party and government leadership. The diatribe against Trotsky had, at best, only a tangential relevance to the jurisprudential issue under discussion, which concerned the legal character and status of party rules and directives. In that relation, Pashukanis argued against requiring that party authorities observe strict legality, criticising unnamed 'arch-leftists' for whom 'formal legality still remains a fetish' and contending that 'legal perfection and legality could not be expected from proletarian power born yesterday'. Somewhat cloudily, he declared: 'Legality is not an empty sack that can be filled with a new class content.'[8]

Pashukanis' central theme in his *General Theory*, often simplistically referred to as a 'commodity-exchange' theory of law,[9] was related to the limited restoration of commercial property and market relations under the 1921 shift to the New Economic Policy. The dangers inherent in this temporary retreat became entrenched in Stalin's bureaucratic elite after 1924.[10] Pashukanis' approach, which regarded commodity exchange as the essence of legal relations, to some extent reconciled Marxist theory with the official revival of economic relations based on private ownership and market forces. In his view, law would remain in the sphere of exchange, while law and the state would continue to fade away, and be replaced by non-legal regulation, throughout society more generally.

Some scholars, notably Fuller, have interpreted Pashukanis' emphasis on commodity exchange as an 'ingenious' development of Marxist theory,[11] implying that it represented an innovative departure from communist orthodoxy. This simplifies a more complex interaction between the doctrinal and practical needs of the emerging Stalinist regime.

Pashukanis' theory was not simply an invention to satisfy the requirements of the NEP or the privileged bureaucracy. Based closely on Marx's method of analysis of the commodity form in *Capital*, it was bound up with a more profound examination of the legal form itself and it correctly rejected the crude instrumentalism expressed at times by some early Soviet theorists, including Stuchka. In his original 1924 publication of his *General Theory* at least, it seems that Pashukanis genuinely sought to make a contribution to Marxist theory, a contribution that he presented in a somewhat preliminary and tentative manner.

8 Beirne and Sharlet, 1980: 143–4.

9 For example, Fuller wrote that Pashukanis' theory 'has been called the "Commodity Exchange Theory of Law" ': Fuller, 1949: 1157. Pashukanis himself did not use that term, or accept that sweeping description. This issue is discussed in the next chapter, under the headings 'Critique of legal form' and 'The commodity exchange theory'.

10 See Chapter 3.

11 Fuller, 1949: 1159.

At the same time, the Stalinist faction still felt obliged to adhere to apparent Marxist orthodoxy in the mid-1920s. Stalin's followers had to work with a population that was imbued with a considerable knowledge of, and loyalty to, Marxism. Despite the manoeuvres already opened up against the Left Opposition from late 1923, the Opposition – which stridently championed Marxism – remained a potent political threat. Pashukanis, whether fully conscious of his role or not, served an essential function in developing a sophisticated Marxist legal doctrine that could facilitate, or at least not challenge, the shifts taking place in the political and legal winds.

Pashukanis and the shifts in Soviet policy

Several writers, including Warrington,[12] present the paradox of Pashukanis' rise and fall as a divorce between (pure) Marxist legal theory and (ruthless) Stalinist practice. While doubtless some gap between theory and practice existed, and Stalin's faction may have cynically tolerated that gap to help provide a theoretical legitimacy for its methods of rule, this oversimplified view is not borne out by an examination of the historical record. In the first place, as we have seen, there were contending tendencies in early Soviet legal theory. Secondly, there were definite connections between the theoretical debates, on the one hand, and the twists and turns of the Stalinist regime, on the other.

More basically, Pashukanis' early prominence and later retractions roughly correspond to the various stages of the struggle against the Left, Joint and Right Oppositions. To make a concrete appraisal of Pashukanis and his role, we explore further the connection between Pashukanis' writings and the following turning points:

(a) The New Economic Policy, adopted in 1921.
(b) The struggle against the Left Opposition from late 1923.
(c) Stalin's adoption of the programme of 'Socialism in One Country' in 1924.
(d) Stalin's 'left turn' to industrialisation and forced collectivisation in the late 1920s.
(e) Stalin's abandonment of the 'revolution from above' and renewed suppression, culminating in the Great Purges of the 1930s.

Pashukanis was born in February 1891 to a Lithuanian family. Details of his early life are sketchy but he only joined the Bolsheviks in 1918, having previously aligned himself with the Mensheviks. Before World War I, he had been a student at the University of St Petersburg and active in the anti-Tsarist movement before being arrested and exiled, as a result of his political activity,

12 Warrington, 1981: 1–22; also reprinted in Varga, 1993: 179–200.

and choosing to complete his studies at the University of Munich, where he specialised in law and political economy.[13] In 1914 he had helped draft a declaration of the Bolshevik faction in the Duma opposing the war in Europe, but in 1917 he was associated with the Menshevik Internationalists.[14]

Initially, from 1918, Pashukanis was a relatively junior figure in the Soviet administration, serving briefly as a local and circuit judge in the Moscow region before spending several years, from 1920 to 1923, as a legal adviser in the People's Commissariat of Foreign Affairs. He then became assistant organiser of the legal section of the Communist Academy of Russia. Based on the lectures he delivered there, in 1924 he published *The General Theory*, which soon earned him promotion to some of the highest posts within the Soviet academic legal institutions.[15]

When the *General Theory* appeared, Pashukanis was a member of Stuchka's Section of Law and State, and of the Institute of Soviet Construction, both parts of the Communist Academy. He soon became a member of the executive committee of the Section and Institute, as well as head of a subsection on the General Theory of Law and State. During 1925, Pashukanis became editor of the new *Revolution of Law* journal, contributing the opening article on Lenin's understanding of law, in which Pashukanis denounced Trotsky. The following year, he joined the law faculty of Moscow State University and the Institute of Red Professors, the Communist Academy's graduate school, and was named chief editor for law of the Soviet Encyclopedia. He became one of the leading authorities in Soviet legal theory, publishing articles in *Encyclopaedia of State and Law* (Moscow 1925–27), editing legal journals, writing many scholarly articles, particularly on international law, and several books. By 1929, Pashukanis reached the pinnacle of the official legal theory establishment, eclipsing Stuchka.

As early as 1927, three editions of his book had been published in Moscow and it had been translated into French, German, Japanese, Serbo-Croatian and English, despite the fact that Pashukanis regarded it as only an outline of the tasks of constructing a Marxist general theory of law. His monograph was subtitled *An Experiment in the Criticism of Basic Juridical Concepts* and Pashukanis emphasised that he had written it primarily for 'self-clarification' and to stimulate further discussion.[16]

As noted earlier, in the Preface to the third Russian edition of 1927, Pashukanis stated that his volume was merely a first draft – 'only briefly sketched' – of a Marxist critique of law.[17] He foreshadowed writing a text on the general theory of law, yet this text does not appear to have seen the light of day. One

13 Warrington, 1981: 17.
14 Kamenka and Tay, 1970: 72.
15 Sharlet, 1974: 112–15.
16 Beirne and Sharlet, 1980: 17–18.
17 Pashukanis, 1978: 36.

initial reason for the wide publication of the book may have been, as Pashukanis suggested in his Preface to the second Russian edition (undated), that it became a teaching text in the absence of other literature presenting a general outline of a Marxist theory of law.[18]

More significant, however, is that Pashukanis' volume appeared in 1924, the year in which Stalin, then part of a triumvirate with Zinoviev and Kamenev, usurped power following Lenin's death, defeating the Left Opposition formed by Trotsky.[19] While insisting on the ultimate Marxist perspective of creating the conditions for the withering away of the state, Pashukanis allowed for a lengthy postponement of this process, a thesis that would have suited Stalin in cementing his grip on power after the 1927 defeat of the Chinese Revolution.[20]

Tracing the links between Pashukanis' initial theoretical positions and the prescriptions of the Kremlin is not without its problems. While there is no doubt that Pashukanis' 1924 *General Theory* was shaped by the conceptions and requirements of the New Economic Policy launched in 1921, Pashukanis barely referred to the NEP. At one point, he made an oblique observation about the NEP. He commented on Marx's warning in the *Critique of the Gotha Program*, that 'the narrow horizon of bourgeois right' will continue for a time in a social order where the means of production are socially owned and the producers do not exchange their products – a stage in the transition from capitalism to communism. Pashukanis simply noted that Marx 'assumes a higher stage of development than the "new economic policy" which we are presently experiencing'.[21] Thus, already in 1924, Pashukanis was suggesting that there would be a lengthy process before communism could be achieved in Soviet Russia.

Schlesinger points to a connection between the NEP, the codification of Soviet law and the development of Pashukanis' work, arguing that the concessions to the free market encouraged Pashukanis and his supporters to identify law with bourgeoisification and project a 'Utopian' disappearance of law when socialism finally arrived:

> To understand the later theoretical disputes about the compatibility of Law and Socialism, quite apart from all the statements of classical Marxism on this issue, it must be remembered that one historical fact stood out before the controversialists: the codification of Soviet Law had been the outcome of the NEP, i.e., of a series of concessions made, if not

18 Pashukanis, 1978: 37.

19 See Carr, 1969; also Trotsky, 1974.

20 On the defeat of the 1926–27 Chinese Revolution and its implication for Stalin's usurpation of power, see Trotsky, 1969b and Trotsky, 1970: 127–76. See also Trotsky's Preface to Isaacs, 1938.

21 Pashukanis, 1978: 61.

> to capitalism, then to certain principles of capitalist economics. And, like most of their colleagues in continental European countries, Soviet legal theorists regarded only codified Law as Law proper. Thus the contemporaneity of the codification of Soviet Law and the NEP was bound to have a strong influence on the sociological interpretation of that Law (Schlesinger, 1945: 92).

Schlesinger's unsubstantiated assertion – that the Soviet scholars shared the view of their Western European contemporaries that only codified law qualified as law proper – may be open to question. Nonetheless, these observations have considerable validity. It was only after the NEP necessitated a retreat from the early hopes of quickly de-legalising life, and required the legal codification of private property rights in the means of production, that Stuchka, Pashukanis and others took up the task of endeavouring to produce general theses on the role of law in socialism.

Arthur discounts Schlesinger's suggestion of an underlying connection between Pashukanis and the requirements of the NEP, without providing any explanation, contending instead that 'this historical conjuncture does not of itself affect Pashukanis' theoretical position, of course'.[22] That may be true if one is confining oneself to considering Pashukanis' analysis in the abstract, but Arthur's approach separates Pashukanis' thought from the contradictions and tasks confronting the Soviet Union, as if these would not have, at the very least, influenced Pashukanis' work. Arthur's assessment presents Pashukanis' ideas as divorced from the material circumstances in which his work developed.

Pashukanis' demise

As early as 1927, Pashukanis made the first of several major 'corrections' to his *General Theory* in order to suit the requirements of Stalin's faction. Responding to criticisms by Stuchka, he dropped his identification of Soviet law as residual bourgeois law and accepted that it could serve socialist purposes in the transitional period to communism.[23] In 1928, he again took up the cudgels against the Joint Opposition, writing an article in the inaugural edition of a new official journal, *Revolution of the Law*, entitled 'The Dictatorship of the Proletariat and the Opposition'.[24]

Nevertheless, in so far as Pashukanis defended the conception that the state must wither away in the transition to communism, the contradiction in his position became ever more acute. After Stalin's declaration of a 'Third

22 Editor's introduction to Pashukanis, 1978: 28.
23 Beirne and Sharlet, 1980: 194.
24 Ibid: 364.

Period' in 1928, which marked the defeat of Bukharin and led to the implementation of brutal forced collectivisation, Stalin soon claimed that socialism necessitated an unprecedented strengthening of the state apparatus. In an address to the Central Committee Plenum of April 1929, Stalin warned against promoting hostile attitudes towards law and the state among the population. He argued that intensifying the struggle against the kulaks, the wealthy peasants, meant strengthening rather than weakening the dictatorship of the proletariat.[25]

In his 1929 article 'Economics and Legal Regulation' Pashukanis adapted to this shift by further revising his position to assert that law is determined by productive relations and the economic policy of the ruling class, not simply by commodity exchange. His adjustment took the form of refuting criticism by economists Preobrazhensky (an early supporter of the Left Opposition), Rubin and Bohm-Bawerk that economic regulation in the first stages of socialism, as in the USSR, was similar to capitalist regulation under conditions of monopoly capitalism. These criticisms echoed Lenin's earlier warning in *The State and Revolution* that capitalist pressures and indeed the bourgeois state would remain in the transition to communism. Pashukanis wrote:

> In every antagonistic society, class relationships find continuation and concretisation in the sphere of political struggle, the state structure and the legal order . . . productive forces [are] decisive in the final analysis (Beirne and Sharlet, 1980: 244).

Pashukanis argued that to hold, as Preobrazhensky did, that the economic law of value continued in the USSR, and therefore capitalist contradictions remained, missed the crucial point that the USSR was a dynamic formation based on 'the economics of cooperation and collectivisation'.[26] But Pashukanis still held out the prospect of law and the legal superstructure playing a less and less important role as the socialist features of the economy developed. The decisive issue was not where the USSR was, but what it would be, he argued. The more nationalisation and firm regulation of production in the common rather than particular interest, the more

> [t]he role of the purely legal superstructure, the role of the law, declines, and from this can be derived the general rule that as [technical] regulation becomes more effective, the weaker and less significant the role of law and the legal superstructure in its pure form (Beirne and Sharlet, 1980: 271).

Pashukanis may have supported Stalin and his canon of 'socialism in one country' in the expectation that the liquidation of the kulaks and other

25 Beirne and Sharlet, 1980: 26.
26 Ibid: 251.

non-socialist forces would clear the way for socialism and the abandonment of state and legal forms. He continued to predict that the elimination of the institutions of private property and the market would see the fading away of private law and the state, to be supplanted by a new category of economic law, consisting of technical rules to enhance collective planning. Pashukanis also advocated the replacement of criminal law with 'criminal policy' in the interests of maximum simplicity and flexibility. This approach was taught in law schools, where students were prepared to administer the gradual disappearance of law as a distinct form.[27] Hazard, then a student at Pashukanis' Moscow Institute of Soviet Law, later reported:

> Law, concerning the rights of individuals, was relegated to a few hours at the end of the course in economic-administrative law and given apologetically as an unwelcome necessity for a few years due to the fact that capitalist relationships and bourgeois psychology had not yet been wholly eliminated (Hazard, 1938: 15).

Instead, Stalin demanded the reinforcement and recognition of 'socialist legality'. In his 1932 article, 'Theory of State and Law', Pashukanis further adjusted to the shifting political wind by drawing back from his analysis of law as an historical product of the equivalent exchange of commodities. He acknowledged that in class societies, legal relations also reflected the forms of labour exploitation that produced surplus value, as well as the policy of the ruling class.

> A legal relationship is a form of production relationship because the active influence of the class organisation of the ruling class transforms the factual relationship into a legal one, gives it a new quality, and thus includes it in the construction of the legal superstructure (Beirne and Sharlet, 1980: 297).

On this basis, Pashukanis reformulated the definition of law from his *General Theory* as 'the form of regulation and consolidation of production relationships and also of other social relationships of class society'.[28] He added that the definition was incomplete without referring to a coercive apparatus, the state, that guaranteed the functioning of the legal superstructure. The essential purpose of this adjustment was to justify the existence of Soviet law, arguing that it was qualitatively different from capitalist law:

> [L]aw in the conditions of the proletarian dictatorship has always had the goal of protecting the interest of the working majority, the suppression

27 Beirne and Sharlet, 1980: 25–6.
28 Ibid: 287.

> of class elements hostile to the proletariat, and the defence of socialist construction . . . As such it is radically different from bourgeois law, despite the formal resemblance of individual statutes (Beirne and Sharlet, 1980: 293).

Pashukanis was now visibly performing doctrinal gymnastics to fulfil the needs of the Kremlin oligarchy, and in the process contributing to his own downfall, as well as the fate of the Old Bolsheviks and their supporters, who were to perish in the great purges from 1936 onwards. Beirne and Sharlet observed:

> In the course of the 'revolution from above' of forced collectivisation and rapid industrialisation, a politically chastened but still theoretically active Pashukanis tried unsuccessfully, as it transpired, to re-define his concept of the state during the transitional period. In effect, Pashukanis superimposed the Stalinist concept of the state in Soviet socio-economic development onto the remnants of his original theory of law. Then by simultaneously presiding over the theoretical articulation of the Stalinist state as well as the practical process of the withering away of criminal law, Pashukanis inevitably contributed to the growth of a jurisprudence of terror (Beirne and Sharlet, 1980: 28–9).

This indictment is justified; except that Pashukanis' service to Stalin's regime began earlier – back in 1924–25. Worse was to come. In a 1935 textbook on Soviet economic law, Pashukanis and L. Gintsburg glorified Stalin and his victories over the Left and Right Oppositions from 1924 to 1929:

> He expanded the Marxist-Leninist doctrine on the dictatorship of the proletariat into a grandiose doctrine of the building of socialism in one country. This occurred under conditions of the delay of the world revolution and of intensified internal class struggle against the capitalist classes and their ideological arms-bearers – bourgeois restorationist theorists, right and left opportunists, and counter-revolutionary Trotskyites (Beirne and Sharlet, 1980: 305).

In their *Course on Soviet Economic Law*, Pashukanis and Gintsburg still refused to accept the concept of 'proletarian law' but engaged in the terminological nicety of upholding the 'class law of the proletariat'. According to the authors, Soviet law served the interests of the working class as the ruling class under socialism, just as bourgeois law served the interests of the capitalist class and its production:

> Bourgeois legality is the will of the ruling class . . . directed at the support of the basic conditions of the capitalist mode of production. Socialist

> (revolutionary) legality expresses the will of the last of the exploited classes, which has taken power, of the proletariat (Beirne and Sharlet, 1980: 314).

Despite his retractions and modifications under mounting official criticism, Pashukanis' refusal to abandon the ultimate goal of the disappearance of the legal form became incompatible with Stalin's purposes. In 1936, Stalin announced incongruously that socialism had already been achieved in the Soviet Union, yet the state apparatus had to be strengthened, not relaxed. Stalin was only able to unveil this self-contradictory travesty of Marxism after a protracted struggle to seal his victory over the Left and Right Oppositions and to crush considerable socialist resistance to his totalitarian regime.

Pashukanis became increasingly abject in his support for Stalin's perversions of Marxism. In 1936 he rushed into print his final self-criticism, essentially repudiating the central thesis of his *General Theory*. His statement, 'State and Law Under Socialism', began by acknowledging the crisis posed for his position by Stalin's pronouncement that classes had been abolished in the USSR:

> The liquidation of the exploiting classes has been completed in our country. This now poses the problem of the Soviet state as the political superstructure of the classless socialist society. Colossal socio-economic advances have led to the creation of a uniform type of socialist relations of production in the towns and countryside, and thus to a new stage in the development of the dictatorship of the proletarian state and Soviet democracy. The question of the role of state and law under socialism now assumes a tremendous theoretical and practical significance ... We must distance ourselves from the mistakes and confusion on these questions, including those errors made by jurists (Beirne and Sharlet, 1980: 348).

If it were indeed the case that the Soviet Union had become a classless society, the writings of Marx, Engels and Lenin were unequivocal: it would also be a stateless society, no longer requiring an apparatus of coercion and repression. But Stalin had insisted on 'consolidating the agencies of the dictatorship of the proletariat'.[29]

Pashukanis sought to attempt to square the circle and provide a thin theoretical cover for Stalin by taking quotes from Lenin's *State and Revolution* out of context. According to Pashukanis, Lenin had directed his pamphlet not only against opportunists who opposed overthrowing the bourgeois state but also 'petty bourgeois and anarchist dreamers' who sought the immediate

29 Beirne and Sharlet, 1980: 350. The phrase is from Stalin, 1933: 580.

elimination of political authority after the socialist revolution. Pashukanis quoted the following passage:

> Without lapsing into utopianism, it is inconceivable that people will immediately learn to work without any legal norms after the overthrow of capitalism. The abolition of capitalism does not immediately provide the economic premises for such a transformation (Beirne and Sharlet, 1980: 349).[30]

But this paragraph is taken from a section of *State and Revolution* where Lenin explained that it was a 'defect' of the first phase of communism, that is, before the abolition of classes and economic inequality, that 'bourgeois law' remained, fundamentally for the purpose of allocating equal shares of production to unequal individuals for unequal amounts of labour. As we saw in Chapter 2, Lenin drew from this conundrum the prescient conclusion that 'bourgeois law' and indeed a 'bourgeois state' would continue to exist until genuine communism, that is a classless, stateless society, had come into existence. In fact, Lenin restated this position in the paragraph following the one quoted by Pashukanis:

> Now, there are no other rules than those of 'bourgeois law'. To this extent, therefore, there still remains the need for a state, which, while safeguarding the common ownership of the means of production, would safeguard equality in labour and in the production of products. The state withers away insofar as there are no longer any capitalists, and classes, and, consequently, no class can be suppressed. But the state has not yet completely withered away, since there still remains the safeguarding of 'bourgeois law', which sanctifies actual inequality. For the state to wither away completely, complete communism is necessary (Lenin, 1970: 132–3).

Lenin's use of the word 'completely' was in line with his insistence that the state formed after the overthrow of capitalism would be, from birth, a very different form of state apparatus to that relied upon by the capitalist class. It would immediately be more democratic and designed to begin withering away from the outset. Yet, Pashukanis, while invoking Lenin's authority, now described that view as a 'false and opportunist theory', without, of course, acknowledging that its author was Lenin:

> Even in our milieu the theory existed that the actual process of withering away had begun with the October Revolution and that, therefore, it

30 The quote can be found, in a slightly different translation, in Lenin, 1970: 132.

> should be proceeding at full speed during the period when classes were being abolished and the classless socialist society was being constructed. But this was a false and opportunist theory. It was false because it did not take into account the fundamental economic premise without which there cannot even be any discussion of the superfluousness of the state (Beirne and Sharlet, 1980: 352).

Pashukanis' sophistry went further. After paraphrasing Lenin's explanation of the need for 'bourgeois law' to remain for distribution of income unequally, again without acknowledging Lenin's authorship, he declared that it was wrong to regard this law as 'bourgeois' rather than as 'the law of the socialist state'. Pashukanis stated: 'The condescending attitude that this law is "bourgeois" benefits only the anarchic theories of the "left wing" and the champions of bourgeois equality.'[31] In that case, Lenin was an anarchic left-winger! Pashukanis completed his apostasy in the most unequivocal fashion:

> Socialist society is organised as a statist society. The socialist state and socialist law will be fully preserved until the highest phase of communism. Only at this phase will people begin to work without overseers and legal norms. It is just as opportunistic to assert that law will wither away under socialism as it is to affirm that state authority should wither away the day after the bourgeoisie was overthrown . . .
>
> However, this question was totally misrepresented in *The General Theory of Law and Marxism.* Law, state and morality were simply declared to be bourgeois forms which cannot be filled with a socialist content and which must wither away in proportion to the realisation of such content. This grossly mistaken position, foreign to Marxism-Leninism, distorts the meaning of the proletarian state, distorts the meaning of proletarian communist morality, and distorts the meaning of Soviet law as the law of the proletarian state which serves as an instrument in the construction of socialism (Beirne and Sharlet, 1980: 354–5).

Having extracted from Pashukanis the repudiation of the classical Marxist and Leninist understanding of the state and law, it was not long before Stalin ordered his execution. Before doing so, he employed Pashukanis' services one last time, on the drafting committee for the 1936 constitution, which ludicrously proclaimed the triumph of socialism. In one of the many tragic ironies of Stalinism, Pashukanis was put to death lawlessly in the name of defending 'socialist legality'.

31 Beirne and Sharlet, 1980: 355.

Conclusion

Pashukanis was a tragic figure. His personal and intellectual fate can only be assessed historically and politically. The NEP, adopted in 1921, made key concessions to capitalist market relations and necessitated a return to traditional legal forms in order to protect private ownership of some of the means of production. This had a profound impact on Soviet legal theory, particularly reflected in the writings of Pashukanis. There was a further distinct shift in content and tone after 1924, signalled by Stalin's usurpation of power and the adoption of the 'socialism in one country' perspective. In the same year, Pashukanis' *General Theory* was published and rapidly became the central legal text. It was followed by Pashukanis' 1925 denunciation of 'Trotskyism' and his subsequent elevation as the doyen of the Soviet legal establishment. A further shift occurred in 1927, amid the defeat of the Joint Opposition, typified by Pashukanis' first 'correction' – his acceptance of 'socialist legality'.

Although Pashukanis made important contributions to the early legal debates, and developed aspects of Marxist legal theory, he played a role in the Stalinist degeneration. As reviewed in the next chapter, Pashukanis shed light on the nature of the legal form, the distinction between law and regulation, the withering away of law and the idea of morality. But by lining up against the Left Opposition, he helped deprive the debates of the analysis and programme that could have combated the political and theoretical degeneration that occurred. In the end, a series of 'corrections' did not save Pashukanis from Stalin's purges because by 1936 his continued view that the state would eventually wither away under communism became incompatible with Stalin's insistence that socialism had already triumphed in the Soviet Union.

After the Twentieth Congress of the Communist Party of the Soviet Union and Khrushchev's secret speech in 1956, Pashukanis was legally rehabilitated in March 1956[32] but his works were not republished. The official view remained opposed to his original Marxist concept of Soviet law as dying bourgeois law.[33] Thus, his analysis remained a threat to the post-Stalin bureaucracy, despite the Kremlin's claims to be de-Stalinising.

How should one assess Pashukanis' legacy? Did he make a contribution to jurisprudence? The next chapter will suggest that, in some respects, he did. But these are complex questions. Given the political and theoretical degeneration underway in the Soviet leadership after 1924, Pashukanis laboured in a very unfavourable climate. It is impossible to separate his strengths and weaknesses from the political pressures at work. He offered some profound insights into the economic roots of the legal form, even if these insights displayed several basic confusions in Marxist economics. However, he was weaker on the ideological and repressive role of law and the state apparatus.

32 Beirne and Sharlet, 1980: 17.
33 See Lapenna, 1964: 55 and 94n.

And key aspects of his theory served the interests of the emerging Stalinist bureaucracy, with whom he aligned himself against the Left Opposition. From 1927, Pashukanis progressively repudiated other prominent features of his theory to appease the ruling clique. Nevertheless, he remained true to some Marxist concepts, including the withering away of the state and law, and pointed to alternative approaches in social organisation, including the treatment of crime.

His writings displayed the potential for a profound theoretical development of the Marxist view of law and the state. But this potential was strangled by the needs of Stalin's regime. In the end, many of the limitations and flaws that can be found in his theorising reflected the requirements of the rising bureaucratic caste.

Chapter 9

Pashukanis' theoretical achievements

> The task of the Marxist critique was not confined to refuting the bourgeois individualistic theory of law, but also consisted of analysing the legal form itself.[1]

Although Pashukanis was writing in a particular environment, in the early transitional period of the Soviet revolution, he undertook a more ambitious task – that of setting out a general theory of law. No doubt, his project was shaped by the more immediate difficulties of the young Soviet state and, increasingly, the requirements of the ruling caste that emerged under Stalin. Nevertheless, his endeavour cannot be judged, let alone dismissed, solely on the basis of the political degeneration that occurred in the Soviet Union. His work deserves to be considered for its potential to illuminate broader and longer-term questions about the role of law under capitalism, socialism and possible future forms of society, including genuine communism.

Pashukanis set out to overcome what he perceived as various shallow and mechanical 'Marxist' interpretations of law. Existing, ostensibly Marxist, approaches generally treated law either as an ideological device, a blunt instrument of class rule or a sociological product of conflicting interests. Pashukanis did not deny that law can have an ideological function – he saw there to be 'no argument about this'[2] – but regarded that as derivative and secondary. Law's roots lay far deeper in economic relations. 'Having established the ideological nature of particular concepts in no way exempts us from the obligation of seeking their objective reality, in other words the reality which exists in the outside world, that is, external, and not merely subjective reality.'[3] Another conception of law, the 'sociological' theories, 'treat[ed] law as the product of conflict of interest, as the manifestation of

1 Pashukanis, 1978: 34.
2 Ibid: 34.
3 Ibid: 75.

state coercion'.[4] This position was essentially positivist, in that law was seen as the will of the state. '[M]any Marxists assumed that by simply adding in the element of class struggle to . . . [positivist] theories, they would attain a genuinely materialist, Marxist theory of law.'[5]

This chapter will outline Pashukanis' main conceptual contributions. Later chapters will consider the criticisms made of Pashukanis, the Marxist alternative to his evolution, and the enduring strengths and contemporary relevance of his observations.

Critique of legal form

While Pashukanis' theory of law has commonly been depicted as a 'commodity exchange' theory, this hardly does justice to the full scope of his intellectual endeavour. He sought, drawing closely on Marx and Engels, particularly Marx's *Capital*, to outline a general theory of law that claimed to go, in Berman's words, 'deeper into the nature of law than any Marxist hitherto'.[6] In the Preface to the 1929 German edition of his *General Theory*, Pashukanis defined his purpose as follows:

> The task of the Marxist critique was not confined to refuting the bourgeois individualistic theory of law, but also consisted of analysing the legal form itself, exposing its sociological roots, and demonstrating the relative and historically limited nature of the fundamental juridical concepts (Pashukanis, 1978: 34).

This perspective challenges not simply the role of law under capitalism but also the very form of law itself as an inherent or eternal instrument of social regulation. Pashukanis' examination of law as a 'relative and historically limited' form necessarily implies the disappearance of law and its replacement by other social relations under genuine socialism.

Pashukanis was critical of Stuchka's definition of law as a system of social relationships. Stuchka defined law as 'the system or order of social relations corresponding to the interests of the ruling class and protected by the organised force of that class'. Pashukanis asked: 'How do social relationships become juridic institutions? How is law converted into itself?'[7] Pashukanis said the definition was useful in disclosing the class content of legal forms and in asserting that law rests on social relations, but it masked the difference between law and all other regulative norms. It did not explain how or why social relations became converted into legal relations. What was peculiar

4 Pashukanis, 1978: 53.
5 Ibid: 53.
6 Berman, 1963: 28.
7 Hazard, 1951: 139.

about the legal form that made it indispensable in enforcing the social relations of class society? Indeed, if law was said to be a form of social relationship, while law regulated social relationships, a tautology resulted: social relationships regulate themselves.

Pashukanis criticised Stuchka for downplaying the 'logical and dialectical development of the form itself'.[8] As Marx had explored in his discussion of commodity fetishism in the first chapter of *Capital*, Volume 1, the relationship between form and content is complex and dynamic. Form is not merely the outward expression of content. On the contrary, once content takes a certain form, the form can impart to the content definite qualities and characteristics. It is through form that content exists and develops. Pashukanis sought to follow Marx's method of analysis, developed in the sphere of political economy, and apply it to law.

In *Capital*, Marx asked: 'Whence, then, arises the enigmatical character of the product of labour, so soon as it assumes the form of commodities? Clearly from the form itself.'[9] Marx explained his answer as follows:

> The equality of all sorts of human labour is expressed objectively by their products all being equally values; the measure of the expenditure of labour power by the duration of that expenditure, takes the form of the quantity of value of the products of labour; and finally the mutual relations of the producers, within which the social character of their labour affirms itself, take the form of a social relation between the products.
>
> A commodity is therefore a mysterious thing, simply because in it the social character of men's labour appears to them as an objective character stamped upon the product of that labour; because the relation of the producers to the sum total of their own labour is presented to them as a social relation, existing not between themselves, but between the products of their labour. This is the reason why the products of labour become commodities, social things whose qualities are at the same time perceptible and imperceptible by the senses. In the same way the light from an object is perceived by us not as the subjective excitation of our optic nerve, but as the objective form of something outside the eye itself. But, in the act of seeing, there is at all events, an actual passage of light from one thing to another, from the external object to the eye. There is a physical relation between physical things. But it is different with commodities. There, the existence of the things *quâ* commodities, and the value relation between the products of labour which stamps them as commodities, have absolutely no connection with their physical properties and with the material relations arising therefrom. There it is a definite

8 Pashukanis, 1978: 53–4, fn 14.
9 Marx, 1970c, vol 1: 76.

> social relation between men, that assumes, in their eyes, the fantastic form of a relation between things. In order, therefore, to find an analogy, we must have recourse to the mist-enveloped regions of the religious world. In that world the productions of the human brain appear as independent beings endowed with life, and entering into relation both with one another and the human race. So it is in the world of commodities with the products of men's hands. This I call the Fetishism which attaches itself to the products of labour, so soon as they are produced as commodities, and which is therefore inseparable from the production of commodities (Marx, 1970c, vol 1: 76–7).

That is, when a product of labour assumes the form of a commodity – a transformation that occurs only at a certain stage of society – it acquires a peculiar, fetishistic quality that it did not previously possess. Once products are exchanged on the market, real social relations between people, of which commodities are themselves the outcome, necessarily assume the appearance of a relation between things. A product of labour is a product of labour; and yet, once it assumes, within the framework of new productive relations, the form of a commodity, it acquires new, fantastic and extraordinary social properties. Marx explained that this transformation took place continuously on the market, whenever commodities were exchanged, even though the participants were oblivious to the real relations between them. The underlying rule of value, produced by human labour, was hidden and indeed mystified, so that considerable analysis was required in order to decipher the true character of the social production taking place:

> Hence, when we bring the products of our labour into relation with each other as values, it is not because we see in these articles the material receptacles of homogeneous human labour. Quite the contrary: whenever, by an exchange, we equate as values our different products, by that very act, we also equate, as human labour, the different kinds of labour expended upon them. We are not aware of this, nevertheless we do it. Value, therefore, does not stalk about with a label describing what it is. It is value, rather, that converts every product into a social hieroglyphic. Later on, we try to decipher the hieroglyphic, to get behind the secret of our own social products; for to stamp an object of utility as a value, is just as much a social product as language (Marx, 1970c, vol 1: 78–9).

Pashukanis sought to carry out this deciphering of the 'hieroglyphic' for law, by examining the legal form as a mystified expression of its content, that is, the social relations formed by commodity production under capitalism. Law as a form acquired fantastic qualities in the eyes of humanity, imparting to law a semi-religious complexion that was not simply an ideological construct, but arose intrinsically and necessarily from the socio-economic relations formed by the capitalist mode of production. Far from being a natural or eternal institution of human society, law was a peculiar form that arose from definite commodity exchange relations that had arisen historically at a certain stage of economic and social development and would die away once that stage had passed.

Pashukanis posed the more general problem of a theory of law as follows: 'Can law as a social relationship be understood in the same sense as that in which Marx called capital a social relationship?'[10] Since law was only one social phenomenon among others, such as morals, religion and art, the question was how to distinguish legal relationships from other social relationships. Pashukanis' answer was that legal relationships are essentially those between possessors of goods. He rejected the view that law can be explained abstractly as a system of norms per se:

> We find that the juridic relationship is generated by the material production relationships of human beings immediately at hand – from which it follows that an analysis of the legal relationship in its simplest form need not start from the concept of a norm as an external authoritative imperative. It is sufficient to take for a basis a juridic relationship 'whose content has been provided by the economic relationship itself' (in the words of Marx) and to investigate the 'legal' form of this juridic relationship as one of the particular cases (Hazard, 1951: 149).

By beginning with commodity exchange, Pashukanis' methodology was also that of Marx in the *Grundrisse* and later, of 'rising from the abstract to the concrete'.[11] In order to understand Pashukanis' approach, it helps to consider a seminal passage from the *Grundrisse*, to which Pashukanis refers in his opening chapter on method. Under the heading 'The Method of Political Economy' Marx gave the example of trying to analyse a country, politico-economically, starting with its population. Beginning the analysis with what appears, on the surface, to be 'real and concrete' led to a false 'chaotic conception' unless more considered determinations were made:

> When we consider a given country politico-economically, we begin with its population, its distribution among classes, town, country, the coast, the different branches of production, export and import, annual production and consumption, commodity prices, etc.
>
> It seems to be correct to begin with the real and the concrete, with the real precondition, thus to begin, in economics, with e.g. the population, which is the foundation and the subject of the entire social act of

10 Hazard, 1951: 131.
11 Marx, 1973: 101.

> production. However, on closer examination this proves false. The population is an abstraction if I leave out, for example, the classes of which it is composed. These classes in turn are an empty phrase if I am not familiar with the elements on which they rest. E.g. wage labour, capital, etc. These latter in turn presuppose exchange, division of labour, prices, etc. For example, capital is nothing without wage labour, without value, money, price, etc. Thus, if I were to begin with the population, this would be a chaotic conception [*Vorstellung*] of the whole, and I would then, by means of further determination, move analytically towards ever more simple concepts [*Begriff*], from the imagined concrete towards ever thinner abstractions until I had arrived at the simplest determinations. From there the journey would have to be retraced until I had finally arrived at the population again, but this time not as the chaotic conception of a whole, but as a rich totality of many determinations and relations (Marx, 1973: 101).

For Marx, the concrete 'appears in the process of thinking . . . as a process of concentration, as a result, not as a point of departure, even though it is the point of departure in reality and hence also the point of departure for observation and conception'.[12] Thus the simplest categories of analysis – commodity, value, labour, money, etc. – were abstractions necessary for the analysis of that concrete. They constituted the essential components of any analysis of the real world, because of, rather than despite, their abstraction. They were the 'determinant, abstract, general relations' from which analysis 'ascends' to more complex and concrete categories. This was 'the scientifically correct method', given that '[t]he concrete is concrete because it is the concentration of many determinations'.[13]

Pashukanis saw these observations as 'directly pertinent to the general theory of law':

> The concrete totality – society, the population, the state – must in this case, too, be the conclusion and end result of our deliberations, but not their starting point. By moving from the most simple to the more complex, from the process in its purest form to its more concrete manifestations, one is following a course which is methodologically more precise and clearer, and thus more correct, than if one were to feel one's way forward with nothing more in mind than a hazy and unarticulated picture of the concrete whole (Pashukanis, 1978: 66).

Pashukanis contended that while the analysis of Marx and Engels had informed Marxist critiques of bourgeois legal ideology, it had not been

12 Marx, 1973: 101.
13 Ibid: 100–1.

applied to studying the legal superstructure.[14] Instead, Marxist scholars had tended to regard the state and law simply as instruments of ruling class power.

> The few Marxists who concerned themselves with legal questions undoubtedly considered the aspect of social (state) coercion as the central, fundamental and only characteristic trait of legal phenomena . . . Hence it was quite natural to think that the Marxian critique of the legal subject which arises directly from analysis of the commodity form, had nothing to do with the general theory of law, since of course external coercive regulation of the relations between commodity owners forms only an insignificant part of social regulation as a whole (Pashukanis, 1978: 39).

There is no doubt that this approach, based on examining the nature and contradictions of the legal form itself, came far closer to a genuinely Marxist analysis than the crude class instrumentalist view that Pashukanis criticised. Pashukanis was correct to probe in a more nuanced manner the relationship between commodity exchange and the legal form. As discussed in Chapter 2, the critique of law developed by Marx and Engels was far from the mechanical economic determinism and bourgeois 'will' theory sometimes ascribed to them. Pashukanis' comment on the source of legal power was also true. Although the coercive powers of the state can be brought to bear to crush infringements of, or challenges to, the rights of private property, these rights are far more pervasively entrenched in the economic and political power exercised by the holders of capital. An employer, for example, may call in the police if employees leak sensitive documents or otherwise appropriate any part of their production for the employer, but more compelling is the employer's capacity to dismiss employees, depriving them of their livelihood. This latter power is derived from the employer's freedom, as a matter of commodity exchange, not to purchase the employee's labour power. Moreover, even if legal regulations temper the employers' power – for example, laws against 'unfair dismissal' – capitalist law does not challenge the underlying freedom to terminate employment on economic or commercial grounds.

As Pashukanis stated, this power relationship is not primarily the result of an ideological process, based on the history of ideas. It is part of an actual process, by which the social relations based on money become legal relations. Pashukanis summed up his conception as follows:

14 I will not attempt to enter the arguably barren debate over whether Pashukanis regarded law as part of the 'base' or 'superstructure' of society mentioned in Marx's Preface to *A Contribution to the Critique of Political Economy*. For a review, see Mieville, 2005.

> Law in its general definitions, law as a form, does not exist in the heads and the theories of learned jurists. It has a parallel, real history which unfolds not as a set of ideas, but as a specific set of relations which men enter into not by conscious choice, but because the relations of production compel them to do so. Man becomes a legal subject by virtue of the same necessity which transforms the product of nature into a commodity complete with the enigmatic property of value (Pashukanis, 1978: 68).

It must be noted that Pashukanis here used the expression 'relations of production' rather than 'relations of exchange'. This demonstrates that he understood commodity exchange as only one part of bourgeois economic relations, or, more accurately, as an essential cell of the capitalist mode of production, which is based on production for exchange. On the other hand, his concise summation is somewhat mechanical compared to the more complex and subtle explanations of Marx and Engels. They emphasised that ideas do indeed play a vital role in legal and other history, but that *ultimately* these ideas reflect, more or less consciously, the prevailing social relations based on production.

Pashukanis attempted to sketch his essential thesis more fully in the preface to the second Russian edition of his *General Theory*. He argued that the significance of Marxian analysis had been limited to exposing the bourgeois ideology of freedom and equality, and criticising formal democracy, without shedding light on the fundamental characteristics of the legal superstructure as an objective phenomenon.

> In the process, people failed to take two things into account: first, that the principle of legal subjectivity (which we take to mean the formal principle of freedom and equality, the autonomy of the personality, and so forth) is not only an instrument of deceit and a product of the hypocrisy of the bourgeoisie, insofar as it is used to counter the proletarian struggle to abolish classes, but is at the same time a concretely effective principle which is embodied in bourgeois society from the moment it emerges from and destroys feudal-patriarchal society. Second, they failed to take into account that the victory of this process is not only and not so much an ideological process (that is to say a process belonging entirely to the history of ideas, persuasions and so on), but rather is an actual process, making human relations into legal relations, which accompanies the development of the economy based on the commodity and on money (in Europe this means capitalist economy), and which is associated with profound, universal changes of an objective kind. These changes include: the emergence and consolidation of private property; its universal expansion to every kind of object possible, as well as to subjects; the liberation of the land and the soil from the relations of domination and subservience; the transformation of all property into moveable property; the

> development and dominance of relations of liability; and, finally, the precipitation of a political authority as a separate power, functioning alongside the purely economic power of money, and the resulting more or less sharp differentiation between the spheres of public and private relations, public and private law (Pashukanis, 1978: 40–1).

In this way, Pashukanis outlined the kernel of an historical materialist approach to the rise and evolution of the legal form.

The 'commodity exchange' theory

It was in this context of probing to the heart and historical origin of the legal form that Pashukanis turned to the reciprocal rights and obligations attached to commodity exchange. He sought to follow the methodology of Marx in *Capital*, who began his exposition of the organic contradictions of the capitalist mode of production by examining the essential contradiction inherent in the commodity itself: that between use value and exchange value.[15]

Pashukanis' essential proposition was that all law was inherently related to the commodity exchange relationship which reaches its highest point under capitalism. The very form of law was derived from the acquisition by individuals of private property interests, which inevitably gave rise to conflicts.

> It is only with the advent of bourgeois-capitalist society that all the necessary conditions are created for juridical factors to attain complete distinctness in social relations . . . A basic prerequisite for legal regulation is the conflict of private interests. This is both the logical premise of the legal form and the actual origin of the development of the legal superstructure. Human conduct can be regulated by the most complex regulations, but the juridical factor in this regulation arises at the point when differentiation and opposition of interests begin (Beirne and Sharlet, 1980: 58, 81).

Pashukanis contended that legal fetishism complements commodity fetishism. Under capitalism, according to Pashukanis, de facto possession was transformed into an absolute and constant right, which adheres to a commodity during exchange. Pashukanis noted Marx's statement in *Capital* that 'commodities cannot send themselves to a market and exchange themselves with one another. Accordingly we must turn to their custodian, to the commodity owner'.[16]

15 Marx, 1970c: 43–53. On the methodological significance of Marx's starting point, see Kemp, 1982 and Ilyenkov, 1982.
16 Beirne and Sharlet, 1980: 9.

Following Marx's outline of commodity production and exchange in *Capital*, Pashukanis traced the legal form to the exchange of commodities on the market:

> The juridic subject is, therefore, the abstract goods-possessor elevated to the heavens. His will – understood in the juridic sense – has its real basis in the wish to alienate as it acquires, and to acquire as it alienates. In order for this wish to be realised, it is essential that the wishes of goods-producers go out to meet each other. This relationship is expressed juridically as a contract or accord of independent wills, and contract is therefore one of the central concepts in the law. In more grandiloquent phraseology, it becomes a constituent part of the idea of law (Hazard, 1951: 169).

Whereas under feudalism 'every right was a privilege',[17] every right was identified with a specific social position vis-à-vis others, capitalist exchange is characterised by the generalisation of 'equal rights'. This is why contract was so vital to Pashukanis' theory of law. Abstract and equal subjects, the atoms of the legal relationship, cannot relate to each other according to principles of 'traditional' privilege, but do so by means of contract, which is the formalisation of mutual recognition of equal subjects. Without a contract, Pashukanis wrote, 'the concepts of subject and of will only exist, in the legal sense, as lifeless abstractions. These concepts first come to life in the contract'.[18]

Pashukanis' argument was that in commodity exchange, each commodity must be the private property of its owner, freely given in return for the other. In their fundamental form, as Marx established in *Capital*, commodities exchange at a rate that is ultimately determined by their exchange value, not because of some other, external, reason or because one party to the exchange demands it. Therefore, Pashukanis suggested, each agent in the exchange must be an owner of private property, and formally equal to the other agent(s). Without these conditions, what occurred would not be commodity exchange. The legal form was the necessary form taken by the relation between these formally equal owners of exchange values. Thus Pashukanis argued that 'reciprocity' and 'mutuality' were integral to the conception of bourgeois private property, as compared to feudal property, which was determined by estate:

> Hauriou, one of the most astute bourgeois jurists, quite rightly emphasises reciprocity as the most effective security for property, which can be brought about with the minimum use of external force. This mutuality, which is ensured by the laws of the market, lends property the

17 Pashukanis, 1978: 119.
18 Ibid: 121.

> quality of an 'eternal' institution. In contrast to this, the purely political security vouchsafed by the coercive machinery of state amounts to nothing more than the protection of specified personal stocks belonging to the owners – an aspect which has no fundamental significance (Pashukanis, 1978: 123).

While Pashukanis' theory has been described as a bold deviation from accepted communist doctrine,[19] Pashukanis was at pains to emphasise his fidelity to Marx's method. In the preface to the second Russian edition, Pashukanis insisted that his general approach of connecting law to commodity exchange presents nothing original but simply fuses the ideas of Marx and Engels. Apart from *Capital*, Pashukanis refers to the chapter 'Morality and Law – Equality' in Engels' *Anti-Duhring*.[20] Engels' chapter did contain, albeit in embryo, the relation between commodity production and formal legal equality. Discussing the drive by capitalism to overturn the local restrictions and status-based inequalities of feudalism, Engels commented:

> Trade on a large scale, that is to say, particularly international and, even more so, world trade, requires free owners of commodities who are unrestricted in their movements and as such enjoy equal rights; who may exchange their commodities on the basis of laws that are equal for them all, at least in each particular place (Engels, 1975: 130).

Engels pointed out that such formal, legal equality did not long satisfy the working class that capitalism had created.

> The proletarians took the bourgeoisie at its word: equality must not be merely apparent, must not apply merely to the sphere of the state, but must also be real, must also extend to the social, economic sphere (Engels, 1975: 131–2).

While, as noted earlier, Pashukanis did not attach the label 'commodity exchange theory' to his analysis, he acknowledged in the preface to the second Russian edition that 'Comrade Stuchka has quite correctly defined my approach to the general theory of law as an "attempt to approximate the legal form to the commodity form".'[21] For Pashukanis, private law was the 'fundamental, primary level of law'.[22] The concept of public law, for example,

19 Fuller, 1949: 1164.
20 Pashukanis quotes a footnote by Engels: 'This derivation of the modern ideas of equality from the economic conditions of bourgeois society was first demonstrated by Marx in *Capital*.' See Pashukanis, 1978: 34 and Engels, 1975: 130.
21 Pashukanis, 1978: 38.
22 Ibid: 103.

'can only be developed through its workings, in which it is continually repulsed by private law, so much that it attempts to define itself as the antithesis of private law, to which it returns, however, as to its centre of gravity'.[23] A complex legal system regulating all levels of social life can be thrown up which appears to differentiate itself from private law, but it ultimately derives from the clash of private interests. Pashukanis sought to find in commodity exchange the ultimate root of labour law (employer–employee contracts), family law (marriage and parent–child relations based on mutual rights and duties), criminal law (punishment measured by exchange equivalents), constitutional law (social contract) and morality (based on seemingly autonomous personalities). As we shall see, these efforts were not as far-fetched as they may sound, and Pashukanis offered numerous valuable insights, particularly in the fields of crime and morality.

In so far as Pashukanis traced law not to production but to exchange, to contract instead of property and to reciprocal relations rather than the exploitation of labour power, it can be argued that he departed from Marxism. However, as discussed in Chapter 11, such criticisms fall short of the mark, primarily because they over-simplify Marx's critique of capitalist economy.

In his *General Theory*, Pashukanis drew certain implications of his theory for the transition to communism:

> In future the vestiges of equivalent exchange in the sphere of distribution, which will be retained even in a socialist organisation of production (until the transition to developed communism), will compel socialist society to enclose within itself the 'narrow horizon of bourgeois law' for a time, as Marx himself foresaw (Pashukanis, 1978: 41).[24]

However, while Pashukanis thus saw 'bourgeois law' continuing under the dictatorship of the proletariat, he did so only in so far as relations, including wage labour and trading between government corporations, remained governed by exchange. He drew a distinction between 'law', which remained bourgeois, and 'regulation', which was socialist. This demarcation has merit to the extent that it postulates the possibility of a future communist society guided by regulation rather than law, but it is highly problematic in the context of seeking to differentiate 'socialist' from 'bourgeois' features of a state, like the Soviet state, supposedly in transition to communism. Marx, and Lenin following him, warned that all transitional law and other forms of social regulation, and indeed the state as a whole, would be tainted by the inability of the socialist state to immediately provide genuine social equality. The legal and political system in its entirety would be obliged to enforce

23 Pashukanis, 1978: 106.
24 Marx's words are from Marx, 1970b: 10.

degrees of inequality until production could be developed sufficiently to overcome this unavoidable capitalist legacy.

Law versus regulation and planning

Both Stuchka and Pashukanis regarded the application of civil law in Soviet society as confined to the regulation of surviving or revived market relations based on commodity exchange. The internal economic relations of the socialist sector of the economy did not need juridical regulation. Pashukanis argued that the Soviet Union already had two systems of economic regulation. On the one hand, administrative-technical rules governed the general economic plan. On the other, legal rules (civil and commercial codes, courts, arbitration tribunals, etc.) governed the commodity exchange, including trading between government corporations, which was the essential feature of the NEP. The victory of the former type of regulation would signify the demise of the latter, and the realisation of Marx's description of human emancipation.

Legal regulation referred to conflicting interests rooted in private property rights; whereas socialism was based on unity of purpose. To law, Pashukanis counterposed the use of technical regulation to achieve common purposes. He gave the examples of the technical rules and timetables for the operation of a railway system and for the provision of medical services. These rules would be devised and revised by technical and scientific experts, not jurists. Pashukanis approached this distinction historically, pointing out that earlier and more primitive forms of social regulation assumed a collective purpose and did not take a legal form, based on opposed interests.

> [U]nder certain conditions the regulation of social relationships *assumes a legal character*. Such a formulation is undoubtedly more correct and, most importantly, more historical. We may not deny that collective life exists even among animals, nor that life there is regulated in one way or another. But it never occurs to us to affirm that the relationships of bees or ants is regulated by law. If we turn to primitive tribes, then although we may observe the origins of law, nevertheless a significant part of the relationships are regulated by a means external to law, e.g. by the prescriptions of religion. Finally, even in bourgeois society such things as the organization of postal and railroad services, military affairs etc. may be assigned entirely to legal regulation only upon a very superficial view which allows itself to be deceived by the external form of laws, charters and decrees. A railroad schedule regulates the movement of trains in a very different sense than, say, the law on the liability of railroads regulates the relationship of the latter with freight shippers (Beirne and Sharlet, 1980: 58).

Any element of official coercion would be determined by technical expedience, and would only become a legal issue in the realm of conflicting individual interests, such as those between a doctor and patient. These conflicting interests would arise in so far as their relations remained dominated by the production and exchange of commodities, rather than by the collective development of medicine, underpinned by social provision for citizens' well-being:

> [T]he treatment of a sick person presupposes a series of rules, both for the patient himself and for the medical personnel; but inasmuch as these rules are established from the point of view of a single purpose – the restoration of the patient's health – they are of a technical character. In conjunction with their application, there may be a certain constraint as regards the patient. But so long as this constraint is regarded from the viewpoint of the same purpose (which is identical for the person exerting the restraint and for the person subjected thereto), it remains a measure which is technically expedient – and nothing more. Within these limits, the content of the rules is established by medical science and changes as that science progresses. There is nothing for the jurist to do here. His role begins where perforce we abandon this basis of unity of purpose and pass to an investigation from another viewpoint – the viewpoint of isolated subjects opposed to each other, each of whom is the bearer of his own private interest (Hazard, 1951: 137).

Technical regulation, which Pashukanis saw as based on the premise of '[u]nity of purpose', 'is undoubtedly strengthened over time through being subjected to a general plan of the economy'.[25] Ultimately, the replacement of market relations by socialised production would mean the 'gradual withering away of the legal form altogether'.[26]

Some Western legal commentators have tended to lightly dismiss the historical validity of this distinction between law and regulation, but it contains the germs of an alternative approach to social and economic life. Both Schlesinger and Kelsen, for example, dismissed the conception of achieving a social unity of purpose as utopian. According to Schlesinger, only a 'rather utopian mind' could visualise complete unity of purpose among members of a society, even after class divisions and social inequalities were eliminated. Schlesinger asserted that it was 'completely wrong' for Pashukanis to give a railway by-law as an example of technical regulation because such measures were addressed to people, not inanimate objects, such as rails and train engines. This was surely obvious to Pashukanis, who did not suggest that technical regulations were addressed to objects. Schlesinger objected: 'Whether it works as mere technical advice which the engine-driver, to whom it is addressed, follows because he is convinced of its reasonableness, depends on

25 Pashukanis, 1978: 131.
26 Ibid: 132.

the general character of the society in the framework of which this railway works.'[27] It seems that Pashukanis would have regarded such a proposition as axiomatic. The real issue is whether a social framework can exist that will inspire such conviction of its 'reasonableness'.

To support his objection, Schlesinger proceeded to list the disciplinary powers and penalties enforced by the railways management in the Soviet Union. The existence of these punitive enforcement mechanisms points to the fact that inequality, oppression and economic hardship continued to exist in Soviet Russia, including for railway workers and train drivers. As seen in Chapter 4, social conditions in the Soviet Union remained harsh, despite the ludicrous self-serving claims of the Stalinist regime to have created socialism. In the context of social ownership, plentiful production, genuine democracy and a widely-held collective approach, it is possible to conceive of a more broadly self-administering society in which engine-drivers and other citizens were economically secure and 'convinced of the reasonableness' of regulations.

Pashukanis confined his argument to so-called technical matters. But it is difficult to see why this vision of a communist future should be so narrow. Over time, on the basis of more advanced social conditions, by democratic agreement and consent, rules could exist not just for regulating technical matters but for clarifying and communicating basic social and moral norms. Of course, this perspective challenges the prevailing conception of human nature as immutably selfish and greedy. But as discussed in Chapter 2, there is good reason to regard human nature as socially conditioned.

The withering away of law (against 'proletarian law')

One of the most important passages from Pashukanis occurs in his Introduction, where he replies to criticisms of his work from those who demanded a theory of proletarian law. In the first place, he points to the ahistorical nature of this objection:

> In raising a demand for new general concepts specific to proletarian law, this line appears to be revolutionary par excellence. In reality, however, this tendency proclaims the immortality of the legal form, in that it strives to wrench this form from the particular historical conditions which had helped to bring it to full fruition, and to present it as capable of permanent renewal (Pashukanis, 1978: 61).

He continued by linking the fate of law to the economic conditions that gave rise to it, suggesting that just as full socialism will supersede production for

27 Schlesinger, 1945: 162.

private profit and all the concepts associated with profit, so will it lead to the withering away of law:

> The withering of certain categories of bourgeois law (the categories as such, not this or that precept) in no way implies their replacement by new categories of proletarian law, just as the withering away of the categories of value, capital, profit and so forth in the transition to fully-developed socialism will not mean the emergence of new proletarian categories of value, capital and so on. The withering away of the categories of bourgeois law will, under these conditions, mean the withering away of law altogether, that is to say the disappearance of the juridical factor from social relations (Pashukanis, 1978: 61).

Quoting a passage from Marx, Pashukanis argued that as long as distribution continues to be governed by exchange, the form of law or 'right' will persist. Since this allocation according to individual contribution takes no account of the natural inequality of individual circumstances, it will still produce inequality. Indeed, distribution by exchange is 'a right of inequality, in its content, like every right'.[28] Pashukanis quoted the passage from *The State and Revolution*, where Lenin draws the conclusion from Marx's view that under socialism there remains for a time not only bourgeois law but also a bourgeois state.[29]

Once, however, production has developed to such a level that scarcity has been overcome and individuals need no incentive to work to their ability – when, in Lenin's words, no one will be forced to 'calculate with the heartlessness of a Shylock whether one has not worked half an hour more than somebody else'[30] – then the legal form will wither away. This was the essential conclusion that Pashukanis refused to relinquish throughout his various corrections and recantations. He eventually abandoned his opposition to the concept of 'socialist law' and embraced the unprecedented boosting of the powers of the Soviet state, but still adhered to the view that legal forms of regulation would disappear under communism.

'Crime', 'guilt' and 'punishment'

Pashukanis attempted to provide a theoretical framework for the Soviet conception of criminal law. By 1924, terms such as 'punishment' and 'guilt' had been dropped from the Criminal Code, replaced by the notion that defined ill-conduct had to be repressed as a matter of social self-defence. Krylenko had explained:

28 Pashukanis, 1978: 62, quoting Marx and Engels, 1973, vol III: 18.
29 Lenin, 1970: 138.
30 Ibid: 139.

> In principle, this view of repression as essentially an act of self-defence by the working people's state is the antithesis of the principle 'an eye for an eye' and the principles of 'retribution' and 'punishment' as they are understood by the classical school of law (Zile, 1970: 220).

Pashukanis went further. He insisted that, 'Changing the terminology does not alter anything in the substance of the matter.'[31] What had to be transformed were the underlying social conditions and class relations that shaped the entire approach of seeking to assess and attach 'guilt' to anti-social behaviour. He recounted that the Criminal Code had rejected the principle of guilt as the basis for punishment, and instead characterised punishment as solely a protective measure. Moreover, the 'Principles of Penal Legislature of the Union' passed by the Central Executive Committee of the Soviet Union had eliminated the term 'punishment' altogether, replacing it with the term 'judicial-corrective measures of social defence'.[32] Such alterations in terminology undoubtedly had a demonstrative value, Pashukanis acknowledged, but the substance of the problems remained, and could not be resolved simply by legal or judicial means.

Pashukanis argued that the social roots of crime lay in capitalist inequality and oppression, and that the juridical notion of punishment was bound up with the commodification of economic and social life:

> Imagine for a minute that the court is actually occupied only with the consideration of how to change the conditions of life of a given person – in order to influence him in the sense of correction, or in order to protect society from him – and the very meaning of the term punishment evaporates (Pashukanis, 1978: 179).

'Crime' could be largely eliminated only by providing economic security for all, and by focusing on proper medical and mental health treatment for those with particular mental or personality disorders. It could not be achieved by artificially assigning degrees of blameworthiness to individuals and seeking to extract retribution, or provide deterrence, by calculations of abstract human labour-time (prison terms) or monetary equivalents (fines, etc.).

> For even bourgeois advanced criminologists are convinced theoretically that the struggle against criminality may itself be regarded per se as a task of medical pedagogy, for whose solution the jurist – with his corpus delicti, his codes, his concept of 'guilt,' his 'unqualified or qualified criminal responsibility' and his subtle distinctions between participation, complicity and instigation – is entirely superfluous (Jaworskyj, 1967: 137).

31 Pashukanis, 1978: 185.
32 Ibid: 185.

Pashukanis contrasted bourgeois criminal law's 'concept of strictly personal liability' that 'corresponds to the radical individualism of bourgeois society'[33] with the collective responsibility of previous socio-economic orders. He described the notion of guilt as unscientific and associated with the concept of retaliation in proportion to injury. From this analysis, Pashukanis concluded that punishment embodied the principle of equivalent recompense in terms of time and money.

Pashukanis examined the prevailing forms of punishment – death, imprisonment and fines – and sought to show that they derived from primitive forms of vengeance. They fixed a monetary value on retribution in terms of labour-time, reflecting a society based on equivalent exchange of commodities, as measured by the expenditure of labour required to produce them. While the re-emergence of the most brutal punishments, such as the death penalty, expressed the need of the capitalist elite to engage in repression to secure its rule, the very *form* of punishment, with its preoccupation with individualising guilt and ranking various levels of culpability, was intrinsic to a society based on market relations.

> If, in place of the punishment, we substitute treatment, that is to say a concept of medical-health, what follows is entirely different, since we would then be interested, not primarily in whether the punishment fits the crime, but in whether the measures taken are adequate to the goals set, that is, whether they are adequate to the protection of society, to having an effect on the offender, and so forth (Pashukanis, 1978: 179).

Law and morality

In his chapter on Law and Morality, Pashukanis outlined but did not fully develop, an underlying relationship between commodity exchange and capitalist morality based on the ethical idea of the equal worth of human personalities. His analysis was signalled in his opening statement: 'For the products of human labour to be able to relate to each other as values, it is necessary for people to relate to each other as autonomous and equal personalities.'[34]

Pashukanis insisted that there are three preconditions for exchange according to the law of value – man as a moral subject, a legal subject and a subject operating egoistically. He explained this as follows:

> The person engaged in exchange must be an egoist, that is to say, he must stick to naked economic calculation, otherwise the value relation cannot

33 Pashukanis, 1978: 178.
34 Ibid: 151.

> be manifested as a socially necessary relation. The person engaging in exchange must be the bearer of rights, that is, he must be able to make autonomous decisions, for his will supposedly 'resides in objects'. Lastly, he embodies the principle of the essential equivalence of human personalities for, in exchange, all forms of labour are equalised and become human labour in the abstract (Pashukanis, 1978: 152).

Pashukanis argued that morality under capitalism was inherently related to individual economic calculation, not necessarily as a matter of ill-intent, but flowing from the entire framework of social relations based on commodity exchange. These concepts are very different from the view of man that prevailed under slavery or feudalism, in which relations were based on status rather than individuality, although Pashukanis notes that the idea of equal worth of personality passed from Stoic philosophy to Roman law, thence to Christianity and natural law doctrines.

In the course of his discussion, Pashukanis offered a critique of Kant's categorical imperative: 'Act only on the maxim through which you can at the same time will that it should become a universal law.'[35] This axiom urges every individual to be guided by a rule that, being absolutely independent of moral content, could become a universal rule of behaviour. Pashukanis established the connection between Kant's precept and the role of the individual in commodity exchange. Kant's categorical imperative was:

> [s]upra-individual because it has nothing to do with natural inclinations at all, with fear, sympathy, pity, the feeling of solidarity. According to Kant, it neither intimidates, nor convinces, nor flatters. At the same time, it appears independently of any external pressure in the direct, crude sense of the word. It is effective by virtue of the consciousness of its universality . . . Kant gave a logically perfected shape to the form which atomised bourgeois society sought to embody in reality . . . (Pashukanis, 1978: 154).

Pashukanis observed that this outlook corresponds to bourgeois propriety.

> There is no place for heroism and heroic deeds within the framework of the Kantian imperative. One is by no means obliged to sacrifice oneself, so long as one does not expect any such sacrifice of others. 'Irrational' acts of self-sacrifice and disregard for one's own interests for the sake of fulfilling one's individual historical destiny, one's social function, acts which stretch the social instincts to its limits, are beyond morality in the strict sense of the word (Pashukanis, 1978: 155).

35 Paton, 1956: 88.

In other words, while Kant sought to divorce the content of the mutual expectation that should guide human conduct from the historically and economically derived norms of capitalism, Kant's individualised conception of social obligations expressed those norms. Pashukanis' observations undermine the accusation, often made against Marxists, that they advocate amorality. Pashukanis did not develop this point, but sympathy, pity, solidarity, self-sacrifice, and consciousness of historical necessity can be regarded as components of truly human ethics.

Pashukanis commented on the deceptiveness of purportedly absolute ethical injunctions, such as Kant's other imperative, 'treat your fellow man as an end in himself'. He observed that in a society torn by class struggles, 'a classless ethic can exist only in the imagination, but not in practice'.[36]

> The large capitalist destroys the small capitalist 'in good faith', without thereby violating the absolute worth of his personality in any way. The proletarian's personality is 'equal in principle' to that of the capitalist; this circumstance is expressed in the fact of the 'free' contract of employment. But all that comes out of this 'materialised freedom' for proletarians is the freedom to die of starvation – without any interference (Pashukanis, 1978: 157).

Pashukanis was making the obvious point that under capitalism, the very existence of economic life based on the profit system requires the capitalist class to treat others – notably their competitors and employees – as objects for their own benefit, rather than as ends in themselves. No matter how much a business operator may wish to treat people well, and with an eye to their personal development, such an attitude would be fatal on the dog-eat-dog battleground of the market and the stock exchange. Profits hinge on extracting surplus value at an ever higher rate, at the expense of competitors and workers alike.

Pashukanis also reiterated the Marxist view that a true human morality could only arise through the complete socialist reorganisation of socio-economic life. 'Eliminating the ambiguity of the ethical form implies the transition to planned, socialised economy,' he wrote.[37] Somewhat more problematically, Pashukanis postulated the abolition of the ethical form altogether, to be replaced by a utilitarian approach of considering the harm and disadvantage to the collective interests of working people. In a footnote to the third Russian edition of the *General Theory*, however, he clarified that he was not arguing that morality would disappear in future society. Rather, morality would reflect 'the development of higher forms of humanity, as the

36 Pashukanis, 1978: 157–9.
37 Ibid: 158.

transformation of man into a species-being (to use Marx's expression)'.[38] 'Species-being' is an expression taken from Marx's early philosophical influence, Ludwig Feuerbach, and used by Marx in early writings such as *Economic and Philosophical Manuscripts of 1844*. By that term, Marx meant not man merely as a natural being, but as a human natural being, that is as a self-conscious social being freed from the alienation and estrangement produced by economic exploitation.[39]

Ideology and legal theory

As part of his critique, Pashukanis responded to criticism by Stuchka[40] that he regarded the legal form as a 'mere reflection of purest ideology'. Pashukanis appeared to bend the stick in the other direction by arguing that law – or at least its enforcement machinery – becomes an objective factor in production, that is part of the productive forces. By contrast, Marx referred to law as part of the political and ideological superstructure shaped by production and within which men ultimately became conscious of the underlying class conflicts and fought them out.[41] Pashukanis argued:

> The more or less unfettered process of social production and reproduction – formally carried out in commodity-producing society through individual legal transactions – is the practical purpose of legal mediation. This purpose cannot be achieved with the help of forms of consciousness alone, that is to say through purely subjective aspects: it requires exact criteria, statutes, interpretation of statute, casuistry, law courts, and the compulsory execution of court decisions. For this reason alone one cannot limit oneself, when analysing the legal form, to 'pure ideology', nor can one disregard the whole of this objectively existing machinery. Every legal action, for example the outcome of a lawsuit, is an objective fact which has its place outside the consciousness of the parties to it in just the same way as the economic phenomenon which it mediates (Pashukanis, 1978: 44).

By treating legal decisions as 'objective facts', this presentation equates the legal result – the outcome of a lawsuit – with the underlying property relations that shaped the law in the first place. Particular legal outcomes may have impacts that reinforce, or at times even contradict or inhibit, existing property rights. But, over time, the law will be modified to conform to the requirements of the prevailing economic order.

38 Pashukanis, 1978: 160–1.
39 Marx, 1977b: 142–7.
40 Stuchka, 1924: Preface.
41 See Marx, 1969.

Stuchka also criticised Pashukanis for recognising the existence of law only in capitalist society. While acknowledging the criticism, Pashukanis maintained that law in previous societies existed only in rudimentary and undeveloped forms.[42] In the preface to the second Russian edition of the *General Theory*, he stated:

> The purport of my analysis was not at all to deny the Marxist theory of law access to those historical periods which were as yet unfamiliar with developed capitalist commodity production. On the contrary, I was and still am concerned to facilitate understanding of the embryonic forms we find in those epochs, and to link them to the more developed forms through a general line of development (Pashukanis, 1978: 45).

Interestingly, Weber, who insisted that law was relatively autonomous from economic forces, came to a similar conclusion. Weber portrayed capitalism as the ultimate realisation of legal rationality – based on 'free' exchange and formal equality – which was incomplete in earlier historical societies.[43]

In the Introduction to his *General Theory*, Pashukanis displayed a working knowledge of bourgeois jurisprudence as well as previous Marxist writings.[44] He referred to the debate between natural law and legal positivism, before dealing with Kelsen.[45] Pashukanis mocked Kelsen's neo-Kantian methodology which reduces law to various norms derived from formal logic and an ill-defined underlying basic norm (*grundnorm*), or defining law of the state. He pointed out that such a conception strips law of all socio-economic content and historical development.

> Such a general theory explains nothing and turns its back from the outset on the facts of reality, that is of social life, busying itself with norms without being in the least interested in their origin (a meta-juridical question!), or in their relationship to any material matters (Pashukanis, 1978: 52).

Turning to sociological and psychological theories of law, Pashukanis criticised them for dismissing the legal form as a series of ideological illusions. As noted earlier, he reproached Marxists, including Stuchka, for 'assuming that by simply adding in the element of class struggle to the above-mentioned theories, they would attain a genuinely materialist, Marxist theory of law'.[46]

42 Pashukanis, 1978: 44.
43 Weber, 1954: 231.
44 Pashukanis, 1978: 47–64.
45 See Kelsen, 1961.
46 Pashukanis, 1978: 53.

Pashukanis maintained that while juridical ideology might be important for the ruling class, in camouflaging class conflict and creating illusions in legal equality, that does not explain how the ideology arose: 'The conscious exploitation of ideological forms is not the same as their emergence.'[47] In other words, while ideology may be a distorted expression of reality, it had a definite connection to that reality. To understand law's ideological role, one had to trace the development of law's actual function. Pashukanis insisted that law is an 'objective social relation' with its history determined by commodity exchange.

47 Pashukanis, 1978: 140.

Chapter 10

Was there an alternative? Pashukanis and the Opposition

> The state assumes directly and from the very beginning a dual character.[1]

The ruling party that Pashukanis joined in 1918 was very different to that which executed him in 1937. From 1917 to 1923, when the struggle against the Left Opposition began, and even to some extent until 1927, when Stalin's machine expelled the Left Opposition, differences continually broke out within the Communist Party in Soviet Russia, accompanied by the formation of opposition groupings. Contrary to the commonly held perception, the Bolshevik Party was far from the monolithic and totalitarian apparatus that it later became in Stalin's grip. Intense debates, conflicts and factional struggles occurred over nearly every major policy. Deep-going discussion and divisions within the leadership accompanied each political and economic turning point.[2] Until the campaign against 'Trotskyism' in 1924, culminating in the 1926–27 defeat of the United Opposition, these debates were conducted with relative freedom and democracy, considering the vicissitudes of economic hardship and foreign military intervention.

The early legal debates took place against a backdrop of conflicts over critical policy dilemmas that had many implications for law. As soon as the Bolsheviks seized power in October 1917, the party was struck by rifts and resignations over three major issues: (1) seeking a coalition government with other Soviet parties (Social Revolutionaries and Mensheviks) or attempting to hold power alone, (2) dissolving the Constituent Assembly, and (3) press freedom for interests aiming to overturn the revolution. By the end of 1917, deep splits occurred over whether to sue for peace with Germany and sign the consequent Brest-Litovsk Treaty.[3]

Even during the years of foreign military intervention and the civil war,

1 Trotsky, 1937: 54.
2 Daniels, 1960: 3–8, and generally: Carr, 1978; Lewin, 1969.
3 Deutscher, 1954: 330ff.

at least two major controversies occurred: the 1919 opposition to Trotsky's professionalisation of the Red Army and the November 1920–March 1921 dispute over the status and role of the trade unions. The March 1921 adoption of the New Economic Policy occasioned considerable political and economic debates, including a sharp conflict in October 1922 over Stalin's support for ending the foreign trade monopoly. From September 1922 to April 1923, Lenin and Trotsky were at loggerheads with Stalin over Georgia and the national question.[4]

Between October 1923, following the crushing of the German revolution, and December 1924, the conflicts assumed a different and more polarised form: the campaign launched by Trotsky and the Left Opposition against the growing bureaucratisation and nationalist perspective of the party at the hands of the triumvirate of Stalin, Zinoviev and Kamenev that emerged following Lenin's incapacitation and death. After suffering serious defeats, and in the face of increasingly anti-democratic measures by Stalin's faction, Trotsky joined with Zinoviev and Kamenev to form the United or Joint Opposition in April 1926. But following further international working class defeats, in Poland, Britain and China, the United Opposition broke apart and the Left Opposition was bureaucratically suppressed from October 1927. Trotsky was removed from the party leadership, expelled from the party, exiled to Central Asia and, in 1929, deported from the Soviet Union.[5]

In 1928 and 1929, Stalin's faction increasingly turned against its allies in Bukharin's Right faction, culminating in the capitulation and crushing of the Right Opposition. That marked the final end of debate within the party, although clandestine oppositions continued to win considerable support, threatening the Stalinist regime.

Throughout these 12 years, there were numerous factions and groupings, as well as independently-minded leading figures, in the Bolshevik Party. The principal factions were the Leninists 1917–23, the Centre (Stalin) 1921–38, the Left Opposition from 1923, the Joint Opposition 1926–27, the Right Opposition 1928–29, and, earlier, the Left Communists 1917–21, the Democratic Centralists 1917–21 and the Workers Opposition 1917–21. Lesser factions included the Workers Group 1921–27 and Workers Truth 1921–27.

How these differences related to the discussions on legal policy and practice is difficult to trace in detail. The early Soviet legal debates featured an array of Bolshevik jurists, lawyers, philosophers and legal scholars. Some may have represented various factions, including opposition tendencies. However, except for Lunacharsky and Krestinsky, neither of whom played an active part in the legal debates after 1918, none of the legal theorists were central party leaders. Except for brief periods, Stuchka and Krylenko were

4 Deutscher, 1959: 1–74.
5 Ibid: 75–394.

secondary party leaders. Pashukanis was never a major figure in the party. None of this is surprising. The key issues in the differences with the opposition factions were political, economic and social. Legal and jurisprudential questions hardly rated alongside the controversies over the NEP, industrialisation, foreign trade and the defeats of the communist parties in Germany and China. The legal debates generally flowed from, rather than directly contributed to, the main conflicts.

No clear evidence seems to exist of any direct influence on the legal debates by the 1923–27 Left and United Oppositions to the Stalinist bureaucracy. One figure identified with the Left Opposition, S. Volfson, participated in the debates, but only fragments of his contributions have been published in English. However, the published views of the Left Opposition did provide an analysis of the economic, political and legal contradictions facing Soviet Russia. Before turning to those documents, and to Volfson's views, it is worth reviewing the extent of the scope that existed for divergent political views in the early years of the revolution.

From democracy to repression

In his work on the communist opposition, Daniels reviews the divergent political biographies of the early Bolshevik leaders and notes their 'highly individualist nature'.[6] Independent spirits abounded in the early leadership. One feature of the politico-legal climate in the early months of the Russian Revolution was the tolerance of dissent, and reluctance to take organisational measures against opponents in the Bolshevik (Communist) Party. For example, the Bolsheviks, having seized power and organised a transitional government headed by Lenin as chairman of the Council of People's Commissars, with majority support in the Second Congress of Soviets, were immediately divided over the issue of whether to form a coalition government representing all the socialist parties.

Negotiations to this end were carried on between the Bolsheviks and other parties for several days. Lenin and Trotsky, the two foremost leaders of the revolution, opposed a coalition with the Mensheviks and Social Revolutionaries, who were demanding Lenin's and Trotsky's removal from office as a precondition for coalition. Support for coalition within the Bolshevik leadership was so strong that five Central Committee members – Zinoviev, Kamenev, Rykov, Miliutin and Nogin – and five People's Commissars – Teodorovich and Shliapnikov, as well as Rykov, Miliutin and Nogin – resigned their posts in opposition to the majority who voted with Lenin and Trotsky. The dispute was finally settled in late November 1917 when the Bolsheviks and the Left Social Revolutionaries reached an agreement on a

6 Daniels, 1960: 30.

coalition. Those who had opposed the majority were quickly reinstated in their positions.[7]

After the stresses and privations of the civil war, party democracy reached a high tide at the ninth party conference in September 1920, by which time the civil war was nearing an end and the immediate danger to Soviet Russia's survival was dissipating. Two 'left' opposition groups, the Workers' Opposition and the Democratic Centralists, were afforded representation on a commission to consider party organisation, and the conference opened with scathing criticisms of the party machinery. Among other things, it was accused of insufficient ties with local organisations, inadequate attention to economic tasks, and lack of centralised direction of educational activities. The conference ended with a manifesto that called for 'broader criticism of the central as well as of the local party institutions', cessation of the appointment of local secretaries by the centre, and rejection of 'any kind of repression against comrades because they have different ideas'. Emphasised above all was 'the need again to direct the attention of the whole party to the struggle for the realisation of greater equality: in the first place, within the party; secondly within the proletariat, and in addition within the whole toiling mass'.[8]

As mentioned in Chapter 4, a regrettable ban on party factions was introduced, together with the NEP, at the Tenth Congress in 1921. Nevertheless, opposition groupings continued to exist. Only one prominent party member, Workers Group leader Gabriel Miasnikov, was expelled from the party in Lenin's time. The Central Committee expelled Miasnikov in February 1922 after he continued to defy party discipline despite a written plea by Lenin.[9] Generally speaking, the ban on formal factions was coupled with the insistence that free discussion and criticism remain protected. Lenin specifically defended the right to dissent on major questions and opposed any attempt to prohibit competing policy platforms within the party.[10]

However, fundamental differences over economic and national policy, as well as the state apparatus, emerged from the second half of 1922. The November 1922 Plenum of the Central Committee, sitting without Lenin and Trotsky, unexpectedly moved to end the state monopoly on foreign trade, which would have created a new layer of NEPmen and opened the still primitive Soviet economy to the direct pressure of international capital. Lenin wrote to Trotsky, urging him to 'take upon yourself at the coming Plenum the defense of our common view as to the unconditional necessity of preserving and enforcing the monopoly'.[11] The alliance was directed

7 Daniels, 1960: 63–8; Deutscher, 1954: 330–41.
8 Daniels, 1960: 115–17.
9 Ibid: 159–64.
10 Ibid: 148–50.
11 Trotsky, 1978: 26.

primarily against Stalin, who had presented the question to the Central Committee. Sensing the danger to his position, Stalin yielded and the decision was revoked at the December Plenum. Over the same months, Lenin and Trotsky combined to defeat a proposal by Stalin, as Commissar for Nationalities, to adopt a bureaucratically centralist policy towards the proposed transformation of the Soviet state into a federated union of national republics.[12]

These struggles provided the backdrop to Lenin's political testament of December 1922 and January 1923, in which he called for Stalin's removal as party general secretary.[13] Concealed by Stalin and his group from the party, the testament was later published and distributed secretly by Oppositionists, hundreds of whom were arrested and exiled for doing so. Thus, Lenin commenced a fight within the party against the growth of the bureaucracy and its usurpation of political power, a fight that was continued by the Left Opposition, formed by Trotsky in late 1923 and, for a time, the Joint Opposition of 1926–27, led by Trotsky, Zinoviev and Kamenev.[14]

The analysis of the Left and Joint Oppositions

The New Course, one of the first documents issued by the Left Opposition in 1923, identified bureaucratism as one of the principal dangers confronting the Soviet state. It demanded a return to the Marxist course of involving the mass of the population in the administration of the state:

> The state apparatus is the most important source of bureaucratism. On the one hand, it absorbs an enormous quantity of the most active party elements and it teaches the most capable of them the methods of administration of men and things, instead of political leadership of the masses. On the other hand, it preoccupies largely the attention of the party apparatus over which it exerts influence by its methods of administration. Thence, in large measure, the bureaucratisation of the apparatus, which threatens to separate the party from the masses. This is precisely the danger that is now most obvious and direct. The struggle against the other dangers must under present conditions begin with the struggle against bureaucratism (Trotsky, 1972: 33).

None of the participants in the legal debates appear to have referred directly to this document or the bitter struggle that it opened up between Stalin's bureaucratic machine and the Left Opposition. Nevertheless, its trenchant

12 Trotsky, 1978: 27–8.

13 For the text of the testament, see Trotsky, 1978: 6–8.

14 For a detailed review of the 1923–27 period, see Deutscher, 1959: 75–394.

defence of the classical Marxist outlook may have influenced some of the objections to the emerging repudiation of the withering away of the state apparatus.

In his 1924 article 'Contemporary Critics of Marxism' Volfson, a supporter of the Left Opposition, appears to have made a critique of various anti-Marxist schools of jurisprudence as a veiled means of defending the classical Marxist programme. On the surface, he examined the writings of three groups. The first consisted of open opponents of Marxism, notably Hans Kelsen. The second grouping, classified by Volfson as 'pseudo-Marxists', sought to 'destroy the revolutionary essence of the Marxist theory of the state'. The third camp, personified by Karl Kautsky and Max Adler, purportedly defended the Marxist theory of the state but distorted it in reformist and opportunist ways.[15]

Volfson introduced his critique by echoing Lenin's words, from the Preface to *The State and Revolution*, emphasising that the question of the state had acquired a special significance following the October 1917 Revolution. Volfson wrote:

> During and after the war, international socialism became confronted with such imperious problems as dictatorship of the proletariat, democracy, participation in governing the state, withering away of the state, liquidation of the state, the state in the transition period, and many other problems connected with the state. Solutions to these problems must be furnished before they get out of hand. The problem of the state has become a demarcation line separating revolutionaries from reformists, Marxism from opportunism. In our epoch the problems of the state are not merely *Zeit und Streitfragen* [timely and contentious issues]; they are literally problems of life and death to political parties (Jaworskyj, 1967: 179).

The urgency of Volfson's language, his argument that positions on the state separated Marxists from opportunists, and his insistence that issues of political life and death were involved, suggest that his concerns were directed not so much against his nominated opponents abroad as against figures at home who were advocating a prolonged strengthening of the state apparatus. Given the heated political atmosphere, with vitriolic accusations hurled against Trotsky and the Left Opposition, such indirect references in politico-legal polemics were hardly surprising. Indeed, from the end of 1924 until mid-1926, Trotsky himself restrained his open criticism of the party leadership, preparing for the conditions to emerge for a further challenge in the wake of his defeat in late 1924.[16]

15 Jaworskyj, 1967: 179–80.
16 Deutscher, 1959: 201.

The central thrust of Volfson's article, reinforced by a key passage from Lenin in *The State and Revolution*, was that the Soviet state was a purely transitional one, required only so long as the capitalist class, revived by the NEP, still remained a threat to Soviet society. This state, Volfson emphasised, was not a state in the old sense of the word under capitalism; it was a state designed to fade away once suppression of the old ruling classes was no longer necessary.

> The Soviet state is struggling against the exploitative tendencies of the capitalist class which has been deprived of its position by the revolution but has not yet been liquidated. Hence, it follows that this class still exists in Soviet society; it seeks to exploit other classes, but the classes that are subject to the threat of such exploitation hold in their hands the power of the state and take measures against the class enemy. This is the state in a period of transition. The proletariat does not exploit anyone. Indeed, the proletariat is the ruling class in the Soviet state, but the goal of this state is neither exploitation nor enslavement – that is, this state is not a state in the Marxist meaning of the term (Deutscher, 1959: 182–3).

The 1927 Platform of the Joint Opposition, which was joined by Zinoviev and Kamenev, resumed the open struggle for a genuinely socialist approach to the state. It emphasised the necessity to restore the ideals of the October Revolution:

> The bureaucratic apparatus of every bourgeois state, no matter what its form, elevates itself above the population, solidifying its rule by cultivating a mutual loyalty among the ruling class and systematically propagating among the masses fear of and subservience to the rulers. The October Revolution, replacing the old state machine by the workers', peasants' and soldiers' soviets, dealt the heaviest blow in history to the old idol of the bureaucratic state.
>
> Our party program says upon this question: Waging the most bitter struggle against bureaucratism, the Russian Communist Party applies for the *complete conquering of this evil* the following measures: (1) The obligatory drawing of every member of a Soviet into some definite work in the administration of the state. (2) A continual rotation of these tasks so that every member is gradually familiarized with all branches of the administration. (3) The gradual attraction of the entire labouring population, to the last man, into the work of State administration.
>
> A full and all-sided carrying out of these measures – which are a further step along the road taken by the Paris Commune – means a simplification of the functions of administration, and together with a rise in the cultural level of the workers will lead to the abolition of the State power (Trotsky, 1973c: 47–8).

The Platform insisted that these tasks, together with the struggle for greater equality, remained among the party's most important challenges during the period of the NEP, in order to ensure that the NEP was a road to socialism, not capitalism. It noted that 'instructions' issued in 1925 extending electoral rights to NEPmen and other employer layers, in violation of the Soviet constitution, had been revoked as a result of criticism from the Opposition. These instructions were 'only one very clear expression of the fact that the bureaucratic apparatus, to its very top, has become responsive to the importunities of the wealthy, accumulating elements of the community'.[17]

The submission of this platform to the Central Committee in early September 1927 sparked a new wave of persecution against Opposition supporters. The Central Committee refused to publish the document, contrary to party traditions, and Oppositionists who claimed responsibility for printing it, including Preobrazhensky, Serebriakov and Mrachovsky, were expelled from the party and later imprisoned.[18] That could explain why none of the contributors to the written legal debates quoted from the forbidden programme.

Nevertheless, the Opposition's analysis of the contradictory character of the Soviet state provided a key to understanding the debates over whether Soviet state and 'law' were bourgeois or proletarian. In essence, the Left Opposition warned that the Soviet state and law had two antagonistic sides. They were socialist in as much as they maintained socialised production and helped develop it towards genuine communism. But they remained bourgeois to the extent that they enforced the continued allocation of products according to market forces, determined by financial capacity to pay. These opposing tendencies were not static – one would inevitably gain ascendancy over the other, depending on the balance of economic and political forces, both within the Soviet Union and on a global scale. Rather than falsely and complacently proclaim the 'socialist' character of the state and law, as did the increasingly privileged officials supporting Stalin's faction, the essential task was to combat the capitalist pressures, while strengthening the ability of the party and the Soviet masses to take real control over economic, political and social life. The emerging Stalinist bureaucracy was the greatest barrier to doing so.

For his part, Pashukanis seemed unable to explain the growing gulf between the Marxist view of the withering away of the state and the increasing authoritarianism of the Kremlin regime. Instead, he appeared to accommodate himself to the official line by extending the time frame for the transition to a classless, stateless society in the light of the political isolation and capitalist encirclement of the Soviet Union. As the Left Opposition argued, however, time was of the essence. It was not a matter of the Soviet

17 Trotsky, 1973c: 49.
18 Ibid: vi–ix.

Union 'holding out' until more favourable circumstances arose internationally. The longer the delay, the stronger the pro-capitalist pressures on the Soviet state.

In his 1931 theses 'Problems of Development of the USSR' written for the Left Opposition, Trotsky warned:

> Absolutely false is the official doctrine of fatalistic optimism prevailing today, according to which the continued speedy growth of the industrialization and collectivization is assured in advance and leads automatically to the construction of socialism in one country . . . At the core of the economic difficulties, the successive crises, the extreme tension of the whole Soviet system and its political convulsions, lie a number of contradictions of diverse historical origin which are interlinked in various ways. Let us name the most important one: (a) the heritage of the capitalist and pre-capitalist contradictions of old tsarist-bourgeois Russia, primarily the contradiction between town and country; (b) the contradiction between the general cultural backwardness of Russia and the tasks of socialist transformation which dialectically grow out of it; (c) the contradiction between the workers' state and the capitalist encirclement, particularly between the monopoly of foreign trade and the world market. These contradictions are not at all of a brief and episodic character; on the contrary, the significance of the most important of them will increase in the future (Trotsky, 1976: 64–5).

Trotsky also warned that these economic contradictions found their most concentrated and dangerous expression within the anti-democratic and repressive regime that had developed within the party and the state machinery. 'Only blind people, hirelings, or the deceived can deny the fact that the ruling party of the USSR, the leading party of the Comintern, has been completely crushed and replaced by the apparatus.' This degeneration of the party, the 'delicate' and absolutely critical instrument of orientation and governance over the Soviet state, threatened the entire state with destruction.[19]

In *The Revolution Betrayed*, published in 1937, Trotsky restated the warnings that the Left Opposition had sounded since 1923 about the dangers at the heart of the Soviet state.

> The bourgeois norms of distribution, by hastening the growth of material power, ought to serve socialist aims – but only in the last analysis. The state assumes directly and from the very beginning a dual character: socialistic, insofar as it defends social property in the means of

19 Trotsky, 1976: 70–1.

> production; bourgeois, insofar as the distribution of life's goods is carried out with a capitalistic measure of value and all the consequences ensuing therefrom. Such a contradictory characterisation may horrify the dogmatists and scholastics; we can only offer them our condolences.
>
> The final physiognomy of the workers' state ought to be determined by the changing relations between its bourgeois and socialist tendencies. The triumph of the latter ought ipso facto to signify the final liquidation of the gendarme – that is, the dissolving of the state in a self-governing society. From this alone it is sufficiently clear how immeasurably significant is the problem of Soviet bureaucratism, both in itself and as a symptom! (Trotsky, 1937: 54)

Trotsky also made a frank assessment of the Bolshevik leadership's lack of preparedness for the economic and class pressures produced by the failure of the Soviet revolution to spread to the more advanced countries of Europe. He stated that Lenin had not fully anticipated the depth of the difficulties that would beset the Soviet state, because Lenin had not envisaged the Russian Revolution standing for any length of time isolated in a capitalist world.

> Basing himself wholly upon the Marxian theory of the dictatorship of the proletariat, Lenin did not succeed, as we have said, either in his chief work dedicated to this question (*The State and Revolution*), or in the program of the party, in drawing all the necessary conclusions as to the character of the state from the economic backwardness and isolatedness of the country. Explaining the revival of bureaucratism by the unfamiliarity of the masses with administration and by the special difficulties resulting from the war, the program prescribes merely political measures for the overcoming of 'bureaucratic distortions': elections and recall at any time of all plenipotentiaries, abolition of material privileges, active control by the masses, etc. It was assumed that along this road the bureaucrat, from being a boss, would turn into a simple and moreover temporary technical agent, and the state would gradually and imperceptibly disappear from the scene (Trotsky, 1937: 58).

In other words, Lenin and the Bolsheviks had seriously underestimated the difficulties presented by the primitivism of the economy they had inherited from Tsarism and the implications of the revolution failing to spread to the more advanced countries of Western Europe. This meant that the measures Lenin had prescribed in *The State and Revolution* for checking the rise of bureaucratic tendencies were inadequate. Organisational safeguards alone could not combat bureaucratism because the root causes lay deeper. These could only be overcome through a difficult combination of mass political participation, rapid industrial development and the completion of the revolution internationally. Trotsky continued:

> This obvious underestimation of impending difficulties is explained by the fact that the program was based wholly upon an international perspective. 'The October revolution in Russia has realised the dictatorship of the proletariat. . . . The era of world proletarian communist revolution has begun.' These were the introductory lines of the program. Their authors not only did not set themselves the aim of constructing 'socialism in a single country' – this idea had not entered anybody's head then, and least of all Stalin's – but they also did not touch the question as to what character the Soviet state would assume, if compelled for as long as two decades to solve in isolation those economic and cultural problems which advanced capitalism had solved so long ago (Trotsky, 1937: 58).

Trotsky's analysis highlighted the doctrinal and political problems that beset the early Soviet legal debates. The unanticipated international isolation of the Soviet state created immense difficulties that could not be remedied in the legal sphere alone. These problems were compounded by Stalin's insistence that socialism could be built in a single country. Regrettably, there are no indications that the Opposition's insights were permitted to inform the legal discussion. Instead, the discourse degenerated into name-calling and scapegoating after 1927, as the grip of Stalin's group tightened.

The prognosis of the Left Opposition was confirmed in the most malignant fashion. Despite subsequent industrial growth, the stranglehold of Stalin's henchmen meant that the capitalist tendencies continued to strengthen at the expense of the socialist tendencies. Stalin's increasingly bureaucratic and repressive regime exterminated its communist opposition in the 1930s. Even before then, genuine Marxist discussion was strangled and replaced by slavish adherence to an official line, falsely presented as Marxism. In the legal sphere this meant ascribing a permanence and sanctity to the 'dictatorship of the proletariat' and 'Soviet law' and the reversal of all the progressive achievements in democratic involvement, family relations and criminal law. Despite often recanting their previous writings, some of the leading figures in the early legal debates were among the victims of Stalin's purges. This brutality laid the basis for a protracted economic and social putrefaction that ultimately culminated in Stalin's heirs, Gorbachev and Yeltsin, dissolving the Soviet state and paving the way for the complete restoration of capitalism after 1991.[20] Over the following decade, this led to a social catastrophe of widespread impoverishment, mass unemployment, gross inequality, collapsing public facilities and a dramatic decline in life expectancy.[21]

20 North, 1989.
21 Beams, 1999.

Chapter 11

Pashukanis and Western theorists

> It is the kind of book that any open-minded scholar can read with real profit, however little he may be convinced by its main thesis.[1]

Having examined the contradictions of Pashukanis' life and work, and, in particular, their relationship to the emergence of Stalinism, we can now probe the two other major enigmas of Pashukanis.

Why has Pashukanis been considered by many Western scholars – both those sympathetic to his views and those who are not – as a leading anti-Stalinist, or at least an exponent of an alternative, arguably more pure, version of Marxism to that adopted by the Stalinist bureaucracy?

Why have many Western scholars praised the quality and originality of Pashukanis' work, yet also drawn the conclusion that his fate illustrates the intrinsic impossibility of the entire communist project?

As noted in Chapter 1, Pashukanis received admiring, or at least sympathetic, reviews in the West in the 1930s, 40s and 50s (Kelsen, Schlesinger, Hazard, Fuller and Berman) and 1970s (Kamenka and Tay, Arthur, Redhead, Beirne and Sharlet). These works appeared in two main periods, and from differing perspectives. The earlier authors reflected attempts by Western governments and academics to understand the emergence and survival of the Soviet Union, and to learn how to co-exist and transact with it. The later interest was bound up with coming to grips with the ever more apparent wreckage of Stalinism in the wake of Krushchev's secret speech at the Twentieth Congress of the Communist Party of the Soviet Union in 1956. In the first period, the writers generally approached Pashukanis from a non-Marxist and more traditional legal positivist perspective. By comparison, those treating Pashukanis in the second period usually wrote from a Marxist or at least partly pro-Marxist point of view.

Regardless of these differences, some common features can be noted. In

1 Fuller, 1949: 1159.

general, these writers portrayed Pashukanis as a more genuine, intellectual or humane Marxist, as against the Stalinist epigones, such as Vyshinsky, who replaced him. At the same time, many of his concepts were dismissed as unrealistic or doctrinaire, as if to prove the hopeless utopianism or crude determinism of classical Marxism. Despite the apparent contradiction between these two approaches to Pashukanis, there is an underlying thread. Overall, these writers largely distorted the relationship between Pashukanis and Marxism, uncritically presenting him as a Marxist scholar and using his fate as proof of the allegedly fatal flaws in Marxist legal and political theory.

Thus, according to Kamenka and Tay, writing in 1970, Pashukanis was 'the foremost and ablest expositor of Marxist jurisprudence'.[2] They attributed to Pashukanis' *General Theory* not only an intellectual prowess and strength of spirit that was to later vanish in the Soviet Union, but also a rescuing of Marxism from the alleged crudities of Engels and Lenin:

> [O]ne finds in the book a freshness of style and of thought that was soon to disappear from Soviet intellectual life. Pashukanis combines a genuine and scholarly involvement in jurisprudence and legal history with an equally genuine feeling for Marx's method and concerns. Not only is he sensitive to the achievements of other scholars – of Laband, Jellinek, Duguit, Maine and Maitland – but he rejects the theoretically crude simplifications of Engels and Lenin to focus on the subtleties of a Marx that most of his contemporaries had not fully appreciated (Kamenka and Tay, 1970: 72).

Such assertions of a contrast between a 'subtle' Marx, on the one hand, and 'crude' Engels and Lenin, on the other, fly in the face of the historical and written record, as we saw in Chapters 2 and 3. An equally significant flaw in the approach taken by Kamenka and Tay is to ignore the connection between Pashukanis' emergence as a leading Soviet theoretician in 1924 and the ultimately successful Stalinist suppression of the Left and Joint Oppositions in 1924–27. Their only cryptic reference to the Marxist opposition to Stalin is to note that Pashukanis was himself denounced in 1937 as a Trotskyite 'liquidator' of socialist law and legality.

Similarly, in an introduction to *The General Theory of Law and Marxism*, Arthur wrote: 'It remains to this day the most significant Marxist work on the subject.'[3] Arthur identified Pashukanis with anti-Stalinism, stating that the revived interest in Pashukanis' theories signalled a 'renaissance of Marxist debate' as 'part of a process of recovery of the heritage Bolshevik thought repressed by the Stalinist bureaucracy and its international supporters'.[4]

2 Kamenka and Tay, 1970: 72.
3 Editor's introduction to Pashukanis, 1978: 9.
4 Ibid: 9.

Arthur made no mention of the genuine socialist opposition to Stalin inside the Soviet Union in the 1920s and 1930s, nor of Pashukanis' alignment with the Kremlin against it. Like Kamenka and Tay, Arthur recorded that Pashukanis was liquidated in 1937 as a 'Trotsky-Bukharin fascist agent'. He further noted that although calls had been made for Pashukanis' rehabilitation in the wake of the 1956 Twentieth Congress, the official Kremlin line still condemned Pashukanis' 'concept of Soviet law as dying bourgeois law'.[5] From this, a reader could wrongly draw the conclusion that Pashukanis was an opponent of the Stalinist bureaucracy.

It is not possible here to review the full range of critiques made of Pashukanis, only some of the most interesting and thought-provoking.[6] In that way, attention can be drawn to some of the strengths and weaknesses of noteworthy representatives of several different political and theoretical schools of thought.[7]

Traditional assessments

In the earlier period, a prominent American scholar of Soviet law, John Hazard emphasised the widespread regard for Pashukanis:

> Pashukanis was an imaginative Marxist, the most imaginative to appear among Soviet lawyers immediately after the October Revolution, or so Harvard's noted legal philosopher, Roscoe Pound, told me when I contemplated entering upon the study of Soviet law in 1934. Pound said he had been so impressed while reading a German translation of Pashukanis' principal work that he had undertaken to study Russian so as to read his works not yet translated. Pound's verdict on Pashukanis' place among Marxist legal theorists was shared by others. Members of a group assembled to suggest what should be included in a volume on Soviet legal philosophy to be published by the American Association of Law Schools said the same thing in 1947. All of them put Pashukanis first among their choices (Beirne and Sharlet, 1990: i).

5 Pashukanis, 1978: 10.

6 Elements of the critiques made by Schlesinger, Arthur, Beirne and Sharlet have been considered in Chapter 8.

7 This treatment by no means attempts to deal with the full range of writings on Pashukanis in the West, let alone the Soviet bloc countries. Rather, an attempt has been made to address the question set at the beginning of this chapter, discussing relevant Western works that either represent wider trends or make particularly critical observations. Among the significant contributions on aspects of Pashukanis' work not treated are Norrie, 1982, Cotterrell, 1979 and Sumner, 1981. Several treatises examining Marxist legal theory, such as Hirst, 1979, have discussed Pashukanis but in isolation from Stalin. For a defence of Pashukanis and an application of his theory to international law, albeit with the same defect, see Mieville, 2005.

Likewise, in a 1949 article, Lon Fuller stated that in his *General Theory*, Pashukanis

> expounds with clarity and coherence an ingenious development of Marxist theory that has been called the 'Commodity Exchange Theory of Law'. His work is in the best tradition of Marxism. It is the product of thorough scholarship and wide reading. It reaches conclusions that will seem to most readers perverse and bizarre, yet in the process of reaching these conclusions it brings familiar facts of law and government into an unfamiliar but revealing perspective. It is the kind of book that any open-minded scholar can read with real profit, however little he may be convinced by its main thesis (Fuller, 1949: 1159).

Fuller's favourable assessment of Pashukanis seems to have been influenced by two related factors. As noted earlier, he was of the opinion that Pashukanis had boldly deviated from accepted Marxist doctrine. Fuller wrote that 'the orthodox communist conception regards law as the expression of the will of the ruling class' whereas Pashukanis 'insisted that this view of law was only a kind of truism, which failed to reveal the real essence of legal phenomena, since it was incapable of explaining how something called "law" could reinforce or sanctify the brute force of domination'.[8] As discussed in Chapter 2, any assertion that Marxism regards law as the expression of the will of the ruling class is based on a simplistic and mechanical interpretation. But for Fuller, the Stalinist regime's repudiation of Pashukanis' view and his replacement by Vyshinsky, who reinstated the 'orthodox view', demonstrated that the Soviet order had been forced to adjust to human nature. Fuller suggested that the Soviet leaders had come to recognise that the principle of legality and other 'bourgeois virtues' were 'indispensable ways of getting things done, rooted in the very nature of the human animal'.[9]

The second related factor was that Fuller's article appeared in the context of the Cold War and its purpose was to examine a volume published by Vyshinsky, who became Stalin's chief legal hatchet man. After convincingly showing Vyshinsky's *The Law of the Soviet Union* to be saturated with mind-numbing vacuity, abusiveness and platitudes, Fuller nonetheless found virtue in the volume. While at first it visited on its reader 'only an acute intellectual nausea' it turned out to 'contain an important message of hope. The hard line of Marxism *can* bend before the compulsions of life [emphasis in original].'[10] Fuller expressed the hope that if the theory (defended by Pashukanis) that all law is capitalist could find its way to the ash heap, so could the theory of

8 Fuller, 1949: 1164.
9 Ibid: 1165.
10 Ibid.

inevitable conflict between capitalism and communism. In the end, then, Fuller, to some extent at least, favoured Vyshinsky's supposed realism against Pashukanis' perceived doctrinaire utopianism. This view, coming from an eminent Western legal theorist, probably helped elevate Pashukanis' status in academic circles as a genuine Marxist theoretician, a reputation that was revived in the 1970s by more left-wing scholars.

One of the most knowledgeable and perceptive traditional, non-Marxist, scholars who expressed appreciation for Pashukanis' intellectual endeavours was Harold Berman. His *Justice in the USSR* remains one of the few academic attempts to examine Pashukanis' theories and their emergence and evolution in the context of the material circumstances confronting the early Soviet Union. Berman credited Pashukanis with being the one Soviet writer in the first two decades after 1917 who developed a theory of law that 'had substantial intellectual content'.[11] He contrasted Pashukanis' 'intricate and scholarly theory' with the 'extremely simple' and 'vituperative' doctrine of Vyshinsky, who replaced him as dean of the Soviet legal fraternity and laid down the basis for subsequent Soviet law.[12]

Berman provided a pithy, if somewhat simplified, summary account of Pashukanis' central thesis, that law's particular unique features as means of class domination lay in its 'reflection of the market'.[13] Berman accurately enough drew attention to the implications of Pashukanis' analysis for the Soviet state:

> To speak of 'proletarian law' is therefore incorrect. The proletarian state may use bourgeois law, and must use it insofar as vestiges of the capitalist economy remain; but it cannot develop proletarian law, since law is by its nature based on individualism and contractualism (Berman, 1963: 28).

Berman pointed out that under the New Economic Policy, 'bourgeois law' was restored, and attempted to trace the actual development of the Soviet legal system from 1917 to 1937 in order to appreciate the significance of the ultimate renunciation of Pashukanis' theories. However, his account of this period is confused by asserting that the central economic and philosophical controversies that proved fateful for the progress of Soviet law were those with the Right Opposition led by Bukharin. Stalin's campaign against Bukharin commenced in 1928, when Bukharin opposed the forced collectivisation of agriculture, and ended in Bukharin's expulsion from the Politburo in late 1929. Regrettably, Berman did not mention the earlier, and much more fundamental 1923–27 conflicts with the Left and Joint Oppositions led by

11 Berman, 1963: 26.
12 Ibid: 53.
13 Ibid: 27.

Trotsky, Zinoviev and Kamenev. During that period, Bukharin's right-wing faction aligned itself with Stalin's 'centre' faction against the Joint Opposition. Indeed, Bukharin was among the first to outline the theory, adopted by Stalin in 1924, that socialism could be developed in a single country, even one as underdeveloped as Russia. This theory led to the conclusion that revolution need no longer be encouraged in the capitalist countries, since Russia could and should achieve socialism alone. As discussed in Chapter 4, the thesis became the linchpin of the Stalin regime's nationalist outlook, bureaucratic privileges and repression. Berman himself stated that the official reason given in 1936 for the departure from the Marxist and Leninist doctrine of socialism as a classless, stateless society was 'the existence of socialism (and eventually communism) in one country; surrounded by capitalist powers'.[14]

Berman appears to have misinterpreted the deepening problems produced for Pashukanis after Stalin's 1930 statement that the withering away of the state was compatible with the strengthening of the dictatorship of the proletariat. According to Berman, strengthening the power of the state did not necessarily involve a concomitant strengthening of the legal system: 'This, in fact, was Pashukanis' point.'[15] He ascribed to Pashukanis the view that law would increasingly give way to other forms of social control under socialism, and communism. Pashukanis certainly wrote of regulation superseding law as private interests were replaced by common interests but this was in the sense of the self-emancipation and self-regulation of society, not of an ever-greater totalitarianism directed against the freedom of ordinary citizens.

Moreover, this totalitarianism ultimately required the reimposition of legal forms of rule because Stalin's regime rested on the revival of propertied interests. As Berman himself documented, from the mid–1930s the Soviet government restored the traditional institutions of social control, including legality and law enforcement, one after the other. For example, by 1935, 'harsh legal measures were taken' against 'juvenile delinquency'; by 1936, 'it was prohibited to perform abortions except in unusual cases'; and in 1936 fees were imposed to discourage divorces. Berman also showed that the encouragement of private property acquisition, reduction of inheritance taxes and incentives given to other forms of individual enrichment with the support of Stalin's repeated denunciations of 'equality-mongering' went hand-in-glove with Stalin's insistence in 1936 that 'we need stability of laws now more than ever'. Berman summed up the shift as follows:

> Soviet law underwent profound changes not only in form and in theory but also in substance and in practice. Here the emphasis on strict legality, the independence of the judiciary, and due process, reflected the effort

14 Berman, 1963: 47.
15 Ibid: 43.

> of the regime to bring about a stabilisation in those areas of social relations in which political power could not be directly affected (Berman, 1963: 53).

It was this shift that sealed Pashukanis' fate. It was no longer possible to argue that law could disappear even as the state apparatus assumed unprecedented power.

'Left-wing' criticisms

An article by Warrington[16] provides a useful starting point to assess various 'left-wing' criticisms of the alleged weaknesses of Pashukanis' theory. Warrington's views have had a certain influence, being cited and substantially reproduced by Freeman in his *Lloyd's Introduction to Jurisprudence*,[17] a widely used Western Jurisprudence text. Like Kamenka, Tay and Arthur, Warrington attempted to provide a critique of Pashukanis in isolation from the struggle waged by the Opposition against the Stalinist regime.

Warrington began by accusing Pashukanis of lacking objectivity, on the basis of the following quote from the *General Theory*:

> The legal form only encompasses us within its narrow horizon for the time being. It exists for the sole purpose of being utterly spent. The task of Marxist theory consists of verifying this general conclusion and of following up the concrete historical material (Warrington, in Varga, 1993: 180).[18]

According to Warrington:

> Pashukanis' enquiry was then in no sense an attempt at an 'objective' theory of law; it was very definitely overlaid with the political demands of orthodox Bolshevism. It was designed to meet a purely political end, the speeding of the revolution which he saw as being in process, the revolution to end property relations entirely (Warrington, in Varga, 1993: 180).

This is a jaundiced and caricatured view. In the first place, the quote from Pashukanis is taken out of context. Pashukanis insisted that his project was to contribute towards establishing a comprehensive theory of law, not one purely applicable to the Russian Revolution. More importantly, Warrington

16 Warrington, 1981: 1–22; reprinted in Varga, 1993: 179–200.
17 See Freeman, 2001: 982–96.
18 Citing Pashukanis, 1978: 133.

presented a false dichotomy between objectivity and engagement in the social and legal processes associated with the Soviet experiment. Pashukanis was involved in the attempt to forge a socialist society, one in which the state and law would no longer be required as instruments of social control and regulation. But that does not automatically invalidate his strivings to draw theoretical conclusions from those experiences. As Trotsky argued in the Preface to *The History of the Russian Revolution*, being an active and partisan participant in great events is no automatic disqualification from objectivity.[19] The validity of one's analysis is neither excluded by partisanship nor guaranteed by indifference. It would have to be shown that Pashukanis' alleged partisanship led to demonstrably false conclusions. By analogy, a biologist who is studying the HIV virus would not, presumably, be disinterested in the consequences of AIDS. He would probably be driven by a 'subjective' motivation: to annihilate the HIV virus. This does not mean that he would be incapable of adopting a scientific attitude towards his work.

Furthermore, it is simplistic to suggest that Pashukanis was seeking to 'speed' the revolution in some artificial sense. Marxists understand that, while social revolutions require conscious and clear-sighted leadership, they remain enormous social transformations that depend, ultimately, on underlying productive, technological, economic and cultural factors, not just in one country but on a global scale. As discussed in Chapter 2, Marx and Engels regarded law and legal relations as important contributors to, and facilitators of, changes in society and social consciousness, and capable of playing a key political role in periods of decisive political contest. Nevertheless, they recognised that the level of legal development remains fundamentally dependent upon and derived from the level of economic, political and social development.

Warrington, apparently relying upon Sharlet, mistakenly referred to Pashukanis as an 'orthodox "Old Bolshevik" '.[20] Pashukanis joined the Bolsheviks in 1918, only after the October 1917 Revolution. He may have been earlier active in the Petersburg student movement and joined the Russian Social Democratic Workers Party in 1908[21] but he was largely identified with the Mensheviks until 1918. The purpose of Warrington's label appears to be to depict Pashukanis as a blind adherent to Bolshevism who proceeded 'according to the orthodoxy of his day (to which Pashukanis adhered with unhealthy rigidity)'.[22]

The chief 'orthodoxy', in Warrington's view, was the two-stage transition to communist society outlined by Marx in the *Critique of the Gotha Program*

19 Trotsky, 1977: 20.
20 Warrington, in Varga, 1993: 181; Sharlet, 1978: 170.
21 Kamenka and Tay, 1970: 72.
22 Warrington, in Varga, 1993: 181.

and developed by Lenin in *The State and Revolution*. Warrington distorted Pashukanis' role as an academic jurist in relation to this transition. Correctly enough, Warrington described two reasons that a transitional process is required. The first task is to raise the productive forces to a sufficient level to make it unnecessary to restrict access to wealth by legal restraints. The second is to overcome the traces of bourgeois mentality in society. But the achievement of this second task will flow predominantly from the first. Warrington asserted that Pashukanis' function related only to the second process. His assignment was to 'overthrow bourgeois attitudes' in general and specifically in relation to legal theory.[23]

It is a caricature to equate legal theorising with 'overthrowing bourgeois attitudes', as if social consciousness could be changed merely by ideological argument, rather than by elevating the social conditions of life. In his *General Theory*, Pashukanis was engaged in seeking to expose the flaws and contradictions in bourgeois legal theory, as Marx, Engels and Plekhanov had done before him. But, as philosophical materialists, Marxists do not conceive of such clarification as a purely pedagogical or theoretical exercise. Indeed, they argue that bourgeois legal theorists essentially reflect, even if only semi-consciously, the constraints of the prevailing socio-economic order. As Engels wrote in his 1890 letter to Schmidt, the reflection of economic relations as legal principles 'happens without the person who is acting being conscious of it; the jurist imagines that he is operating from *a priori* principles, whereas they are really only economic reflexes; so everything is upside down'.[24]

On a related issue, Warrington distorted one of Pashukanis' core theses. Because Pashukanis observed that formal juridical concepts continued to exist in Soviet statute books and commentaries, Warrington concluded that this was the basis for Pashukanis' characterisation of Soviet law remaining bourgeois: 'Thus for Pashukanis, Russia in the 1920s was still dominated by a recognizable bourgeois legal system.'[25] In reality, Pashukanis ascribed the bourgeois nature of law not to ideological befuddlement but to its very form, which was historically rooted in commodity exchange. The continued reliance on law as a central instrument of social regulation reflected the continued need to resort to capitalist norms of private production and distribution, given the poor and primitive level of the Soviet economy – the danger that Lenin had warned of in *The State and Revolution*.

Warrington set out to establish that Pashukanis' 'central insight' – 'the commodity form theory' – has merits but is marred by 'several major flaws'.[26] Five defects identified by Warrington provide a means of reviewing some of

23 Warrington, in Varga, 1993: 181.
24 Engels, Letter to Conrad Schmidt, 27 October 1890, in Marx and Engels, 1975: 482.
25 Warrington, in Varga, 1993: 181.
26 Ibid: 187.

the inherent weaknesses in Pashukanis' jurisprudence. They are that Pashukanis (1) wrongly denied pre-capitalist law, (2) over-emphasised commodity exchange and misread Marx, (3) ignored the role of state coercion and the class struggle, (4) overlooked the interactive role of law in shaping economic life and (5) failed to recognise certain contradictions in his commitment to the withering away of law. There is force in each of these propositions. Yet Warrington's critique is often superficial, whereas the problems in Pashukanis' theory are usually more profound than Warrington indicates.

Denial of pre-capitalist law

Warrington insisted that Pashukanis' view that law was a uniquely capitalist institution was central to Pashukanis' argument that legal forms are not eternally necessary and can therefore wither away under communism. Warrington contended that Pashukanis undermined his conclusions by later abandoning his contention about law and capitalism.

According to Warrington, Pashukanis held law to be a peculiarly capitalist institution and denied its existence under previous modes of production:

> As Pashukanis defined all law as merely the outgrowth of the exchange of commodities, it follows that to be consistent social arrangements prior to the commodity form of society were not legal. Thus he wrote of the Middle Ages having 'no abstract concept of the legal subject' and of slavery not being a legal relation and thus requiring no specifically legal formulation (Warrington, in Varga, 1993: 194).[27]

This somewhat simplifies and distorts Pashukanis' view. In fact, Pashukanis' view was less absolute than Warrington suggested. Pashukanis did acknowledge that his argument needed clarification. As already mentioned, he qualified his conclusions as early as the writing of the preface to the second Russian edition of the *General Theory*. However, Pashukanis' subsequent corrections did not alter his argument that capitalism clothes all essential social relations in legal form for the first time in human civilisation. Nor did his modifications alter his view that law would wither away under genuine communism. In the preface to the second Russian edition, Pashukanis conceded 'with certain reservations' the criticism made by Stuchka that he had recognised the existence of law only in bourgeois society, but added:

> I have indeed maintained, and still do maintain, that the relations between commodity producers generate the most highly developed, most universal, and most consummate legal mediation, and hence that every

27 Warrington refers to Pashukanis, 1978: 110, 170.

> general theory of law, and every 'pure jurisprudence' is a one-sided description, abstracted from all other conditions, of the relations between people who appear in the market as commodity owners. But a developed and consummate form does not of course exclude undeveloped and rudimentary forms, rather to the contrary, it presupposes them (Pashukanis, 1978: 44).

Nevertheless, the problems thrown up by Pashukanis' initial rather schematic attempt to deny that the legal form arose before capitalism cannot be overcome simply by suggesting that embryonic legal forms existed in earlier epochs. How those elemental forms corresponded to the emergence of commodity exchange would have to be explored. This was an enterprise that Pashukanis did not subsequently undertake. In his own defence, he argued that it was not his task to solve all, or even only a few, of the problems of legal theory. 'I merely wished to show how one should approach them, and how the questions should be put.'[28]

Commodity exchange over-emphasised

Warrington accused Pashukanis of illogically maintaining that commodity exchange pre-dated law and of ignoring the process of production. His second criticism has some force, but not the first.

On the first point, Warrington was hardly original. He took the formal position that it is simply untenable to postulate the existence of any form of property prior to law. Pashukanis' 'concept of property existing prior to law is unacceptable'.[29] This view appears to be based on the circular proposition that property consists of a legal right, and therefore cannot exist unless it is defined by law. However, Marxists, and indeed other historians, have drawn the conclusion that the concept of private property, based upon the exclusion of others, arose out of definite economic and productive requirements that were reflected ultimately in evolving legal definitions.[30] Among these writers was Macpherson, whose analysis was considered in Chapter 2.

On the second point, Warrington contended that Pashukanis wrote production out of the law, whereas capitalism is a process of production, and exchange is merely part of that process. Warrington did not offer any suggestions as to how this alleged defect deforms Pashukanis' theory or point to how considerations of production would affect legal theory. Nevertheless, Warrington made a valid point, albeit abstractly. Others, including Schlesinger, have pointed out that Pashukanis contradicted the Marxist explanation of social

28 Pashukanis, 1978: 45.
29 Ibid: 187.
30 See, for example, Engels, 1942 and Lafargue, 1975.

phenomena, which refers primarily to the relations that people enter into in production, as distinct from distribution, which Marxism analyses as secondary.[31]

Similarly, Warrington accused Pashukanis of misreading Marx by confining his analysis to the exchange of commodities in simple commodity production, a process that Marx began with in *Capital*, Volume 1.[32] By simple commodity production, Marx meant the elementary production of goods for exchange on a small, one-to-one, basis – for example, a farmer bringing produce to market. In Volume 1 of *Capital*, Marx commenced his analysis by examining the contradiction inherent in this rudimentary process.

Simple commodity production did not commence with capitalism; it occurred under slavery and feudalism, but only marginally. As others, including Fine[33] and Picciotto,[34] have pointed out, in Volumes 2 and 3 of *Capital*, Marx examined the production, circulation and distribution of surplus value under a much more developed and complex economic system – that of capitalism. It is only with capitalism that commodity production becomes predominant and that wage working – the buying and selling of labour-power as a commodity – becomes the means of surplus value creation.

According to Pashukanis: 'The legal system differs from every other form of social system in that it deals with private isolated subjects.'[35] While capitalism began with the atomisation of the old collective social relations of feudalism into relations between individuals, and this is an important starting point for jurisprudential analysis, it did not stop there. Capitalism gave rise to the formation of giant companies, the necessity for credit and the dominance of financial institutions and the development of workers' organisations (trade unions, political parties).[36] It socialised production, while individualising appropriation.[37]

However, as Picciotto argued, Pashukanis' failure to follow Marx in developing his analysis of the expanded reproduction of capital as a whole, does not negate his entire enterprise.[38] In so far as law under capitalism is largely concerned with mediating social relations in the sphere of circulation, analysis at the level of commodity exchange can reveal much about the forms developed by capitalist law.

To grasp the real problem with Pashukanis' theory it is necessary to go further. Under capitalism, production is undertaken almost entirely for the

31 Schlesinger, 1945: 152.
32 Marx, 1970c, vol 1.
33 Fine, 1979: 41.
34 Picciotto, 1979: 170.
35 Pashukanis, 1978: 100.
36 See generally Lenin, 1976.
37 See Engels, 1982: Part III.
38 Picciotto, 1979: 170.

purposes of exchange. As Marx explained, the capitalist must make money, not products. Marx began *Capital* by drawing out how commodities – that is, products produced for exchange – contain within them an inherent contradiction between use value and exchange value, a contradiction that is central to the capitalist mode of production.[39] Pashukanis, by seeking to apply Marx's analysis of this contradiction to legal theory, made some important observations about the legal form.

Yet, as Marx also showed, the source of surplus value under capitalism lies not in exchange but in production. While capitalists must find markets for their commodities – and their immediate profits may be affected spectacularly by success or failure in that quest – the only source of surplus value in the economy as a whole is the labour power of the working class, which is consumed in production. Given that, in general and on average, commodities will be exchanged for equivalent value in the market, the capitalist must find a commodity that can create value over and above the value embodied within it. As Marx put it:

> Moneybags [Marx's embryonic capitalist] must be so lucky as to find, within the sphere of circulation, in the market, a commodity whose use-value possesses the peculiar property of being a source of value, whose actual consumption, therefore, is itself an embodiment of labour, and, consequently, a creation of value. The possessor of money does find on the market such a special commodity in capacity for labour, or labour-power (Marx, 1970c: 164).

Therefore, the essential role of law must relate to the extraction of surplus value in the production process. It is true that, in order to retain the ability to exploit labour-power, the capitalists rely substantially on market forces, that is, on the process of exchange, rather than on legal or physical coercion. Capitalism differs from previous forms of class exploitation, such as slavery and feudalism, in that the bond between the exploiter and the exploited is not fixed formally by status but instead appears to be based on individual freedom. In the main, the worker is not compelled by law or force to sell his labour-power to the employer. On the contrary, he is 'free' to do so – or go hungry. Because the capitalist class has acquired a monopoly over the basic productive forces – the large factories, mines, agribusinesses, media outlets, banks and other financial and commercial corporations – the working masses, the vast majority of the population, have, in reality, little choice but to become wage-workers. The illusion of freedom is an important component of capitalist ideology, including legal theory.

Nonetheless, capitalists do resort to both violence and law to enforce their

39 Marx, 1970c: Chapter 1.

position when market forces prove inadequate. Some of the most obvious examples include the use of security guards and strikebreakers to combat collective resistance by workers,[40] and the master – servant laws (more latterly workplace relations legislation) to enforce the powers of employers. Ultimately, in times of economic, social or political breakdown, the full force of the state is mobilised – police riot squads, military special forces and intelligence agencies – to restore or maintain order, protect capitalist property and ensure the continued existence of the socio-economic structure.

Absence of coercion and the class struggle

Warrington states that Pashukanis ignored the role of coercion, something that Pashukanis' contemporaries, including Stuchka,[41] commented upon. Yet, as Warrington acknowledges, Pashukanis did write a chapter on the state, in which he discussed its coercive nature. Pashukanis regarded the state as having a dual character – political and legal – with political power not necessarily wielded through a legal form.

> The state as an organisation of class rule, and for waging external wars, neither needs nor admits of any legal interpretation. This is an area where the *raison d'etat* holds sway, which is nothing but the principle of naked expediency. In contrast to this, power as a guarantor of market exchange not only employs the language of law, but also functions as law and law alone, that is, it becomes one with the abstract, objective norm (Pashukanis, 1978: 137).

Particularly at critical points, when the political establishment was under threat, the state was the authority for the organised force of one class against others. On the other hand, Pashukanis argued, the legal state embodied the mutual guarantees that commodity owners gave each other.

> In a society of commodity owners, and within the limits of the act of exchange, coercion is neither abstract nor impersonal – hence it cannot figure as a social function. For in the society based on commodity production, subjection to one person, as a concrete individual, implies subjection to an arbitrary force, since it is the same thing, for this society, as the subjection of one owner of commodities to another. That is also why coercion cannot appear here in undisguised form as a simple act of expediency. It has to appear rather as coercion emanating from an abstract collective person, exercised not in the interest of the individual

40 For instance, the 1998 waterfront dispute in Australia. See Davies and Trinca, 2000.
41 Stuchka, 'My journey and my errors', in Zile, 1970: 230.

> from whom it emanates ... but in the interest of all parties to legal transactions (Pashukanis, 1978: 143).

Pashukanis was concerned to refute some distorted interpretations of Marxism, which depicted its analysis as based upon crude force. Warrington himself was guilty of this distortion. He wrote:

> The dominant Leninist view of the time included the conception that all law is but the expression of the will of the ruling class to crush other classes and that in the revolutionary period of the dictatorship of the proletariat the role of law was to help crush the bourgeoisie (Warrington, in Varga, 1993: 191).

As discussed in earlier chapters, the Marxist and Bolshevik view of law was more nuanced and complex. It recognised that, while law ultimately reflected ruling class interests, it did so imperfectly.

In 1932, in one of his recantations, Pashukanis wrote of his error in not referring to coercion and personal subordination as essential to all legal systems.[42] Warrington and others[43] have linked Pashukanis' weakness in this sphere to his failure to relate his theory to the struggle between the contending classes in society.

One-sided view of law

Warrington charged Pashukanis with 'taking a fairly unsophisticated approach to the base-superstructure metaphor' and hence ignoring 'the potential of law for shaping economy' and reducing 'law to the mere reflex response of the given economic'.[44] As discussed earlier, if this were true, Pashukanis' approach would be mechanical and one-sided. Pashukanis did not ignore the ideological role of law, but insisted that its ideological trappings were derived from its underlying economic function. Nevertheless, his reference to legal outcomes as 'objective facts' belittled the dialectical role of law analysed by Marxists. Law fundamentally reflects and serves the needs of the prevailing economic order, but often does so incompletely or in contradictory ways, and can have a considerable impact on economic life.

The withering away of law

Warrington quoted Stuchka from 1927: 'Communism means not the victory of socialist law, but the victory of socialism over any law, since with the

42 Pashukanis, 'Exchange and Law', in Zile, 1970: 235.
43 See, for example, Fine, 1979 and Picciotto, 1979.
44 Warrington, in Varga, 1993: 192.

abolition of classes with their antagonistic interests, law will die out altogether.'[45] Warrington suggested that this summarises Pashukanis' view, which constitutes 'his most important contribution to legal theory'.[46]

Warrington acknowledges that 'the most heated legal debate in the 1920s in Russia' related to the characterisation of the legal system of the transition period. He does not raise any criticism of Pashukanis on this issue, quoting him as follows:

> The proletariat may well have to utilise these forms [bourgeois legal forms], but that in no way implies that they could be developed further or be permeated by socialist content. These forms are incapable of absorbing this content and must wither away in an inverse ratio with the extent to which this content becomes reality (Warrington, in Varga, 1993: 160).

But Warrington charged Pashukanis with being 'not totally consistent' in arguing that crime, state and morality would disappear under communism. Following Korsch,[47] he claimed that Pashukanis contradicts himself by writing: 'Only the complete disappearance of classes will make possible the creation of a system of penal policy which lacks any element of antagonism.'[48] On the face of it, this seems a strained argument, based on interpreting 'the creation of a system of penal policy' as meaning the continuation of punishment by law. Rather Pashukanis, following Marx, Engels and Lenin, suggested that under communism members of society will find ways to deal with social problems and individual conflicts in non-punitive ways that focus on remedying their sources.

Warrington accused Pashukanis of adding a chapter on criminal law only 'to attempt a spurious theoretical consistency', an effort Warrington found 'faintly comic'.[49] Without elaborating, Warrington asserted that Pashukanis displays a far more sophisticated approach to criminal policy elsewhere. He does not attempt himself to examine the possibility of organising society's responses to social problems, currently labelled as 'crime', on a more humane, curative and non-legal level.

Law and force

In *Lloyd's Introduction to Jurisprudence*, Freeman appended to Warrington's critique two further 'puzzles' with Pashukanis' theory. Both Freeman's

45 Warrington, in Varga, 1993: 194, citing Berman, 1963: 26.
46 Ibid: 194.
47 Korsch, 'An Assessment', in Pashukanis, 1978: 189–95.
48 Pashukanis, 1978: 175.
49 Warrington, in Varga, 1993: 197.

questions reveal a shallow view of Pashukanis. First, Freeman asked why the capitalist class uses law, when it could use brute force.[50] Pashukanis also asked, and answered, this question:

> [W]hy does class rule not remain what it is, the factual subjugation of one section of the population by the other? Why does it assume the form of official state rule, or – which is the same thing – why does the machinery of state coercion not come into being as the private machinery of the ruling class; why does it detach itself from the ruling class and take on the form of an impersonal apparatus of public power, separate from society?
>
> It is not enough to confine ourselves to pointing out that it is advantageous to the ruling class to erect an ideological smokescreen, and to conceal its hegemony beneath the umbrella of the state. For although such an elucidation is undoubtedly correct, it still does not explain how such an ideology could arise, nor, therefore, does it explain why the ruling class has access to it. For the conscious exploitation of ideological forms is of course something separate from their emergence, which usually occurs independently of people's will. If we wish to expose the roots of some particular ideology, we must search out the material relations which it expresses (Pashukanis, 1978: 139–40).

Freeman ignored not only the ideological function of law in mystifying the real class relations in capitalist society but also, more profoundly, the very basis of capital accumulation in the 'free' (unfettered) purchase and consumption of labour power as a commodity. As Pashukanis went on to explain, 'The legal view is one-dimensional; its abstractions are the expression of only one of the facets of the subject as it actually exists, that is, of commodity-producing society.'[51]

Second, Freeman asserted that 'if law is so central, one would have expected Pashukanis to believe not in revolution but in legal reformism'.[52] This misses the fundamental point that Pashukanis, like all Marxists, regarded law as a secondary, albeit sometimes influential factor, in social relations, derived from economic relations. Pashukanis also viewed law as a transient phenomenon, elevated to a prominent role under capitalism, but destined to fade away if and when a communist society could be created. Before that task could even be approached, capitalism first had to be overturned. Pashukanis frequently cited Lenin's *The State and Revolution*, which insisted on the necessity of the overthrow of the capitalist state.

50 Freeman, 2001: 984.
51 Pashukanis, 1978: 140.
52 Freeman, 2001: 984.

Alan Hunt

Another Western scholar who paid some attention to Pashukanis from a self-declared Marxist or semi-Marxist standpoint is Alan Hunt. In *Explorations of Law and Society*, Hunt attempted the ambitious task of outlining 'a general framework for a Marxist theory of law'.[53] He devoted several pages to Pashukanis, after asserting that, at first sight, it appears 'most strange' that early debates and controversies in the young Soviet Republic, notably Pashukanis' writings, should have attracted so much attention in the 1970s. Hunt attributed the interest to a general tendency in contemporary Marxist theory to return to Marx's major theoretical texts and to 'avoid the accusations of simple economic and/or class reductions so frequently directed against Marxism by its critiques'.[54]

In my view, the renewed interest in Pashukanis, and to a lesser extent, the wider early controversies, was related to the increasingly evident political and doctrinal crisis within the Stalinist regime and its affiliated parties around the world after Khrushchev's 1956 'secret speech' and ensuing attempts to distance the Kremlin bureaucracy from the most grotesque features of Stalinism. The confusion and disorientation in these circles was aggravated by Krushchev's implausible attempts to separate Stalin's crimes, which he attributed to a 'cult of the individual', from the underlying bureaucratised regime and its repudiation of fundamental Marxist tenets. The guiding line of Krushchev's report to the Twentieth Congress of the Communist Party of the Soviet Union was that until 1934, Stalin 'actively fought for Leninism, against the opponents and distorters of Lenin's teachings'. Stalin had led the 'fight against those who tried to divert the country from the only correct, Leninist path – against Trotskyists, Zinovievists, rightists and bourgeois nationalists'. It was only after the murder of Sergei Kirov that Stalin 'increasingly abused power and began to victimise prominent members of the party and state, applying terrorist methods against honest Soviet people'.[55] Moreover, even in unleashing massive state terror, Stalin had been guided by defending

> the interests of the working class, the interests of the labouring people, the interests of the victory of socialism and communism. It cannot be said that these were the actions of a bully. He felt that he had to do this in the interests of the party and the workers, in the interests of defending the gains of the revolution. Herein lies the real tragedy! (Rogovin, 1998: xii).

Krushchev's incoherent explanation, designed to preserve the Kremlin regime,

53 Hunt, 1993: 265.
54 Ibid: 79–80.
55 Cited in Rogovin, 1998: xii.

not only sought to sanctify the defeat of the genuine Marxist opposition to Stalin but implicitly blamed Marxism for the 'tragedy'. The result was severe demoralisation and renunciation of Marxism among those in the ranks or orbits of the official communist parties worldwide. What had predominantly passed for Marxist theory in the West, as in the East, was presented within the framework of, and under the ideological influence of, Stalinism and its underlying doctrines of 'socialism in one country', 'peaceful coexistence' with capitalism, the 'peaceful road to socialism' and the 'two-stage' theory (first democracy, then socialism) for the colonial and semi-colonial countries. With Krushchev's admissions of some of the gross political abuses under Stalin, followed by the bloody Soviet suppression of the 1956 Hungarian revolution, the Sino-Soviet split and the Moscow-backed repression in Czechoslovakia in 1968, the pro-Moscow line began to unravel. However, the underlying bewilderment also affected those left-wing activists and intellectuals who sought to fashion a more acceptable Marxist alternative to the official line without coming to grips with its political and ideological origins under Stalin. Hence, the attraction to Pashukanis, who was seen as a less rigid or, to use Hunt's terminology, 'class reductionist', Marxist.

Significantly, in his treatment of Pashukanis, Hunt made no attempt to assess Pashukanis' theories and rise to official prominence in relation to the struggle against the Left Opposition. Indeed, he did not mention the socialist opposition to Stalin. At one point, Hunt opined that it was difficult to determine the extent to which Pashukanis' subsequent modifications and self-criticisms were made to accommodate 'Stalinist pressure'.[56] Without elaborating on his observations (apart from making general references to works by Beirne and Sharlet, and Redhead), Hunt contended in a footnote that although criticism of Pashukanis' positions 'became more vociferous after 1927, he remained a very powerful figure well into the 1930s'. However, after 1932, 'his writing [sic] degenerate and are completely incompatible with his general theory'.[57] These speculations raise obvious unanswered questions. What is meant by the polite term 'Stalinist pressure'? Against whom and what political positions was it directed? Why did Pashukanis remain 'a very powerful figure' for the first eight years or so after Stalin took control? What happened after 1932 to produce a stark degeneration and reversal? Is there no continuity between the two periods? Isn't it necessary to probe more seriously the relationship between Pashukanis and Stalinism?

Despite his failure to address these issues, Hunt attributed considerable significance to Pashukanis in the context of contemporary socialist and Marxist debates about law, arguing that one central feature of these debates 'revolves around the problem of the place of law in socialist society'. Hunt

56 Hunt, 1993: 81.
57 Ibid: 337, fn 14.

described those who had revived the work of Pashukanis, and his insistence on the withering away of law and development of a non-legal social order, as one of the two most important poles of the modern debates. The other pole was E.P. Thompson and his commitment to the rule of law, in whose view socialist legality would complete the mission of bourgeois legality by overcoming the formalism of its concepts of individual rights and justice.[58] This counterposing of Pashukanis to Thompson as the principal protagonists in the law–state–socialism debate is interesting.

In considering Pashukanis' critique and contribution to that debate, however, Hunt eschewed any examination of the kernel of Pashukanis' analysis – his attempt to derive the inherently bourgeois character of the legal form from the commodity exchange relationship and the creation of formally equal legal subjects. Hunt stated: 'It is not my intention to examine the problems associated with Pashukanis' derivation of the legal form from commodity relations, but rather to examine its relation to the dualism of coercion and consent.'[59] To assess Pashukanis' arguments on the ultimate withering away of the legal form without treating the foundation stone of Pashukanis' approach is artificial. As Hunt himself acknowledged, Pashukanis sought to 'found his theorisation of law on a sophisticated understanding and application of the methodology elaborated by Marx in the opening chapters of *Capital*'.[60] Attempting to evaluate Pashukanis without discussing the central premise of his work, which is set out in his Introduction to *The General Theory*, entitled 'The Tasks of General Legal Theory', parallels the fundamental error made by those who dismiss or brush aside the famous Chapter 1 of *Capital* on 'Commodities'.[61]

Hunt concluded that Pashukanis had failed to overcome the dichotomy that Hunt considered to be presented by 'coercion–consent dualism'. Hunt observed that Pashukanis had directed his critique against two Marxist trends: one that placed primary emphasis on the ideological dimensions of law and the other that highlighted the instrumental or coercive element. Hunt admitted that Pashukanis had not expressed his aim in the terminology of coercion–consent, yet came to a verdict of failure in this enterprise:

> For him no mere combination of the contradictory elements of coercion and consent adequately provides a basis for the theorisation of bourgeois law. To what extent did Pashukanis succeed in providing a theory that overcame the limitations of the dichotomous conceptions of law? With due recognition for the wider heuristic significance of Pashukanis'

58 Hunt, 1993: 61–2.
59 Ibid: 80.
60 Ibid: 80.
61 See Rubin, 1973: 61–2.

> analysis of the legal form it can only be concluded that not only did he fail, but that albeit in amended form he reproduces the same dualism (Hunt, 1993: 80).

Thus, having erected a straw man – that Pashukanis was endeavouring to overcome a dichotomy identified by Hunt – Hunt relegated the 'wider heuristic significance' of Pashukanis' analysis to something akin to a scenic background. Hunt asserted that Pashukanis was probably aware of the problematic implications of his commodity form analysis because of his subsequent modifications and self-criticisms. Hunt did not examine these either, beyond commenting that it was difficult to determine the extent to which Pashukanis had been accommodating himself to Stalinist pressure.

Hunt skipped to Pashukanis' separation of private law and state law (which is outlined in the final chapter of Pashukanis' *General Theory*), contending that it reproduced the 'dualistic' analysis of law. In the sphere of private law, Hunt suggested that Pashukanis' commodity exchange approach bore marked similarities to Eugen Ehrlich's sociological conception of the origin of law in spontaneous customary norms, although without the latter's metaphysical conception of the essence of law residing in the social or popular will of a people. This unexplained comparison points to a superficial view of Pashukanis' (and Marx's) analysis of commodity exchange, and how its appearance in social relations is highly distorted by commodity fetishism. Ehrlich's observations about how Austrian courts recognised and respected commercial usage and custom may have been germane to the development of the sociological school of legal theory, and perhaps American realist jurisprudence, but had little in common with Marxism.[62]

Hunt asserted that Pashukanis introduced a sharp polarity between civil law, governing relations between atomised legal subjects, and criminal law, a means of securing class domination. Hunt did so on the basis of an isolated quote from Pashukanis, and leaving off a reservation expressed by Pashukanis. After reviewing aspects of the historical development of class society, Pashukanis wrote:

> Basically, that is to say from the purely sociological standpoint, the bourgeoisie maintains its class rule and suppresses the exploited classes by means of its system of criminal law . . . Criminal justice in the bourgeois state is organised class terror, which differs only in degree from the so-called emergency measures taken in civil war (Pashukanis, 1978: 173).

Hunt's rendition of this quote left off the opening clause referring to 'the purely sociological standpoint'. According to Hunt, Pashukanis sought to

62 See Ehrlich, 1936. See also Hertogh, 2004: 457–81.

overcome the dualism between private law and state law by introducing 'what is undoubtedly the weakest feature of his general theory'.[63] That was, Pashukanis erected a correspondence between the 'equivalence' inherent in commodity exchange, enshrined in the labour theory of value, and the 'equivalence' established in punishment by the use of imprisonment and monetary fines. Hunt accused Pashukanis of making 'nothing more than a verbal equation'.[64] Yet, consistent with his omission of Pashukanis' caveat about a 'sociological standpoint', Hunt ignored the crux of Pashukanis' critique of bourgeois criminal law, which was its 'concept of strictly personal liability' that 'corresponds to the radical individualism of bourgeois society'.[65] Pashukanis contrasted the capitalist concept with the collective responsibility of previous socio-economic orders and the socialist emphasis on remedial treatment of offenders, combined with social protection. He also challenged the notion of guilt, describing it as unscientific and associated with the concept of retaliation in proportion to injury. It was from this analysis that Pashukanis derived his conclusion that capitalist punishment embodied the principle of equivalent recompense in terms of time and money:

> For it to be possible for the idea to emerge that one could make recompense for an offence with a piece of abstract freedom determined in advance, it was necessary for all concrete forms of social wealth to be reduced to the most abstract and simple form, to human labour measured in time (Pashukanis, 1978: 181).

Hunt concluded that Pashukanis' 'failure' to overcome the dualism between private and state law should not detract from the importance of his analysis of the legal form – an analysis that Hunt did not examine. In Hunt's view, 'his failure is testimony to the intractable nature of the problem'.[66] This conclusion served as a link for Hunt to review the work of Thompson, who is perhaps the best-known late-twentieth-century 'Marxist' exponent of the 'rule of law' and opponent of the classical Marxist conception, upheld by Pashukanis, that the state and law should wither away with the advent of genuine communism.

Hugh Collins

A further critic of the Marxist 'withering away' thesis, Hugh Collins, paid short shrift to Pashukanis in his *Marxism and Law*. In Collins' case it is clear

63 Hunt, 1993: 81.
64 Ibid: 81.
65 Pashukanis, 1978: 178.
66 Hunt, 1993: 82.

that his target is not so much Pashukanis but the Marxist doctrine itself, at least to the extent that Pashukanis defended it. With little explanation, Collins accused Pashukanis of adopting a 'crude materialist explanation' of how law expressed the capitalist mode of production's mutual respect for property rights as the basis of commodity exchange. Collins purported to sum up Pashukanis' essential theory in three short sentences:

> He said that the concept of a juridical subject reflected the practice of individuals holding property rights. Bourgeois law, therefore, focused upon individuals as the subjects of the law, and its function was to vindicate and enforce individuals' rights. This theory has since become known as the commodity exchange theory of law (Collins, 1984: 108).

We have already noted that the label 'commodity exchange theory' hardly does justice to Pashukanis' analysis. It is even less plausible to compress his thesis into three essentially circular propositions. Having branded Pashukanis a crude materialist, Collins referred to his own previous conclusion that such an outlook is fatally flawed because it lacks an account of how social practices determine conscious action. Without going into detail about Collins' earlier identification of 'crude materialism' as one of two Marxist 'camps' – the other was 'class instrumentalism' – it must be noted that his description of 'crude materialism' was itself crude. One example he gave for its alleged deficiencies was that it could not account for family law legislation concerning marital status, ownership of property and custody of children. Collins asserted that it was implausible to suppose that such laws performed functions directly related to the economic basis of society. By using the word 'directly' Collins also erected a straw man. Such laws are related to the requirements of production, albeit indirectly, as Engels traced out in the *Origin of the Family, Private Property and the State*. As compared to the communal family of pre-class societies, the nuclear family of capitalism serves definite functions in maintaining and reinforcing productive relations, such as providing for individual wealth accumulation, inheritance and future supplies of labour power.

Collins' central indictment of 'crude materialism' was the supposedly 'deeper problem' that it did not explain how conscious action is determined by the material base. In support of this objection, Collins simply asserted that 'In order to complete the crude materialist explanation it has to be demonstrated that individuals and groups are somehow constrained by their material circumstances so that they will only create laws which reflect the relations of production.'[67] Once again, this 'straw man' methodology leaves no room for the slightest nuance. If this test were applied to Pashukanis, as

67 Collins, 1984: 25.

Collins apparently intended, he would have to prove that law makers were virtual mental prisoners of their material circumstances. As we saw earlier, however, Pashukanis argued that the legal form, not every precise aspect of its content, was rooted in commodity exchange and production. Moreover, as Engels explained in *Ludwig Feuerbach and the End of German Classical Philosophy*, a Marxist analysis was perfectly compatible with the fact that bourgeois law could take on many different styles, depending on various intellectual and jurisprudential traditions, and even national traits. As we saw in Chapter 2, Engels compared the English common law with the Western European civil code and the Prussian version of civil law, and concluded: 'If, therefore, bourgeois legal rules merely express the economic life conditions of society in legal form, then they can do so well or ill according to circumstances.'[68]

Collins charged that because of his crude materialism, Pashukanis indulged in all the vices of 'reductionism', that is, he 'purported to explain all legal rules as reflections of commodity exchange'. Like others, Collins sought to sheet home his argument by suggesting that Pashukanis made a valiant but unsuccessful bid to explain criminal law in this way. Collins argued that to analyse criminal law in terms of the mutual recognition of rights ignored its role as 'vindicator of the dominant values and standards of a community'. Sanctions were imposed because offenders had 'violated established norms' and this was 'startlingly illustrated in cases of victimless crimes', such as illicit drug use.[69] Two major assumptions are made here. The first is that the criminal law expresses community values, rather than the property, financial and other interests of ruling circles. No doubt, in contemporary mass democratic societies, penal provisions must be packaged politically to appear responsive to and consonant with popular sentiment. But, as the constant promotion of 'law and order' scare campaigns by media owners and politicians illustrates, this amounts to manipulating opinion to suit the prevailing economic and political agenda.[70] The second assumption relates to 'victimless crimes'. Like some other offences, such as those against the state (sedition, treason, etc.), these are traditionally regarded as being directed both at protecting potential victims of resulting harm and averting threats to social and political stability. Here too, the focus is on punishing the miscreant with some equivalent retribution, usually in length of deprivation of liberty, rather than on addressing the social and psychological causes of the conduct in question.[71]

Having written off Pashukanis, Collins proceeded to pour scorn on the idea – the 'dogma' he branded it – of law withering away under socialism.

68 Engels, 1978: 54.
69 Collins, 1984: 109.
70 See Chapter 12.
71 See also Chapter 12.

Both his language and his methods were crude. First, he simply ridiculed the notion as 'smacking of anarchism and a naïve belief in the ability of men to act justly and to cooperate without coming into conflict occasionally'. Second, he accused Lenin of reducing the thesis to a tautology by insisting that laws were instruments of class oppression, which by definition would vanish in classless society. Third, Collins charged Pashukanis with manipulating a narrow definition of law to substantiate the claim that law would wither away with commodity exchange, leaving other forms of social control intact.[72] On each count, Collins distorted and oversimplified the issues involved.[73]

Underpinning these assertions are basic assumptions about human nature and law that have been tackled throughout this book. Interestingly, in the end, Collins admitted that his objections to the Marxist thesis were based on 'liberal presuppositions about the limited altruism of human nature and the limited possibilities of political organisation' and not on 'any incoherence within the Marxist position'. Ultimately, his chief objection to the withering away prognosis was that 'Marxism provides only a few foggy notions about the organisation of a Communist society'.[74] But, as discussed earlier, Marxists reject the conception of laying down a watertight blueprint for the construction of communism as essentially anti-democratic and contrary to the essential character of human self-emancipation: mass participation in charting society's course.

Finally, Collins contended that it would be 'overly hasty' to argue that legal regulation would disappear in a communist society because 'probably elementary rules of cooperation and mutual respect could not be abandoned without destroying the community entirely'. Legal rules and judicial institutions of some kind would be required to enforce 'fundamental norms of behaviour'.[75] Again, this assertion is based on no more than a 'liberal presupposition' that excludes the very possibility of a truly classless society, bound together by mutual self-interest, in which basic ethical and behavioural norms would not need to be policed by a state apparatus standing above society's members.

72 Collins, 1984: 104–11.
73 See Chapters 1, 2 and 8.
74 Collins, 1984: 122.
75 Ibid: 122.

Chapter 12

Is Pashukanis still relevant?

> Only when the real, individual man re-absorbs in himself the abstract citizen. . . will human emancipation have been accomplished.[1]

Naturally, any attempt to apply, or even draw lessons from, Pashukanis' writings of the 1920s and 1930s must take account of great differences in circumstances today. Pashukanis initially sought to help lay the foundations for a Marxist understanding of the role of law and the state in early Soviet Russia. By the time Pashukanis was executed, however, the first attempt to construct a socialist and ultimately communist society had thoroughly degenerated. Partly as a result of that bitter experience, which severely damaged the reputation of Marxism, capitalist market relations currently dominate the globe, even in the major countries that claim to adhere to some form of Marxism, namely China and Vietnam. No one would suggest a mechanical or simple application of Pashukanis' ideas.

Nevertheless, it would be premature and short-sighted to conclude that the present state of world affairs will last indefinitely. Just as powerful economic processes and contradictions produced the 1917 Russian Revolution, and the French, American and English Revolutions of the seventeenth and eighteenth centuries, there will undoubtedly be profound social, economic and political convulsions in the century ahead. Seen in this light, many of the debates and experiences of Pashukanis' time remain acutely relevant to contemporary society, particularly in view of several underlying trends.

One of these trends is the overturning of traditional civil liberties and the growth of executive power, most apparent since the United States government's declaration of the 'war on terror' in 2001. Many of the previous legal and democratic norms identified with the capitalist state – such as free speech, habeas corpus, freedom of association and the presumption of innocence – have been eroded. Why is this break from traditional principles

1 Marx, 'On the Jewish Question', in Marx and Engels, 1975b: 167–8.

taking place and what are its implications? Pashukanis' writings can assist in probing these questions. Moreover, his defence of the perspective of the withering away of the state stands in stark contrast to the turn to arguably more authoritarian forms of rule.

Another disturbing development is the rise of 'law and order' politics and legal measures. In many countries, most notably the United States, arguably the most powerful nation-state and also a model of 'free market' policy, the growth of police powers and institution of tougher approaches to punishment have seen imprisonment rates rise dramatically since the 1970s. This phenomenon suggests that the supposed triumph of the market has not produced social harmony and contentedness. On the contrary, it seems to have intensified economic inequality and exacerbated the resulting social and class tensions. Pashukanis' analysis of the roots of 'crime' and 'punishment' and his arguments for abolishing those concepts could suggest more enlightened approaches.

A third tendency is the increasing dismantling of public and welfare provisions and the growing privatisation, deregulation and outsourcing of economic activity, often facilitated by legal changes. Everywhere, social and public care, monitoring and responsibilities are being replaced by individual 'freedom' and family or personal burdens. These processes raise afresh Pashukanis' distinction between law, as a form shaped by private interest, and regulation, as rules guided by social interests, and his approach may suggest alternatives.

Finally, there is another contemporary relevance to certain features of Pashukanis' work, as well as his fate. They point to the tragic cost of bending Marxist theory to fit perceived pragmatic requirements, let alone to the pressures, and later the dictates, of an emerging ruling caste. At the same time, Pashukanis' series of 'self-corrections' in the late 1920s and 1930s, ever more repudiating his earlier principles, underlines the incompatibility between Marxism and Stalinism. This clarification itself may be critical in understanding the challenges of the twenty-first century.

Pashukanis and the assault on civil liberties

As we saw in Chapter 11, Pashukanis argued that the development of the bourgeois state itself was bound up with the principle of commodity exchange. Commodity exchange, based on the emergence and domination of private interests, required public power for the mutual protection of those interests.

> [N]either of two people exchanging in the market can regulate the exchange relation unilaterally; rather this requires a third party who personifies the reciprocal guarantees which the owners of commodities mutually agree to as proprietors, and hence promulgates the regulations

> governing transactions between commodity owners (Pashukanis, 1978: 149).

Thus, the character of the state as a seemingly independent apparatus standing above society was not a purely ideological construct for duping ordinary people; the appearance was rooted in the reality of maintaining an *impersonal* guarantor of *personal* rights. To best achieve that end, the state could not be the plaything of this or that tycoon or even dictator. Pashukanis quoted Marx and Engels' famous characterisation of the bourgeois state as a 'committee for managing the common affairs of the whole bourgeoisie'.[2]

However, in times of crisis, particularly when capitalist interests as a whole were threatened from below, the ideal of the constitutional state would be swept aside.

> For the bourgeoisie has never, in favour of purity of theory, lost sight of the fact that class society is not only a market where autonomous owners of commodities meet, but is at the same time the battlefield of a bitter class war, where the machinery of state represents a very powerful weapon. On this battlefield, relations do not appear to be in the least in the spirit of Kant's definition of law as a minimal limitation of the freedom of the personality indispensable to human coexistence . . .
>
> The state as a power factor in internal and foreign policy – that is the correction which the bourgeoisie was forced to make to the theory and practice of its 'constitutional state'. The more the hegemony of the bourgeoisie was shattered, the more compromising these corrections became, the more quickly the 'constitutional state' was transformed into a disembodied shadow, until finally the extraordinary sharpening of the class struggle forced the bourgeoisie to discard the mask of the constitutional state altogether, revealing the nature of state power as the organised power of one class over the other (Pashukanis, 1978: 149–50).

Pashukanis also noted that in the face of exceptional revolutionary upheaval, the impersonal nature of public power could give way to the private or semi-private wielding of power, via the mobilisation of fascist and other violent militias.

> In our times of heightened revolutionary struggle, we can observe how the official machinery of the bourgeois state retires into the background as compared with the volunteer corps of the fascists and others. This further substantiates the fact that, when the balance of society is upset, it

2 Pashukanis, 1978: 147, fn 18, quoting from the *Communist Manifesto* (Marx and Engels, 1973, vol 1: 110–11).

> seeks salvation not in the creation of a power standing above society, but in the maximal harnessing of all forces of the classes in conflict (Pashukanis, 1978: 139, fn 10).

These observations were highly pertinent in the 1920s and 1930s, when fascist thugs, and later stormtroopers, were let loose in Italy and Germany, and totalitarian forms of rule emerged in other major countries, such as Spain and Japan. But Pashukanis' analysis also remains relevant today. There has been a marked ratcheting up of the repressive powers of the state machinery and the accompanying assault on civil liberties in the early years of the twenty-first century. Outright fascist or military dictatorships have not yet resurfaced in Western capitals. Yet, around the world, the alleged threat of terrorism has been used, particularly since the attacks in the United States on 11 September 2001, as a pretext to make far-reaching inroads into basic democratic rights, including free speech, freedom of political association, protections against arbitrary detention, and the right to open and public trial for any serious offence.

Moreover, these measures have been matched by the unilateral unleashing of military forces, complete with unprecedented doctrines of pre-emption, including the unprovoked invasions of Afghanistan and Iraq, in violation of international law. Indeed, one legal scholar has documented the creation of a 'lawless world' in which the leading global powers, notably the United States, have overturned fundamental precepts of international law, in domestic and foreign policy alike, both with regard to unprovoked military aggression and civil and political rights.[3] These developments are causing intense judicial ructions. In 2006, the US Supreme Court decision in *Hamdan v Rumsfeld* was split, with a slender majority ruling that the Bush administration's flouting of the Geneva Conventions in relation to trying Guantánamo Bay detainees in military tribunals was illegal.[4]

Despite criticisms by civil liberties groups, the three governments that spearheaded the 2003 invasion of Iraq – the American, British and Australian – also introduced severe domestic measures, including detention without trial and proscription of organisations.[5] Amnesty International condemned the Bush administration for breaching the International Covenant on Civil and Political Rights and other international protocols against arbitrary detention and inhuman treatment of prisoners.[6] In Britain, the Blair government introduced anti-terrorism legislation that derogated from the European Convention on Human Rights in order to authorise the indefinite detention without charge or trial of non-citizens who could not be deported. The

3 Sands, 2006, especially 143–257.

4 548 U.S. ____ (2006); 126 S.Ct 2749.

5 For a comparison of the US and British legislation, see Hancock, 2001: 2–8.

6 Amnesty, 2002.

legislation allowed indefinite detention to be decided by a person whose identity remained secret, and on grounds that could not be disclosed. The judges of the House of Lords ruled these provisions discriminatory and in breach of Britain's international law obligations, with one judge describing them as 'the stuff of nightmares'.[7] In Australia, more than 30 pieces of legislation were introduced to substantially increase the surveillance, detention and proscription powers of the government and its security and intelligence agencies. The legislation (1) defines terrorism in vague terms; (2) permits the banning of political groups; (3) allows for detention without trial; and (4) shrouds the operations of the intelligence and police agencies in secrecy and provides for semi-secret trials.[8]

Elsewhere, governments came under Western pressure to converge or conform to the proclaimed indefinite 'war on terror'. Human rights organisations accused Asian governments, together with other governments, of exploiting the 'war on terror' to justify political repression and attacks on democratic rights. In its 2004 annual report, Amnesty International outlined many violations of civil liberties implemented by the United States and other countries, including human rights violations related to the American-led wars against Iraq and Afghanistan, including the torture of prisoners.[9] It reported that in Asia:

> The belief of several governments that human rights could be curtailed under the 'war on terror' was particularly apparent in China, India, Malaysia, Pakistan and Thailand. Hundreds of people suspected of 'terrorism' found themselves condemned to legal black holes as authorities ignored national and international legal frameworks (Amnesty International Report, 2004).

Under President George W. Bush's doctrine, the 'war on terror' is not a temporary state of affairs. It is an endless 'long war' against an intangible enemy. Terrorism is an amorphous concept, divorced from any concrete ideological or political cause. It has existed for centuries. In the contemporary world, it is a reactionary set of tactics, to which resort can be had by a multitude of disaffected political currents. Moreover, the classification is susceptible to abuse for political purposes. In the hands of a president or prime minister, the label 'terrorist' can be applied to anyone from a suicide bomber to a member of a national resistance movement fighting foreign occupation, to a political activist involved in a demonstration that ends in violent clashes with police. Today's primary 'terrorist' targets – Al Qaeda-linked

7 Sands, 2006: 233.
8 For full details, see Head, 2002 and Head, 2004.
9 Amnesty International Report, 2004.

groups – were yesterday's 'freedom fighters' in the guerrilla war against the Soviet-backed regime in Afghanistan. Billions of dollars were siphoned into Osama bin Laden's Islamic fundamentalist movement by the Carter, Reagan, and George Bush senior administrations until as recently as the early 1990s.[10] Likewise, Saddam Hussein was once a close ally of Washington, particularly during the fratricidal Iran–Iraq war of the 1980s.[11]

The collapse of the reasons used to justify the United States-led invasion of Iraq – 'weapons of mass destruction', and Saddam Hussein's supposed links to Al Qaeda-backed terrorism – suggests that lies were told to divert attention away from the real motives of the 'war on terror', both domestically and internationally. The Middle East and Central Asia, as is well known, contain the largest proven concentrations of oil and natural gas reserves in the world. Whether or not the Bush administration knew in advance of plans for terrorist acts on September 11 – and that question still has to be answered[12] – the outrages in New York and Washington provided the pretext for the implementation of plans prepared much earlier – during the 1990s – for the conquest of Afghanistan and Iraq.[13] For all their claims to be introducing democracy to the Middle East, Washington and its allies have for decades financially, diplomatically and militarily propped up dictatorships like the Saudi monarchy and Gulf kingdoms, in the interests of controlling access to the region's oil wealth.[14]

Equally, the claims of exporting democracy are belied by the erosions of democratic rights at home. On the face of it, none of the new powers were necessary to protect ordinary people against terrorism. In most jurisdictions, any conceivable terrorist activity, such as murder, bombing, hijacking, kidnapping and arson, was already a serious crime under existing law. Moreover, the police and intelligence services hardly needed new powers to detect terrorists. They already had vast arrays of powers to tap phones, install listening devices

10 Blum, 2002: 155.

11 Ibid: 133–4, 145–6.

12 A multitude of works have called into question the official explanations of 9/11 and the lack of a credible official investigation into the events. See, for example, Ahmed, 2005. The report of the US national commission investigating the terrorist attacks of September 11 was filled with criticisms of the Bush and Clinton administrations and the performance of the government agencies responsible for intelligence, national security and emergency response. But the commission attributed all of these failures to incompetence, mismanagement, or 'failure of imagination'. The fundamental premise of its investigation was that the CIA, the FBI, the US military and the Bush White House acted in good faith. The report thus excluded, *a priori*, the most important question raised by the events of 9/11: did US government agencies deliberately permit – or actively assist – the carrying out of this terrorist atrocity, in order to provide the Bush administration with the necessary pretext to carry out its programme of war in Central Asia and the Middle East and a huge build-up of forces of state repression at home. See United States 9/11 Commission, 2004.

13 Bacevick, 2002.

14 Shalom, 1993: 63–88.

in offices and homes, intercept telecommunications, open people's mail, monitor on-line discussion, break into computer files and databases, seize computers and use personal tracking devices. Intelligence officials could already issue emergency search and entry warrants, allowing officers wide scope to conduct operations against political activists and organisations, as well as to infiltrate them. In addition to the anti-terrorism measures, many states have since 2000 adopted far-reaching measures to strip asylum seekers of basic legal rights and to facilitate the calling out of the armed forces domestically.[15]

The official justifications for the anti-terrorism measures assert that the 'war on terrorism' requires a 'new framework' for considering civil liberties and the rule of law. For example, in 2004, Australian Attorney-General Philip Ruddock stated:

> The war on terror is like no other war in living memory. This is a war which may have no obvious conclusion, no armistice and no treaty. Victory in this war will not necessarily be measured by territory gained or regimes toppled. In this war victories will be measured by disasters averted and democracy strengthened. This war's victories will be measured by citizens feeling safe in their homes. This war's victories will be measured in the steadfastness and resolve of Australians to be cognisant of, but not to fear, a potential terrorist threat . . .
>
> Our Constitution, one of the world's oldest and most stable, provides us with a mechanism to protect our country and at the same time protect civil liberties through human security laws. In enacting such laws we are not only preserving traditional notions of civil liberties and the rule of law, but we are recognising that these operate in a different paradigm. If we are to preserve human rights then we must preserve the most fundamental right of all – the right to human security (Ruddock, 2004).

While insisting that his government was upholding the Australian Constitution, civil liberties and the rule of law, the minister asserted that these operated in a new paradigm: the right to human security, which was said to be the most fundamental right of all. Citing remarks by then-UN Secretary-General Kofi Annan, Ruddock loosely defined 'human security' as encompassing human rights, good governance, access to education and health care and opportunities for individuals to fulfil their potential. All these, the minister asserted, depended upon a secure environment. Thus, in the name of defending civil liberties and the rule of law, these bedrock principles were said to no longer have any independent or absolute existence. Instead, they were subsumed under another concept, human security. Making 'citizens feel safe in their homes' had become the chief criterion for the unknown duration of the 'state of war'.

15 For details, particularly regarding Australia, see Head, 2004b.

Despite the sweeping breadth of such claims, much of the debate and analysis in academic publications concerning the 'anti-terrorism' legislation begins with the proposition that a balance must be struck between 'national security' and 'civil liberties'. According to this approach, the only disagreement concerns where the balance should lie. By this measure, some inroads into civil liberties must be accepted. There is good cause to question this assumption, however. For powerful historical reasons, fundamental democratic rights should be regarded as paramount. They embody centuries of deep-going political struggles. In Anglo-Saxon law, civil liberties – such as habeas corpus, the presumption of innocence, the requirement of proof beyond reasonable doubt for a criminal conviction, freedom of association and free speech – were substantially forged in the conflict against the absolutist monarchy, from the Magna Carta of 1215 onwards and culminating in the English Civil War of the 1640s and the so-called Glorious Revolution of 1688.

Among these fundamental rights is freedom from detention without trial, as the US Supreme Court, by a 6 to 3 majority, commented in June 2004, in ruling that Guantánamo Bay detainees could seek writs of habeas corpus in US courts. While not freeing any of the prisoners, the majority judgment, delivered by Stevens J, suggested that at stake were democratic conceptions dating back nearly 800 years to the Magna Carta of 1215:

> Executive imprisonment has been considered oppressive and lawless since John, at Runnymede, pledged that no free man should be imprisoned, dispossessed, outlawed, or exiled save by the judgment of his peers or by the law of the land. The judges of England developed the writ of habeas corpus largely to preserve these immunities from executive restraint (*Rasul v Bush*, 2004).[16]

Similar statements were uttered in *A & Ors v Secretary of State for the Home Department*,[17] when the British House of Lords, in the case mentioned earlier, ordered the release of eight individuals who had been certified and detained for more than two years under the Anti-terrorism, Crime and Security Act 2001 (UK). Lord Bingham referred to:

> [T]he long libertarian tradition of English law, dating back to chapter 39 of Magna Carta 1215, given effect in the ancient remedy of habeas corpus, declared in the Petition of Right 1628, upheld in a series of landmark decisions down the centuries and embodied in the substance and procedure of the law to our own day (*A & Ors v Home Secretary*).[18]

16 *Rasul v Bush; Al Odah v United States* 542 US 466 (2004), quoting Jackson J in *Shaughnessy v United States ex rel. Mezei*, 345 US 206, 218–19 (1953) (dissenting opinion).

17 [2004] UKHL 56.

18 [2004] UKHL 56 at [36].

That these fundamental conceptions are today under serious attack points to an historical regression in the face of rising international and social tensions. The utilisation of an alleged terrorist threat to overturn traditional civil liberties raises disturbing historical experiences. It should never be forgotten that Adolf Hitler cited the 1933 Reichstag Fire, which the Nazis falsely attributed to communists, as the reason for insisting that the parliament agree to rule by decree.[19] The morning after the fire, Hitler's cabinet adopted the emergency decree, 'For the Protection of the People and State'. In the words of historian Ian Kershaw:

> With one brief paragraph, the personal liberties enshrined in the Weimar Constitution – including freedom of speech, of association and of the press, and privacy of postal and telephone communications – were suspended indefinitely . . . The hastily constructed emergency decree amounted to the charter of the Third Reich (Kershaw, 1998: 459).

A month later, on 23 March 1933, the Nazi-controlled Reichstag passed 'enabling' legislation declaring that the executive had the power to make laws. 'The Act to Relieve the Distress of the People and the Reich' cemented dictatorial power in Germany under Hitler. It essentially transformed into legislation legal opinions previously prepared by the leading Nazi jurist Carl Schmitt. These authorised executive rule because of the 'state of exception' in Germany, namely its economic and political crisis and the alleged threat of revolution. Schmitt set out a 'legal defence' of the enabling legislation in the *Deutsche Juristen Zeitung*, in which he opined that the executive prerogative was unlimited at a time of national crisis.[20]

This is not to say that contemporary Western societies face the imminent danger of fascist dictatorship. Nevertheless, the very fact that governments and security authorities are citing 'national security' threats, especially of indefinite duration, as the justification for suspending or overturning constitutional norms and basic legal rights, is a cause for grave concern. Once more, to borrow Pashukanis' phrase, the 'constitutional state' is being discarded by key sections of the bourgeoisie, revealing 'the nature of the state power, the organised power of one class over the others'. Any attempt to explain this trend as a temporary aberration in order to defeat 'terrorism' also fails to address the issue of why terrorism has become such an allegedly all-pervasive threat. Exploring the roots of disaffected movements engaged in violent attacks is beyond the scope of this book. However, there seems little doubt that they lie, ultimately, in deepening global inequality and the increasingly aggressive military activities of the major powers themselves, notably the

19 Kershaw, 1998: 456–60.
20 Cited in Neumann, 1942; see also Meier, 1988; Muller, 2003.

United States. Moreover, the 'war on terror' is not an isolated development. Similar processes can be seen in the field of 'crime' and 'punishment'.

'Crime' and 'punishment'

Pashukanis posed the necessity for a more humane and effective approach to anti-social behaviour. He probed the roots of the capitalist legal system's fixation on the concepts of guilt, crime and punishment. In his *General Theory*, he pointed out the inherent connection between these three concepts, each rooted in the 'radical individualism' of bourgeois society, which translated into the notion of 'strict personal responsibility' in criminal law.[21] If the focus were shifted entirely, to an examination of the social and personal causes of misconduct, and the best measures to alleviate those causes and protect society, the approach would be fundamentally different.

> If we replace punishment with *Behandlung* ('method of influence'), i.e. a legally neutral, medical-pedagogical concept, we reach very different results. This is so because primarily we will be interested *not in the proportionality*, but in the *correspondence* of the measures taken to the goals which are placed before it, i.e. to the goals of protecting society from the criminal etc. From this point of view the relationship may appear as the opposite; that is, in the case of the least responsibility the most intensive and long-lasting measures of influence may seem necessary (Pashukanis, 1978: 179).

On the latter issue, Pashukanis gave the examples of children and people with psychiatric abnormalities. In law their responsibilities may be regarded as diminished. Nevertheless, long-term and extensive measures of education or treatment may be needed to lessen the likelihood of individual and social harm. However, this rational approach could not be pursued without tackling the notion of equivalence.

> The idea of responsibility is necessary if punishment is to appear as a method of payment. The criminal answers for the crime with his freedom, and he answers with an amount of his freedom which is proportional to the gravity of what he has done. This idea of responsibility is unnecessary when punishment is liberated from the character of equivalence; and when no remnant of this remains, punishment ceases to be punishment in the legal sense of the word (Pashukanis, 1978: 178).

Pashukanis further explored the linkage between this retributive paradigm

21 Pashukanis, 1978: 178.

and the rise of imprisonment as the predominant form of punishment with the emergence of capitalism, in which social relations were based on commodity production, measured in terms of human labour time.

> Punishment proportionate to guilt chiefly represents the same form as revenge related to damage. Above all, it is characterized by the numerical, mathematical expression for 'severity' of the sentence: the number of days, months etc., of deprivation of freedom, the amount of monetary fine, deprivation of various rights.
>
> Deprivation of freedom – for a definite term previously indicated in the judgment of a court – is the specific form in which modern, that is, bourgeois capitalist criminal law, realizes the basis of equivalent retribution. This method is deeply, but unconsciously connected with the concept of the abstract man and of abstract human labour time. It is not accidental that this form of punishment grew strong and eventually seemed natural and expected, in the nineteenth century, i.e. when bourgeois society was fully developed and had consolidated all its particular features. Prisons and dungeons, of course, existed even in ancient times and in the Middle Ages, alongside other means of physical coercion. But at that time prisoners were usually confined until their death or until the payment of a ransom. A necessary condition for the appearance of the notion that payment for a crime should be by a previously determined amount of abstract freedom, was that all concrete forms of social wealth had to be reduced to the simplest and most abstract form – to human labour time (Pashukanis, 1978: 180–1).

This analysis remains essentially correct. For contemporary capitalist law, criminal culpability remains understood primarily in terms of supposedly free individual decision and action. Punishment is conceived as deprivation of liberty for periods of time proportionate to culpability. In the Anglo-American common law, as Hart states, 'the principle of punishment should be restricted to those who have voluntarily broken the law'.[22] This emphasis upon free individual choice, as ground of culpability, finds expression in the requirement to establish that the accused's guilty mind, or *mens rea*, has caused a particular criminal action, or *actus reus*. *Mens rea* has come to refer to a range of states of mind. But the underlying idea is that of a responsible agent who has freely chosen to break the rules, or at least undertaken action knowing there is a chance of causing a prohibited result.

The notion of free will presupposes that an individual is in a position to make a real choice between genuine alternatives on the basis of rational and informed deliberation. Apart from narrowly construed defences of

22 Hart, 1968: 181.

self-preservation such as duress and self-defence, the law refuses to examine the real constraints and pressures under which most people live their lives, notably the socio-economic factors that may severely affect their behaviour and also restrict the choices they have. Motive is generally regarded as irrelevant, as far as guilt is concerned, even if 'mitigating circumstances' may be later taken into account, to some extent and as a matter of discretion, in sentencing. As Norrie observes: 'It is as firmly established in legal doctrine as any rule can be that motive is irrelevant to responsibility – crime may be committed from the best of motives and yet remain a crime.'[23]

Punishment is typically regarded as a response to deviant behaviour produced by the free choice of individual violators, involving some sort of decision about the costs and benefits of such actions to themselves. All such wrongdoing is supposedly treated in a consistent fashion, so as to allow rational decision-making, and effectively influence such individual cost-benefit analysis, in the direction of crime reduction. Such privation and suffering are also meant to serve the function of both individual and general deterrence, dissuading the individual concerned from committing further offences (on the basis of a revised calculation of costs and benefits) and similarly dissuading others from committing any such offence for fear of similar punishment.

These calculations are also understood in terms of retribution – infliction of suffering commensurate with the seriousness of the wrong the perpetrator has inflicted upon others. This takes the form of deprivation of property (fines), of liberty (imprisonment) and – in some jurisdictions – of life (execution). Rehabilitation remains an official rationale of imprisonment but the primary factors in determining the length of detention are those of equivalence of suffering. Another factor is incapacitation, depriving the imprisoned individual of the opportunity for further crimes (at least in the wider community) by confining them to the precincts of the prison.

Pashukanis argued that a non-juridical approach would far more effectively protect society. Instead of an artificial preoccupation with proving individual culpability, attention would shift to the social and psychological symptoms, and the methods to be used to address them.

> A consistent realisation of the principle of social protection would not require the establishment of particular *evidence* (with which the *degree of punishment* determined by law or by the court is logically connected), but would require an exact description of the *symptoms* characterising the socially dangerous situation, and an exact elaboration of the *methods* to be used in each individual case in order to avert the danger to society (Pashukanis, 1978: 186–7).

23 Norrie, 2001: 36.

The gulf between Pashukanis' approach and the situation prevailing in contemporary capitalism is illustrated by data on the rising imprisonment rate in the United States. According to the US Justice Department's Bureau of Justice Statistics (BJS) annual report, 'Prison and Jail Inmates at Midyear 2005', the nation's prisons and jails held 2,186,230 prisoners – an increase of 56,428, or 2.6 per cent over midyear 2004.[24] This was an average of nearly 1,100 new inmates each week – more than twice the rate of population growth for the US, according to Census Bureau data. The BJS statistics indicated that 738 per 100,000 of the population were incarcerated in 2005, up from 725 per 100,000 the year before. According to the report, as of midyear 2005, 1 in every 136 US residents were imprisoned. If this ratio excluded children from the total population, the percentage of those incarcerated would likely be closer to 1 in every 100 residents.

The US imprisoned the largest proportion of its population of any country in history, accounting for a quarter of the world's inmates in its corrections system. On any given day in America, more than 7 million of its residents were under some form of penal supervision, such as imprisonment, community detention, suspended sentence and parole. Since the late 1970s, when many 'tough on crime' measures were adopted, the national prison population has increased sixfold. The most dramatic increase occurred in the decade from 1995 to 2005, in which 'welfare to work' and other measures to dismantle social entitlements were combined with aggressive mandatory sentences for petty theft, property and drug crimes. According to the BJS report, the incarcerated population increased at an average rate of 3.4 per cent annually in the decade between 1995 and 2005. The incarceration *rate* rose more quickly: overall, the state incarceration rate rose by about 14 per cent, and the federal rate by 72 per cent.

The incarceration demographics pointed to entrenched social inequality. African-Americans continued to suffer a disproportionate rate of incarceration, just as they suffer disproportionate rates of social disadvantage. In 2005, blacks were five times as likely as whites to be jailed in local facilities. Consistent with rates over the past decade, an estimated 12 per cent of young black men were incarcerated in 2005. Over the course of a lifetime, nearly a third of all black men in America were imprisoned at some point.

More broadly, the rise in incarceration – like the prevalence of drug addiction – can be linked to the erosion of economic opportunities, industry, access to education, health care, and drug treatment programmes, and the consequent despair of many working-class people. This deterioration was coupled with changes in the legal system. Funding was significantly shifted away from public defence and rehabilitation towards more aggressive prosecution and policing. Simultaneously, legislatures imposed rigid, severe sentencing

24 US Justice Department, 2005.

policies, removing much of the discretion previously administered by the judicial system.

With the soaring imprisonment rate came overcrowding and deleterious conditions for inmates. The BJS statistics showed that capacity rates exceeded 95 per cent at the local level, 99 per cent at the state level, and 140 per cent at the federal level, often forcing violent and non-violent offenders into close contact. Serious diseases such as HIV/AIDS, mental illness, physical and sexual assault were rampant and unmanaged in the large penitentiaries. The punitive approach has led to high levels of recidivism, particularly for those committing non-violent offences such as drug possession, shoplifting and non-payment of child support. Various 'three strikes' laws effectively funnelled prisoners found guilty of minor offences into crowded, dangerous and oppressive conditions. Upon release, many were confronted with permanent discrimination in seeking employment.

More generally, the evidence indicates no consistent deterrent effect from punishment in society, and that the use of imprisonment, in particular, is not an effective deterrent to crime. The US is not the only country where recidivism rates have remained high among those who receive custodial sentences. In one year, in England, approximately 50 per cent of adults and 66 per cent of juveniles were reconvicted within two years of a prior sentence. And there was no evidence that longer custodial sentences produced better results than shorter sentences.[25] Similarly, in Australia, 'on prison census night 2000, 56 per cent of prisoners were known to have served a prison sentence on a previous occasion'.[26]

The 'law and order' framework repudiates the basic conception, held since the Enlightenment of the eighteenth century, that the intellectual and personal development of individuals is fundamentally a product of their social, cultural and economic environment. From this it flows that it is impossible to overcome the problems of crime, substance abuse, ignorance or mental illness without eliminating poverty and uplifting the conditions of social life. In the early years of the labour movement, throughout the nineteenth and early twentieth centuries, this understanding was at the centre of the fight for equality and democratic rights. It animated every struggle for higher wages, shorter working hours, safe working conditions, free public education, good health care, quality housing, state funding of the arts and public ownership of basic services.

Multitudes of studies demonstrate myriad connections between poverty, social tensions and crime.[27] Increasingly, however, the primary official response

25 Norrie, 2001: 203.

26 Hogg, 2002: 11.

27 This discussion leaves aside another issue – the prevalence of corporate and 'white collar' crime, which together far outweigh other crime in human and social costs. See Croall, 2001: 23; Korten, 2001: 304; Hogg and Brown, 1998; 93; Box, 1983: 30.

to social deprivation is stepped-up police repression, targeted against young people in particular. During 2005, for example, Bob Carr, the Labor Party Premier of Australia's most populous state, New South Wales, claimed that the streets were 'safer' because the state's prison population had topped the 9,000 mark for the first time, a 50 per cent increase in a decade.

The question needs to be asked: what kind of society measures progress in terms of growing imprisonment? It is one that increasingly cannot or will not provide the most basic requirements for the intellectual, physical and cultural development of its younger generation. Around the world, the jobs, wages, conditions and welfare entitlements of working people have been slashed in order to satisfy the demands of global corporations and wealthy investors for lower tax rates, cheaper labour and greater profits. Through downsizing, outsourcing and privatisation, full-time, permanent jobs have been replaced increasingly by insecure, temporary and part-time employment. Vast economic changes bound up with the globalisation of production have shattered the former trade union and social democratic programme of placing pressure on employers and governments for improvements within nationally protected and regulated economies. Driven by relentless global competition for markets and profits, transnational corporations demand, as the price for their investment, continual cutbacks to working-class wages and basic rights.

A common response to suggestions of less punitive approaches to antisocial conduct is to argue that human nature, rather than social relations, is the major cause of criminal wrongdoing. It follows that crime, in the sense of selfish behaviour causing serious harm to others, will continue to exist, regardless of the prevailing social relations. Some sort of retributive punishment will still be required, the argument goes, as the morally respectful and the practically effective means of keeping criminal activity within acceptable bounds.

Yet a wealth of everyday and historical experience tells us that treating people with respect encourages them to treat others with respect. Giving them non-criminal opportunities for rewarding and socially useful life activities is the best way to reduce criminal activity. Where they are unable to take advantage of such opportunities for one reason or another, comprehensive social welfare is crucial in protecting them from the need for criminal acts.

Human nature is a problematic concept, as discussed in Chapter 2. But even if genetic propensities or predispositions cause irresponsible and harmful behaviour, it must still be triggered by some environmental stimuli. Any harm could be reduced by removing such triggers and rearranging circumstances to lessen the harmful impact of such conduct, as well as by ensuring proper treatment of psychological and social disorders. Restructuring society along egalitarian and genuinely democratic lines would remove the enormous pressures produced by the individual scramble for existence. If all members of society had free and guaranteed access to first-class education, health care, public housing and other welfare services, as envisaged in a truly socialist or communist society, many causes of crime would fade away.

Law and regulation

One of the central propositions of Pashukanis' *General Theory* was that the legal form would gradually wither away as the dominance of commodity exchange and market relations was overcome and replaced by social production and distribution. To the extent that purely private interests became superseded by collective interests, it would no longer be necessary for society to be governed by formal legal instruments. Social regulation would increasingly take the form of technical coordination and management.

> The basic assumption of legal regulation is thus the opposition of private interests. At the same time the latter is the logical premise of the legal form and the real cause of the development of the legal superstructure. The conduct of people may be regulated by the most complex rules but the legal element in this regulation begins where the individualization and opposition of interests begins. 'Controversy', says Gumplowicz, 'is the basic element of everything legal.' Unity of purpose is, on the contrary, the premise of technical regulation. Therefore the legal norms concerning the liability of railroads presume private claims, private individualized interests; the technical norms of railroad movement suppose a single purpose, e.g. the achievement of maximum freight capacity (Beirne and Sharlet, 1980: 60).

As discussed in Chapter 9, Western legal theorists have tended to lightly dismiss this analysis as ludicrously utopian. Again, complex questions of human nature arise. But is it impossible to conceive of a different kind of society, in which the conflict of individual interests would substantially give way to a common interest? What if people not only had abundant resources, eliminating the everyday scramble for individual existence, but also meaningfully controlled society in a genuinely democratic and collective manner? In order to do justice to Pashukanis' argument, it is important to understand that it was based on a deeper conception of human emancipation, which Marx maintained from his earliest writings. Pashukanis quoted from Marx's 1844 article, 'On the Jewish Question'.

> Only when the real, individual man re-absorbs in himself the abstract citizen, and as an individual human being has become a *species-being* in his everyday life, in his particular work, in his particular situation, only when man has recognised and organised his '*forces propres*' as *social forces*, and consequently no longer separates social power from himself

> in the shape of political power, only then will human emancipation have been accomplished (Marx and Engels, 1975b, vol III: 167–8).

As far back as 1843, Marx centred his critique of Hegel's doctrine of the state on the separation of the state from civil society. He saw that this split could only be healed with the establishment of genuine democracy, conceived not merely as a system of political representation but as a society in which all citizens are actively involved, as a condition of their social existence, in its administration and development.[28]

Marx explained that liberal democracy – representative government grounded on a free market capitalist economy – contained a fundamental cleavage between the political state and civil society, between the conduct of politics and everyday life. In the sphere of politics, the citizen functions as a member of a political community. On the other hand, in civil society, he functions as a private citizen, pursuing his own individual interests in conflict with his fellow citizens. The citizen of the free state leads a double life. In his imaginary life, as a citizen of the state, he is part of an integrated community, integrated, at least, in theory, but not in practice. For, in his real life, in civil society, that is, in the real world of economic life, he is an isolated individual, pursuing his own goals.

In other words, liberal democracy is based on a fundamental contradiction. While it offers to every citizen the prospect of shaping and determining the political state, in practice, the political state is separated from civil society, real life, which is shaped not by the political decisions of the members of society, but by the laws of the capitalist market. The right to vote every few years means little when a financial oligarchy dictates the most important issues of daily life: whether people will have a job, how much they will be paid, under what conditions they will work. Increasingly, thanks to the prevailing privatisation and 'user pays' agendas, the market also dictates access to essential human services, such as health, education, housing and welfare.

This contradiction, which appeared to subside in the wealthy industrialised countries during the period of rising living standards of the 1950s and 1960s, has become increasingly apparent again since the 1970s. Within the framework of the nationally regulated capitalism of the 1950s and 1960s there existed the possibility, albeit limited, to improve the conditions of everyday life through political struggles – not only via elections, but through trade union and other social struggles. Since then, however, the processes of economic globalisation have raised to a new peak of intensity all the contradictions within liberal democracy. Some of the most obvious manifestations are the widening gulf between the rich and the poor, and 'free-market' measures such as privatisation, outsourcing and contracting out. In addition to lining

28 Marx, 1970a.

the pockets of the wealthiest layers of society – those able to capitalise on the carving up of previously state-owned enterprises or government-run services – these processes have led to the ever-greater commodification of social relations and domination of market forces. Regardless of whichever party is elected to office, their economic and social policy is increasingly dictated by the global market.

If one takes the United States, the free-market model, as an example, there has been a staggering concentration of wealth since the late 1970s. In 1960, the average CEO salary at a Fortune 100 company was 41 times that of an average factory worker. Such a stark disparity was already at odds with the rationale of democracy, which is said to provide each member of society with equal political power. But by 1990, CEO pay had risen to 85 times that of an average worker. By 1996, it was 209 times, and by 2000 it was 531 times.[29] US statistics for the distribution of wealth in 2001 revealed an even greater social polarisation. The richest 1 per cent of the population owned 33 per cent of the national wealth. The top 10 per cent owned 71 per cent. The next 10 per cent below owned 13 per cent, and the 20 per cent below that owned 11 per cent. The middle 20 per cent owned just 4 per cent, while the next 22 per cent owned 0.3 per cent, leaving the bottom 18 per cent with zero or negative net worth.[30]

Such a yawning chasm is hardly compatible with any meaningful notion of democracy. Rather it points to the existence of a plutocracy – rule by the rich. Multi-millionaires literally buy their way into office at all levels of government. Others rely on the largesse of corporate sponsors. To win the mayoral post of a major American city costs tens of millions of dollars in campaign funds; the presidency involves an outlay of hundreds of millions.

To overcome the divorce between the state and civil society, the very concept of democratic rights must be expanded beyond the narrow framework of equality before the law and due process. It must encompass the social realities of life for the broad mass of people, beginning with the democratisation of the workplace, where most people spend the bulk of their time and effort. Industrial democracy means real control by working people over their working lives. Decisions affecting conditions of work, safety, salaries, hiring and hours must be subject to the democratic voice of the workforce. That means replacing the capitalist system, in which all the basic forces of industry and finance are privately owned and controlled, by a socialist system of public ownership and democratic control of the economy.

Then Pashukanis' vision of going beyond the conflict of individual interests would be far less utopian. For the first time, the mass of people would fully control their own lives, as well as the economic, political, social and

29 North, 2004: 83–4.
30 Wolff, 2004.

cultural direction of society. In that context, the 'unity of purpose' that Pashukanis postulated could be genuinely democratically determined and mutually agreed upon.

Marxism and Stalinism

As outlined in Chapter 8, from 1925 onwards, Pashukanis aligned himself with Stalin's faction against the Left and Joint Oppositions and increasingly abandoned his theoretical positions in a series of humiliating self-criticisms. By 1935, in his text on Soviet economic law, co-authored with Gintsburg, Pashukanis asserted that Stalin, alongside Marx, Engels and Lenin, was one of the 'greatest theorists of scientific communism'. Stalin had 'enriched the heritage of Marxism-Leninism with the analysis and development of the basic questions of the theory and practice of the building of socialism'. Among his other doctrinal achievements, Comrade Stalin had 'exhaustively characterised' the 'new content of revolutionary legality'.[31]

Pashukanis' self-abasement was crowned by his 1936 article, 'State and Law Under Socialism', in which he lauded Stalin for explaining that 'the path to the future communist, stateless society lies in the all-round consolidation of state power' and for speaking out 'most sharply against the opportunists who, on the occasion of the approach to the classless society, had tried to project their ridiculous ideas concerning the suppression of the class struggle and the weakening of the dictatorship of the proletariat'.[32] Such 'ridiculous ideas' – that a classless society, genuine communism, would involve the disappearance of the temporary post-revolution dictatorship of the proletariat and the emergence of a stateless society – were essentially those that Pashukanis had defended until 1936.

Pashukanis' unedifying capitulation to the requirements of Stalin's order was not simply an individual question. Far more prominent figures, who had played a leading role in the 1917 Revolution, capitulated to Stalin and eventually issued grovelling confessions to have committed all manner of 'counter-revolutionary' crimes in ultimately futile attempts to avoid execution in the show trials of the late 1930s. Among them were Zinoviev, Kamenev, Bukharin, Rykov, Radek and Piatakov. Their ludicrous confessions, after life-long dedication to the cause of socialism, to having functioned as agents of fascism were the end-product of years of political and theoretical back-tracking, self-criticisms and humiliations in order to prove their devotion to the Soviet state.

Only one group distinguished themselves by their refusal to participate in the charade of Stalin's trials. In the words of one Russian historian, they were:

31 Beirne and Sharlet, 1980: 304–5, 317.
32 Ibid: 349, 350.

> [U]nbroken oppositionists who had never capitulated and could not be made to 'cooperate' with the investigators no matter what means were employed. Such people, who had not stained themselves by renouncing their views, and who considered Stalin the gravedigger of the revolution, openly told their jailers that they hated Stalin and his regime, or else that they refused to give any testimony in general (Rogovin, 1998: 166).[33]

From 1924, every oppositionist, dissident or person simply out of favour was presented with the demand to distance themselves from Trotsky, and the more vulgar the denunciation the better. Long before they came under investigation and interrogation for the Moscow Trials, the chief defendants were led to a state of complete demoralisation as a result of ceaseless self-criticisms of 'errors' that had led them into the 'counter-revolutionary swamp'. All these people had renounced themselves several times, and repudiated their political convictions, while heaping praise on Stalin and his version of 'socialism'.[34]

One underlying lesson is that the sacrifice of carefully considered theoretical propositions and principles for expedient, short-term considerations leads inexorably to disaster. Initially, adaptation to the prevailing political winds may be seen as a manoeuvre, undertaken in the hope of tempering the shifts taking place, or even of buying time for more favourable circumstances to emerge on a national or international scale. But such accommodation to the perceived stronger or more popular forces – the true meaning of opportunism – only reinforces the descent into political reaction. In the Soviet context, the historical record shows that those who opposed Stalin and remained true to their principles against the degeneration into terror and horror were those who continued to develop a Marxist analysis. As Leopold Trepper, a famous defector from Stalin's counter-intelligence service, put it, the Trotskyists had 'the enormous advantage over us of having a coherent political system capable of replacing Stalinism'.[35]

More broadly, these experiences show that the Stalinist degeneration was not based on Marxism, nor was it inevitable. It involved the reversal of the genuinely Marxist approach to law all down the line, not only practically but also theoretically. From being impregnable, Stalin feared any survival of classical Marxist doctrine. Pashukanis could not be regarded as a political threat but his theoretical writings remained subversive of the Kremlin bureaucracy's grip over the Soviet state. Pashukanis had rendered invaluable services to the ruling strata by providing a veneer of Marxism for a decade, but in the

33 See also Rogovin, 1998: 374–92, which documents the deaths of thousands of oppositionists who went to their deaths shouting their support for Trotsky and hostility to Stalin.

34 Rogovin, 1998: 172.

35 Trepper, 1975: 56–7.

end his past adherence to Marxist orthodoxy meant that he had to be replaced by a new breed of jurists personified by Vyshinsky, who would ruthlessly execute Stalin's orders in the great purges of 1936–38.

The Stalinist degeneration of the Bolshevik Party and the Soviet state was, in the final analysis, the product of unfavourable objective conditions – principally, the historic backwardness of Russia, the economic devastation produced by seven uninterrupted years of world war, revolution and civil war, and, finally, the protracted isolation of the Soviet state that resulted from the defeats suffered by the European, and especially the German, working class after World War I. Under these powerful adverse pressures, the Stalinist regime arose on the basis of a Russian nationalist reaction against the internationalism that was embodied in the Bolshevik government under the leadership of Lenin and Trotsky. The programme of 'socialism in one country' provided a banner for all those elements within the bureaucracy who identified their own material interests with the development of the USSR as a powerful national state. The bureaucracy obtained its privileges through the mechanism of state ownership of the means of production. The more it became conscious of the national-state foundations of its privileges, the less willing it was to place these at risk in the interest of world revolution.

However, the objective material foundations of Stalinism did not dictate that there could only be one political outcome – the irreversible bureaucratic degeneration of the USSR and its ultimate collapse in 1991. Any such conception ignores the role of politics, of programme, of the struggle of tendencies, of consciousness – the significance of the decisions made by individuals, motivated by a greater or lesser degree of political insight into the historical process, about what they intended to do. The growth of the bureaucracy and its usurpation of political power were consciously and systematically opposed from within the Bolshevik Party. The most significant opposition was that which arose in 1923 under the leadership of Leon Trotsky. Trotsky and the Left Opposition were subjected to a degree of repression that was as brutal as it was relentless. Always conscious of the dubious character of his own claim to the continuity of Bolshevism, Stalin himself believed that Trotsky represented the most dangerous political opposition to his regime.[36] In the end, Stalin could not defeat the opposition without recourse to police-state measures.[37] Thus, there was an alternative to the Stalinist variant of Soviet development, and the Stalinist terror was the means by which it was annihilated. What was destroyed in the cellars of the Lyubianka and countless other execution chambers throughout the Soviet Union were hundreds of thousands of revolutionary socialists who had contributed to the October 1917 Revolution.

36 A vivid portrayal of Stalin's fear of Trotsky is to be found in Volkogonov, 1988: 254–9.
37 See also Reiman, 1987: 19–29.

For all his recantations, Pashukanis also ended up in one of these execution chambers. His efforts to tailor Marxist theory to suit the Kremlin hierarchy only strengthened its hand, making it easier for his own death warrant to be signed. This tragic fate, however, does not negate his initial theoretical contribution. Indeed, in its own way his brutal elimination underscores the power and potential of some of Pashukanis' work, which Stalin and his acolytes certainly felt threatened by. Such are the unresolved problems, and reactionary trends, of global capitalism that this author is confident that in the future the circumstances will appear for this potential to be realised.

Bibliography

[Note: Several works by Marx, Engels and Trotsky are cited from more than one edition.]

Ahmed, N (2005) *The War on Truth*, Northampton, Mass: Oliver Branch Press.

Akhapin, Y (1970) *First Decrees of Soviet Power*, London: Lawrence and Wishart.

Althusser, L (1969) *For Marx*, Harmondsworth: Penguin.

Amnesty International (2002) *Amnesty International's concerns regarding post September 11 detentions in the USA*, Amnesty International (http://web.amnesty.org/library/Index/engAMR510442002).

Amnesty International (2004) *Amnesty International Report 2004*, Amnesty International (http://www.amnesty.org/report2004/index-eng).

Aronson, R (1995) *After Marxism*, New York: Guildford Press.

Arthur, C (1976–77) 'Towards a Materialist Theory of Law', *Critique* 7, p 31.

Arthur, C (1978) Editor's introduction to E Pashukanis, *Law and Marxism, A General Theory*, London: Ink Links.

Atiyah, P (1990) *Essays on Contract*, Oxford: Clarendon Press.

Bacevick, A (2002) *American Empire: The Realities and Consequences of US Diplomacy*, Cambridge, Mass: Harvard University Press.

Balbus I (1977) 'Commodity Form and Legal Form: An Essay on the "Relative Autonomy" of the Law', *Law & Society* 11, p 571.

Ball, A (1987) *Russia's Last Capitalists. The Nepmen, 1921–1929*, Berkeley and Los Angeles: University of California Press.

Bauer, R (1959) *The New Man in Soviet Psychology*, Cambridge, Mass: Harvard University Press.

Beams, N (1999) 'UN report on Eastern Europe and the former USSR: The "free market's" social catastrophe', *World Socialist Web Site*, 5 August 1999 (http://www.wsws.org/articles/1999/aug1999/un-a05.shtml).

Beirne, P (1990) (ed) *Revolution in Law, Contributions to the Development of Soviet Legal Theory, 1917–1938*, Armonk, New York: M.E. Sharpe.

Beirne, P and Hunt, A (1990a) 'Law and the Constitution of Soviet Society: The Case of Comrade Lenin' in Beirne (1990).

Beirne, P and Hunt, A (1990b) 'Lenin, Crime, and Penal Politics, 1917–1924', in Beirne (1990).

Beirne, P and Sharlet, R (1980) (eds) *Pashukanis: Selected Writings on Marxism and Law*, London: Academic Press, 1980.

Beirne, P and Sharlet, R (1990) 'Toward a General Theory of Law and Marxism: E. B. Pashukanis' in Beirne, 1990.

Berman, H (1963) *Justice in the USSR: An Interpretation of Soviet Law*, Cambridge, Mass: Harvard University Press.

Bettelheim, C (1976) *Class Struggles in the USSR. The First Period: 1917–1923*, London: Monthly Review Press.

Blum, W (2002) *Rogue State: a guide to the world's only superpower*, London: Zed Books.

Bonnell, V (1984) *Roots of Rebellion: Workers' Politics and Organizations in St. Petersburg and Moscow, 1900–1914*, Berkeley: University of California Press.

Box, S (1983) *Power, Crime and Mystification*, London: Tavistock.

Butler, W, Maggs, P and Quigley, J (eds) (1988), *Law After Revolution*, New York: Oceana.

Butler, W (1988), 'Necessary Defense, Judge-Made Law, and Soviet Man' in Butler, Maggs and Quigley, 1988.

Cain, M and Hunt, A (1979) *Marx and Engels on Law*, London: Academic Press.

Carr, E (1969) *A History of Soviet Russia, The Interregnum, 1923–1924*, Baltimore: Pelican.

Carr, E (1971), *A History of Soviet Russia*, 14 vols, London: Macmillan.

Carr, E (1978) *A History of Soviet Russia, The Bolshevik Revolution 1917–1923*, London: Macmillan.

Clements, B (1989) 'The Effects of the Civil War on Women and Family Relations', in Koenker, D, Rosenberg, W and Suny, R (eds), *Party, State and Society in the Russian Civil War*, Bloomington, Indiana University Press.

Cohen, S (1985) *Rethinking the Soviet Experience: Politics and History Since 1917*, New York: Oxford University Press.

Collins, H (1984) *Marxism and Law*, Oxford: Oxford University Press.

Conquest, R (2000) *Reflections on a Ravaged Century*, New York: Norton.

Cotterrell, R (1979) 'Commodity Form and Legal Form: Pashukanis' Outline of a Materialist Theory of Law', *Ideology and Consciousness* 6, p 111.

Croall, H (2001) *Understanding White Collar Crime*, Buckingham: Open University Press.

Davies, A and Trinca, H (2000) *Waterfront: The Battle that Changed Australia*, Sydney: Doubleday.

Daniels, R (1960) *The Conscience of the Revolution: Communist Opposition in Soviet Russia*, Cambridge, Mass: Harvard University Press.

Daniels, R (1991) *Trotsky, Stalin and Socialism*, Boulder, Colorado: Westview.

Deutscher, I (1954) *The Prophet Armed, Trotsky: 1879–1921*, London: Oxford University Press.

Deutscher, I (1959) *The Prophet Unarmed, Trotsky: 1921–1929*, London: Oxford University Press.

Dobson, C and Miller, J (1986) *The Day They Almost Bombed Moscow: The Allied War In Russia, 1918–1920*, New York: Atheneum.

Draper, H (1971) 'The Principle of Self-Emancipation in Marx and Engels', *The Socialist Register 1971*, pp 81–109.

Engels, F (1942) *The Origin of the Family, Private Property and the State*, New York: International Publishers.
Engels, F (1948) *The Origin of the Family, Private Property and the State*, Moscow: Progress Publishers.
Engels, F (1959) *Anti-Duhring*, Moscow: Foreign Languages Publishing House.
Engels, F (1969) 'Preface to the 1888 English edition of the *Communist Manifesto*' in Marx and Engels, *Selected Works*, vol 1, Moscow: Progress Publishers.
Engels, F (1975) *Anti-Duhring: Herr Eugen Duhring's Revolution in Science*, Moscow: Progress Publishers.
Engels, F (1975b) *The Condition of the Working Class in England*, in Marx and Engels, *Collected Works*, vol IV, London: Lawrence and Wishart.
Engels, F (1978) *Ludwig Feuerbach and the End of German Classical Philosophy*, Moscow: Progress Publishers.
Engels, F (1982) *Socialism: Utopian and Scientific*, Moscow: Progress Publishers.
Ehrlich, E (1936) *Fundamental Principles of the Sociology of Law*, Cambridge, Mass: Harvard University Press.
Farnsworth, B (1978) 'Bolshevik Alternatives and the Soviet Family: The 1926 Marriage Law Debate', in Atkinson, D, Dallin, A and Lapidus, G (eds) *Women in Russia*, Hassocks, Sussex: Harvester Press.
Fine, B (1979) 'Law and class' in Fine, 1979b.
Fine, B (1979b) (et al) (eds) *Capitalism and the Rule of Law: From Deviancy Theory to Marxism*, London: Hutchinson.
Fitzpatrick, S (1978) (ed) *Cultural Revolution in Russia 1928–1931*, Bloomington: Indiana University Press.
Frankel, E, Frankel, J and Knei-paz, B (eds) (1992) *Revolution in Russia: Reassessments of 1917*, Cambridge: Cambridge University Press.
Freeman, M (2001) *Lloyd's Introduction to Jurisprudence*, London: Sweet & Maxwell.
Fukuyama, F (1992) *The End of History and the Last Man*, London: Penguin.
Fuller, L (1949) 'Pashukanis and Vyshinsky: a study of the development of Marxist Legal Theory', *Michigan Law Review* 47, p 1157.
Fuller, L (1964) *The Morality of Law*, New Haven, CT: Yale University Press.
Goldman, W (1984) 'Freedom and its Consequences: The Debate on the Soviet Family Code of 1926', *Russian History* 11, pp 364–6.
Goldman, W (1991) 'Working-Class Women and the "Withering Away" of the Family: Popular Responses to Family Policy', in Fitzpatrick et al (eds) *Russia in the Era of NEP: Explorations in Soviet Society and Culture*, Bloomington: University of Indiana Press.
Gouldner, A (1977) 'Stalinism: A Study of Internal Colonialism', *Telos* 34, p 5.
Graves, W (1931) *America's Siberian Adventure, 1918–1920*, New York: Jonathan Cape & Harrison Smith.
Gsovski, V (1948) *Soviet Civil Law*, Ann Arbor: University of Michigan Press.
Hancock, N (2001) *Terrorism and the Law in Australia: Supporting Materials*, Canberra: Parliament of Australia, Department of Parliamentary Library, Research Paper No. 13.
Hart, H (1968) *Punishment and Responsibility*, Oxford: Oxford University Press.
Hazard, J (1938) 'Housekeeping in Soviet Law', *American Quarterly on the Soviet Union* 1.
Hazard, J (1948) (ed) *The Law of the Soviet State*, New York: Macmillan.

Hazard, J (1951) *Soviet Legal Philosophy*, Cambridge, Mass: Harvard University Press.

Head, M (2002) ' "Counter Terrorism" Laws: A Threat to Political Freedom, Civil Liberties and Constitutional Rights', *Melbourne University Law Review* 26, p 666.

Head, M (2004) 'Another threat to democratic rights: ASIO detentions cloaked in secrecy', *Alternative Law Journal* 29, p 127.

Head, M (2004b) 'The Global "War on Terrorism": Democratic Rights Under Attack' in Brownsword, R and Lewis, N, *Global Governance and the Quest for Justice*, London: Hart Publishing, vol IV, pp 11–32.

Hertogh, M (2004) 'A "European" Conception of Legal Consciousness: Rediscovering Eugen Ehrlich', *Journal of Law and Society* 31, pp 457–81.

Hill, C (1972) *God's Englishman: Oliver Cromwell and the English Revolution*, London: Harper & Row.

Hill, C (2001) *The Intellectual Origins of the English Revolution – Revisited*, Oxford: Oxford University Press.

Hirst, P (1979) *On Law and Ideology*, London: Macmillan.

Hobsbawm, E (2003) *Interesting Times: A Twentieth-Century Life*, New York: Pantheon.

Hodgskin, T (1832) *The Natural and Artificial Rights of Property Contrasted*, London: B. Steil.

Hogg, R (2002) 'Prisoners and the Penal Estate in Australia' in Brown, D and Wilkie, M (eds) *Prisoners as Citizens*, Sydney: Federation Press, Sydney.

Hogg, R and Brown, D (1998) *Rethinking Law and Order*, Sydney: Pluto Press.

Hunt, A (1993) *Explorations in Law and Society: Toward a Constitutive Theory of Law*, London: Routledge.

Huskey, E (1986) *Russian Lawyers and the Soviet State: The Origins and Development of the Soviet Bar, 1917–1939*, Princeton: Princeton University Press.

Huskey, E (1990) 'Vyshinsky, Krylenko, and Soviet Penal Politics in the 1930s' in Beirne, 1990.

Ilyenkov, E (1982) *The Dialectics of the Abstract and the Concrete in Marx's Capital*, Moscow: Progress Publishers.

Isaacs, H (1938) *The Tragedy of the Chinese Revolution*, London: Secker and Warburg.

Jaworskyj, M (1967) *Soviet Political Thought – An Anthology*, Baltimore: Johns Hopkins.

Juviler, P (1976) *Revolutionary Law and Order. Politics and Social Change in the USSR*, New York: Simon & Schuster.

Kaiser, D (ed) (1987) *The Workers' Revolution in Russia, 1917: The View From Below*, Cambridge: Cambridge University Press.

Kamenka, E and Tay, A (1970) 'The Life and Afterlife of a Bolshevik Jurist', *Problems of Communism*, January–February 1970, p 72.

Kautsky, K (1920) *Terrorism and Communism: a contribution to the natural history of revolution*, London: Allen & Unwin.

Kelsen, H (1955) *The Communist Theory of Law*, London: Stevens.

Kelsen, H (1961) *General Theory of Law and State*, New York: Russell and Russell.

Kemp, T (1982) *Karl Marx's 'Capital' Today*, London: New Park Publications.

Kershaw, I (1998) *Hitler, 1889–1936 Hubris*, London: Allen Lane.

Korten, D (2001) *When Corporations Rule the World*, San Fransisco: Kumarian Press.

Kucherov, S (1970) *The Organs of Soviet Administration and Justice: Their History and Operation*, Leyden: E.J. Brill.

Lafargue, P (1975) *The Evolution of Property from Savagery to Civilization and Social and Philosophical Studies*, London: New Park Publications.

Lapenna, I (1964) *State and Law: Soviet and Yugoslav Theory*, New Haven: Yale University Press.

Lapenna, I (1968) *Soviet Penal Policy*, London: The Bodley Head.

Lenin, V (1964) *Collected Works*, Moscow: Progress Publishers.

Lenin, V (1970) *The State and Revolution*, Moscow: Progress Publishers.

Lenin, V (1976) *Imperialism, the Highest Stage of Capitalism*, Moscow: Progress Publishers.

Lewin, M (1969) *Lenin's Last Struggle*, London: Faber and Faber.

Lewin, M (1985) *The Making of the Soviet System. Essays in the Social History of Interwar Russia*, New York: New Press.

Locke, J (1984) *Two Treatises of Government*, Cambridge: Cambridge University Press.

McDaniel, T (1988) *Autocracy, Capitalism and Revolution in Russia*, Berkeley: University of California Press.

Macpherson, C (1962) *The Political Theory of Possessive Individualism: Hobbes to Locke*, Oxford: Clarendon Press.

Macpherson, C (1990) *Democratic Theory*, Oxford: Oxford University Press.

Malia, M (1994) *The Soviet Tragedy: A History of Socialism in Russia, 1917–1991*, New York: Free Press.

Marx, K (1948) *The Civil War in France*, Moscow: Progress Publishers.

Marx, K (1964) 'Provisional Rules of the Association' in *The General Council of the First International; Minutes, 1864–66*, Moscow: Foreign Languages Publishing House.

Marx, K (1969) Preface to *A Contribution to the Critique of Political Economy*, in Marx and Engels, *Selected Works*, vol 1, Moscow: Progress Publishers.

Marx, K (1970a) *Critique of Hegel's Philosophy of Right*, Cambridge: Cambridge University Press.

Marx, K (1970b) *Critique of the Gotha Program*, New York: International Publishers.

Marx, K (1970c) *Capital*, vol 1, London: Lawrence and Wishart.

Marx, K (1971) 'Capital Punishment' in Marx and Engels, *Articles on Britain*, Moscow: Progress Publishers.

Marx, K (1972) 'The Bourgeoisie and the Counter-Revolution', in Marx and Engels, *Articles from 'Neue Rheinische Zeitung' 1848–49*, Moscow: Progress Publishers.

Marx, K (1973) *The Grundrisse (1857–1858)*, New York: Random House.

Marx, K (1976) 'On the Jewish Question', *Collected Works*, vol 3, London: Lawrence and Wishart.

Marx, K (1977) *A Contribution to the Critique of Political Economy*, Moscow: Progress Publishers.

Marx, K (1977b) *Economic and Philosophical Manuscripts of 1844*, Moscow: Progress Publishers.

Marx, K and Engels, F (1942) *Selected Correspondence*, New York: International Publishers.

Marx, K and Engels, F (1952) *The Communist Manifesto*, Moscow: Progress Publishers.

Marx, K and Engels, F (1973) *Selected Works*, Moscow: Progress Publishers.
Marx, K and Engels, F (1975) *Selected Correspondence*, Moscow: Progress Publishers.
Marx, K and Engels, F (1975b) *Collected Works*, Moscow: Progress Publishers.
Marx, K and Engels, F (1975c) *The Holy Family*, in Marx and Engels (1975b), vol IV.
Marx, K and Engels, F (1976) *The German Ideology*, Moscow: Progress Publishers.
Marx, K and Engels, F (1980) *On the Paris Commune*, Moscow: Progress Publishers.
Marx, K and Engels, F (1987) *Collected Works*, New York: International Publishers.
Meier, H (1988) *The Lesson of Carl Schmitt*, Chicago: University of Chicago.
Mieville, C (2005) *Between Equal Rights: A Marxist Theory of International Law*, Leiden and Boston: Brill.
Moscow Trials Anthology (1967) London: New Park.
Muller, J (2003) *A Dangerous Mind; Carl Schmitt in Post War European Thought*, New Haven, CT: Yale University Press.
Neumann, F (1942) *Behemoth; The Structure and Practice of National Socialism*, London: Victor Gollancz.
Norrie, A (1982) 'Pashukanis and the "Commodity Form Theory": A Reply to Warrington', 10 *International Journal of the Sociology of Law*, p 419.
Norrie, A (2001) *Crime, Reason and History*, London: Butterworths.
North, D (1989) *Perestroika Versus Socialism, Stalinism and the Restoration of Capitalism in the USSR*, Detroit: Labor Publications.
North, D (1996) *Equality, the Rights of Man and the Birth of Socialism*, Sheffield: International Worker Books.
North, D (2004) *The Crisis of American Democracy*, Detroit: Mehring Books.
Nove, A (1969) *An Economic History of the USSR*, London: Penguin.
Pashukanis, E (1978) *Law and Marxism, A General Theory*, London: Inks Links.
Pathfinder (1987) *Founding the Communist International – Proceedings and Documents of the First Congress, March 1919*, New York: Pathfinder Press.
Paton, H (1956) (ed) *The Moral Law or Kant's Groundwork of the Metaphysics of Morals*, London: Hutchinson's University Library.
Petrazhitsky, L (1909) *The Theory of Law and State in Connection with the Theory of Morality*, St Petersburg.
Phillips, P (1980) *Marx and Engels on Law and Laws*, Oxford: Martin Robertson.
Picciotto, S (1979) 'The theory of the state, class struggle and the rule of law', in Fine, 1979b.
Pipes, R (1993) *Russia Under the Bolshevik Regime*, New York: Alfred A. Knopf.
Plekhanov, G (1976) *Selected Philosophical Works*, Moscow: Progress Publishers.
Pogrebinskii, A, Motylev, V, Pazhitnova, T and Podkolzin, A (1964) *History of the National Economy of the USSR*, Moscow: Progress Publishers, cited in Zile, 1970: 96–7.
Quigley, J (1979) 'The 1926 Soviet Family Code: Retreat from Free Love', *Soviet Union* 6, pp 166–74.
Quigley, J (1988) 'The Impact of Soviet Law in the West: Boon or Bane' in Butler, W, Maggs, P and Quigley, J (eds), *Law After Revolution*, New York: Oceana.
Redhead, S (1978) 'The Discrete Charm of Bourgeois Law: A Note on Pashukanis', *Critique* 9, p 113.
Reiman, M (1987) *The Birth of Stalinism: The USSR on the Eve of the Second Revolution*, Bloomington: Indiana University Press.

Robertson, G (2005) *The Tyrannicide Brief: The Story of the Man who sent Charles I to the Scaffold*, London: Chatto & Windus.

Rogovin, V (1998) *1937: Stalin's Year of Terror*, Detroit: Mehring Books.

Rubin, I (1973) *Essays on Marx's Theory of Value*, Montreal: Black Rose Books.

Ruddock, P (2004) 'A New Framework: Counter Terrorism and the Rule of Law', Address to the Sydney Institute, 20 April 2004 (http://152.91.12/www/MinisterRuddockHome.nsf/Alldocs/RWPB046617DB0869).

Sands, P (2006) *Lawless World*, London: Penguin.

Schlesinger, R (1945) *Soviet Legal Theory, Its Social Background and Development*, London: Routledge and Kegan Paul.

Schlesinger, R (1949) (ed) *Changing Attitudes in Soviet Russia: The Family in the USSR, Documents and Readings*, London: Routledge and Kegan Paul.

Schlesinger, R (1951) Soviet Legal Theory, London: Routledge.

Selsam, H and Martel, H (1963) *Reader in Marxist Philosophy*, New York: International Publishers.

Shalom, S (1993) *Imperial Alibis: Rationalizing US Intervention After the Cold War*, Boston: South End Press.

Sharlet, R (1974) 'Pashukanis and the Rise of Soviet Marxist Jurisprudence, 1924–1930', *Soviet Union* 1.

Sharlet, R (1977) 'Stalinism and Soviet Legal Culture', in Tucker, 1977.

Sharlet, R (1978) 'Pashukanis and the withering away of law in the USSR' in Fitzpatrick, 1978.

Sharlet, R, Maggs, P and Beirne, P (1988) *P.I. Stuchka Selected Writings on Soviet Law and Marxism*, New York: M.F. Sharpe.

Shub, D (1948) *Lenin*, New York: Doubleday & Co.

Shukman, H (ed) (1994) *The Blackwell Encyclopaedia of the Russian Revolution*, Oxford: Blackwell Reference.

Siegelbaum, L (1992) *Soviet State and Society Between Revolutions, 1918–1929*, Cambridge: Cambridge University Press.

Stalin, J (1933) *Problems of Leninism*, Moscow: Progress Publishers.

Stuchka, P (1924) *The Revolutionary Part Played by Law and the State: A General Doctrine of Law*, Moscow: Progress Publishers.

Sumner, C (1981) 'Pashukanis and the Jurisprudence of Terror', *Insurgent Sociologist* 10, p 99.

Thompson, E (1975) *Whigs and Hunters*, London: Allen Lane.

Trepper, L (1975) *The Great Game*, New York: McGraw-Hill.

Trotsky, L (1925) *Lenin*, New York: Blue Ribbon Books.

Trotsky, L (1937) *The Revolution Betrayed: What is the Soviet Union and Where is it Going?* New York: Pathfinder.

Trotsky, L (1938) 'Hue and Cry over Kronstadt', *The New International* 4.

Trotsky, L (1945) 'The Character of the Russian Revolution', *The New International* 11.

Trotsky, L (1961) *Terrorism and Communism*, Ann Arbor: University of Michigan Press.

Trotsky, L (1962) *The Permanent Revolution and Results and Prospects*, London: New Park.

Trotsky, L (1969) *Writings 1932–33*, New York: Pathfinder Press.

Trotsky, L (1969b) *Problems of the Chinese Revolution*, London: New Park Publications.

Trotsky, L (1970) *The Third International After Lenin*, New York: Pathfinder Press.

Trotsky, L (1970b) 'Address to the Third All-Union Conference on Protection of Mothers and Children' (December 1925), translated in Trotsky, *Women and the Family*, New York: Pathfinder Press.

Trotsky, L (1971) *War and the International (The Bolsheviks and World Peace)*, London: Wesley Press.

Trotsky, L (1971b) *1905*, London: Penguin.

Trotsky, L (1972) *The New Course*, London: New Park Publications.

Trotsky, L (1973), 'Three Conceptions of the Russian Revolution' (August 1939), *Writings of Leon Trotsky [1939–40]*, (eds) Allen, N and Breitman, G, New York: Pathfinder.

Trotsky, L (1973b) *Problems of Everyday Life*, New York: Pathfinder Press.

Trotsky, L (1973c) *The Platform of the Joint Opposition* (1927), London: New Park Publications.

Trotsky, L (1974) *The Stalin School of Falsification*, London: New Park Publications.

Trotsky, L (1974b) *The Third International After Lenin*, London: New Park Publications.

Trotsky, L (1975) *Terrorism and Communism*, London: New Park Publications.

Trotsky, L (1975b) *Social Democracy and the Wars of Intervention in Russia 1918–1921*, London: New Park.

Trotsky, L (1976) *Towards Socialism or Capitalism?* London: New Park Publications.

Trotsky, L (1977) *The History of the Russian Revolution*, London: Pluto Press.

Trotsky, L (1978) *On the Suppressed Testament of Lenin*, Sydney: Allen Books.

Trotsky, L (1979) *The Military Writings and Speeches of Leon Trotsky, Vol 1: 1918 How the Revolution Armed*, London: New Park Publications.

Trotsky, L (1980) *The Challenge of the Left Opposition 1923–25*, New York: Pathfinder Press.

Tucker, R (1975) *The Lenin Anthology*, New York: Norton.

Tucker, R (1977) (ed) *Stalinism*, New York: Norton.

Turner, B (1993) Preface to Lowith, K, *Max Weber and Karl Marx*, London: Routledge.

United Nations (1998) *Human Development Report*, New York: Oxford University Press.

US Justice Department (2005) *Prison and Jail Inmates at Midyear 2005*, Bureau of Justice Statistics annual report (http://www.ojp.usdoj.gov/bjs/prisons.htm).

United States 9/11 Commission (2004) *The 9/11 Commission Report*, Washington: Government Printing Office.

Varga, C (1993) *Marxian Legal Theory*, London: Dartmouth.

Vinogradov, P (1915) *Ocherki po Obshchei Teory Prava* [Introduction to the General Theory of Law], Moscow.

Volkogonov, D (1988) *Stalin: Triumph and Tragedy*, New York: Grove Weidenfeld.

Voronsky, A (1998) *Art as the Cognition of Life*, Detroit: Mehring Books.

Vyshinsky, A (1948) 'The XVIIIth Congress of the CPSU and the Tasks of the Theory of Socialist Law', in Hazard, 1948.

Warrington, R (1981) 'Pashukanis and the Commodity Form Theory', *International Journal of the Sociology of Law* 9, p 1.

Weber, M (1954) *Max Weber on Law in Economy and Society*, Cambridge, Mass: Harvard University Press.

Wolff, E (2004) *Changes in Household Wealth in the 1980s and 1990s in the U.S.*, New York: Jerome Levy Economics Institute.

Wood, G (1993) *The Radicalism of the American Revolution*, New York: Vintage Books.

Zile, Z (1970) *Ideas and Forces in Soviet Legal Theory: Statutes, Decisions and Other Materials on the Development and Processes of Soviet Law*, Madison, Wisconsin: College Printing & Publishing Inc.

Index

Please note that references to Notes will have the letter 'n' following the reference. References to publications beginning with 'The' are entered under the first significant word, e.g. *The Civil War in France* is entered under *Civil.*

For Product Safety Concerns and Information please contact our EU representative GPSR@taylorandfrancis.com
Taylor & Francis Verlag GmbH, Kaufingerstraße 24, 80331 München, Germany

www.ingramcontent.com/pod-product-compliance
Ingram Content Group UK Ltd.
Pitfield, Milton Keynes, MK11 3LW, UK
UKHW010956180926
475701UK00004B/402
9781904385752